The German Student Movement and the Literary Imagination

Protest, Culture and Society

General editors:
Kathrin Fahlenbrach, Institute for Media and Communication
Martin Klimke, New York University Abu Dhabi
Joachim Scharloth, Technical University Dresden

Protest movements have been recognized as significant contributors to processes of political participation and transformations of culture and value systems, as well as to the development of both a national and transnational civil society.

This series brings together the various innovative approaches to phenomena of social change, protest and dissent which have emerged in recent years, from an interdisciplinary perspective. It contextualizes social protest and cultures of dissent in larger political processes and socio-cultural transformations by examining the influence of historical trajectories and the response of various segments of society, political and legal institutions on a national and international level. In doing so, the series offers a more comprehensive and multi-dimensional view of historical and cultural change in the twentieth and twenty-first century.

Volume 1
Voices of the Valley, Voices of the Straits: How Protest Creates Communities
Donatella della Porta and Gianni Piazza

Volume 2
Transformations and Crises: The Left and the Nation in Denmark and Sweden, 1956–1980
Thomas Ekman Jørgensen

Volume 3
Changing the World, Changing Oneself: Political Protest and Collective Identities in West Germany and the U.S. in the 1960s and 1970s
Edited by Belinda Davis, Wilfried Mausbach, Martin Klimke, and Carla MacDougall

Volume 4
The Transnational Condition: Protest Dynamics in an Entangled Europe
Edited by Simon Teune

Volume 5
Protest Beyond Borders: Contentious Politics in Europe since 1945
Edited by Hara Kouki and Eduardo Romanos

Volume 6
Between the Avant-garde and the Everyday: Subversive Politics in Europe from 1957 to the Present
Edited by Timothy Brown and Lorena Anton

Volume 7
Between Prague Spring and French May: Opposition and Revolt in Europe, 1960–1980
Edited by Martin Klimke, Jacco Pekelder, and Joachim Scharloth

Volume 8
The Third World in the Global 1960s
Edited by Samantha Christiansen and Zachary A. Scarlett

Volume 9
The German Student Movement and the Literary Imagination: Transnational Memories of Protest and Dissent
Susanne Rinner

The German Student Movement and the Literary Imagination

Transnational Memories of Protest and Dissent

Susanne Rinner

berghahn
NEW YORK • OXFORD
www.berghahnbooks.com

First published in 2013 by
Berghahn Books
www.berghahnbooks.com

© 2013 Susanne Rinner

All rights reserved. Except for the quotation of short passages for the purposes of criticism and review, no part of this book may be reproduced in any form or by any means, electronic or mechanical, including photocopying, recording, or any information storage and retrieval system now known or to be invented, without written permission of the publisher.

Library of Congress Cataloging-in-Publication Data

Rinner, Susanne.
 The German student movement and the literary imagination : transnational memories of protest and dissent / Susanne Rinner.
    p. cm. – (Protest, culture, and society)
 Includes bibliographical references.
 ISBN 978-0-85745-754-7 (hardback) – ISBN 978-0-85745-755-4 (e-book) 1. German fiction–20th century–History and criticism. 2. Student movements in literature. 3. Opposition (Political science) in literature. 4. Social conflict in literature. 5. Memory in literature. 6. Literature and transnationalism. 7. Social change in literature. 8. Literature and society–Germany–History–20th century. 9. Influence (Literary, artistic, etc.)–History–20th century. I. Title. II. Title: Transnational memories of protest and dissent.
 PT772.R54 2012
 83'.91409–dc23

2012025542

British Library Cataloguing in Publication Data

A catalogue record for this book is available from the British Library

Printed in the United States on acid-free paper

ISBN 978-0-85745-754-7 hardback
ISBN 978-0-85745-755-4 ebook

Contents

Acknowledgements		vi
INTRODUCTION.	Trans/National Memories of 1968	1
CHAPTER 1.	Remember? 1968 in German Fiction	31
CHAPTER 2.	Forget it? 1968 in East Germany	57
CHAPTER 3.	Transatlantic Encounters between Germany and the United States as Intercultural Exchange and Generational Conflict	94
CHAPTER 4.	Transnational Memories: 1968 and Turkish-German Authors	121
CONCLUSION.	Continued Taboos, Confirmed Canons	147
Bibliography		155
Index		171

Acknowledgements

This book, like most others, has a long history. Therefore, I would like to express my gratitude to all those who supported its publication. In my youth, I participated in many demonstrations, and organized some, in order to protest against the obstacles that stand in the way of living in peace and creating a more just and sustainable world for all. I was fortunate to be able to immerse myself in the study of protest, rebellion, and revolution in the context of the literary imagination at the Freie Universität in Berlin, at Washington University in St. Louis, and at Georgetown University in Washington DC. I would like to thank my teachers and fellow graduate students for their inspiration with which they fostered my intellectual pursuits.

I thank the organizers of the research project "European Protest Movements since the Cold War: The Rise of a (Trans-)national Civil Society and the Transformation of the Public Sphere," in particular Martin Klimke for the invitation to present and discuss my research at numerous conferences. My academic home, The University of North Carolina at Greensboro, provided institutional support that enabled me to deliver lectures at national and international conventions and meetings. I was able to publish aspects of my research on the cultural and transnational memories of the 1960s student movement in Germany in earlier versions. The feedback I received on these occasions substantially advanced my thinking about the 1960s student movement in the context of German fiction and culture and encouraged me to connect these threads to one coherent narrative. I would like to extend my thanks to the many colleagues, on campus in Greensboro and elsewhere, who took an active interest in my research, commenting on my work and providing encouragement when needed. I am also grateful for the staff in Jackson Library at The University of North Carolina at Greensboro who provided support in many ways and without whom I could not have written this book.

Last, but not least, I would like to thank my family and friends. Their patience and generosity seemed to be limitless throughout the years in which this book was conceived, written, and finally published. I continue to ask myself whether writing about protest is not a contradiction per se since the act of writing gives form and shape to something that is inherently unruly. Hence, writing about rebellion and revolution exercises a disciplinary power over something that set out to defy conventional norms and expectations. With this book, I illuminate some of the historical and aesthetic perspectives of the 1960s student protest with the hope to engage critical readers and future protestors.

Susanne Rinner

Introduction

Trans/National Memories of 1968

> Der Erzähler nimmt, was er erzählt, aus der Erfahrung;
> aus der eigenen oder berichteten.
> Und er macht es wiederum zur Erfahrung derer,
> die seiner Geschichte zuhören.
> *Walter Benjamin*[1]

Wladimir Kaminer's *Schönhauser Allee* is a collection of short stories that depict the everyday life of Berlin after 1989.[2] The Schönhauser Allee, a boulevard located in the former East Berlin, and its surrounding neighborhood serve as the narrator's stomping ground and as the site of exploration of contemporary Germany and its past through the lens of immigrants' experiences. In one of the vignettes the narrator describes how he is sifting through the remnants of what looks like someone's personal library. Mirroring a scene already described in the 1977 novel *Der Schleiftrog* by Hermann Kinder, where the protagonist, disillusioned after the end of the student movement, discards his collection of Marx's volumes next to rotten potatoes and old tires, Kaminer's narrator leaves some books in the trash, including the works of Marx and Lenin, while taking the rest to his apartment in order to decide which ones are readable and useful and which ones truly belong in the trash.[3] He finds, among books by cultural icons such as Günter Grass and Wolf Biermann, two novels by Peter de Lorent, *Die Hexenjagd: Ein Berufsverbotsroman* and *Bin ich Verfassungsfeind?*[4] The narrator comments: "Der Autor und gleichzeitige Herausgeber war Redakteur der Hamburger Lehrerzeitung HLZ, hatte Berufsverbot bekommen und es auch sonst nicht leicht gehabt. Man merkt, dass damals in Hamburg tierisch was los gewesen sein muss" (The author and publisher was also editor of the journal for teachers in Hamburg, he had been banned from being a teacher and suffered numerous other setbacks. The reader noticed right away that Hamburg was the place to be during that time).[5]

Kaminer, one of the leading literary voices of Russian descent in Germany today, evokes the 1960s student movement while at the same time rendering the event insignificant by suggesting that "1968" happened a long time ago ("damals") and somewhere else ("in Hamburg"). So, does the narrator really propose to dispose of the student movement and its legacy? By creating historical, as well as spatial, distance Kaminer counters a trend in the 1990s that propelled 1968 into a mythos that, in the decades in between, had produced only cycles of repetitive anniversary commemorations and stalemate memory contests. From an immigrant's perspective, Kaminer inserts his voice into a seemingly internal German debate and participates in the historicization of 1968 in order to determine its significance for contemporary Germany. After all, the discourse on 1968 erupted with full force in the 1990s and served as an indicator for the major and minor shifts that occurred after 1989 in Germany and elsewhere.

This monograph traces the emergence of a cultural memory of the 1960s student movement, subsequent social movements, and terrorist groups in Germany in fiction published after the fall of the Berlin Wall. Through a close reading of seminal novels by Ulrike Kolb, Irmtraud Morgner, Emine Sevgi Özdamar, Bernhard Schlink, Peter Schneider, and Uwe Timm, the study unearths layers of remembering and forgetting reaching beyond conventional boundaries of time and space. Chronologically, the novels construct a palimpsest of memories that reshape the reader's understanding of the 1960s with respect to the end of the Cold War and to the legacy of the Third Reich. Topographically, these novels refute assertions that East Germans were isolated from the political upheaval that took place in the late 1960s and 1970s in the West and the East. Rereading so-called GDR (German Democratic Republic) fiction that was considered obsolete after the fall of the Wall creates a new understanding of the European web of relations that existed among social movements during the Cold War. Given the increasing significance of global flows of people, goods, and ideas, and the vulnerability these global flows create as exemplified by the terrorist attacks in the United States on September 11, 2001 and subsequent political developments, the cultural memory of the 1960s student movement in Germany also proves to be a site of identity struggle. Authors with bilingual and multicultural backgrounds who write and publish in German insert themselves into this seemingly German memory contest by writing about the significance of the 1960s and 1970s and the complicated relationship between members of the student movement and those who were responsible for the Third Reich and the Holocaust. Through their aesthetic appropriations and subversions, these multicultural contributions challenge conventional understandings of German identity and at the same time lay down claims of belonging within a German society that is more openly diverse than ever before.

The term "1968" marks nearly two decades of unrest, rebellion, and civil disobedience in Germany. The height of the movement lies between June 2, 1967, when the first death of a student protestor named Benno Ohnesorg at the hands of police officer Karl-Heinz Kurras occurred, and April 11, 1968 when student leader Rudi Dutschke was wounded by gun shots in an attempted assassination.[6] This ultimately short period of unrest and rebellion is embedded in the long 1960s and as such has roots in the 1950s and stretches into the 1970s.[7] A variety of events in the early and mid 1960s in Germany triggered a renewed public interest in the Nazi past which led to the German student movement's indictment of their parents' generation, which they believed had not done enough to deal with the Holocaust and its legacy.[8] At the same time, like other young people across the globe, young Germans rejected the complacency of Western capitalist society and its so-called fascist tendencies by pointing to the hypocrisy of the Vietnam War and the various instances of exploitation of humans and their natural environment, in particular in colonial and postcolonial societies.

At the onset of the movement, the students adopted protest techniques from the American Civil Rights and student movements in order to strengthen their critique of the German university system and to push university reforms. Drawing on a mix of ideological sources, including unorthodox Marxism, anti-authoritarianism, and notions of participatory democracy, students expanded their protest to topics such as social inequalities in the distribution of wealth, the inner emptiness of consumer society, the dangers of the nuclear arms race, and threats to human rights. In the beginning, the students adhered to nonviolent forms of protest; however, with the death of Benno Ohnesorg the movement radicalized by embracing the notion of revolutionary counter-violence, which would at least justify the use of violence against things. After the attempted assassination of Rudi Dutschke, the core of the movement, the German student organization SDS quietly dissolved in 1969, leaving unresolved the question of violence. While some activists became terrorists, or actively supported terrorism, others joined the new social movements that emerged in the 1970s with the goal of changing society from within.

As a contribution to cultural studies and literary criticism this study is less interested in reconstructing the historical events in an attempt to write yet another history of the time period and to assess its legacy. Instead, this study is concerned with the analysis of why this particular historical moment gained this astonishing significance after 1989 and how its literary representations contribute to the memory contests of the 1990s. Maybe it is not surprising that the fall of the Berlin Wall that was preceded by countless demonstrations in the former GDR triggered an interest in the history of protest and rebellion and its many failures to radically change society in Germany in general. What is noteworthy, however, is the fact that within this context, literary contributions, in particular novels, took on an active role negotiating this history within the fictional realm. Hence, the goals of this study are twofold: to establish that fiction forms an integral part of the cultural memory of 1968 and to explore the specific ways literary texts contributed to the construction of this memory in the 1990s. This study rescues 1968 from oblivion in Kaminer's trash-heap and proposes to read 1968 through its literary representations within a cultural and transnational memory in Germany in the new millennium. I argue that fiction published in Germany in the 1990s serves as an archive for personal as well as culturally mediated recollections. This cultural memory of 1968 entails numerous temporal layers of remembering and various strategies of forgetting whereby the Third Reich and the Holocaust play the most significant points of reference.[9] The novels explored in this book thus position 1968 as the central event in the historiography of the formerly divided Germany, constructing a chronological and causal connection between the years 1933, 1945, 1968, and 1989.[10]

In addition to serving as an archive, this cultural memory enables the retrospective reassessment of the 1960s student movement in order to shape its significance for the future. 1968 memory novels contribute significantly to the structure of this archival cultural memory by expanding its scope to include a spatial dimension. This transnational memory reaches beyond Germany and embeds the German 1960s within a global context, reflecting on concurrent historical events in numerous countries. This transnational dimension of the student movement mirrors the changing nature of Germany's engagement with Europe and the world after 1945, an engagement that is increasingly also shaped by contacts and encounters outside those determined by governmental and economic relations. Philipp Gassert and Martin Klimke assert that "the motives for protests varied from country to country," yet "people readily imagined themselves as part of a global community of protest."[11] This study asks how these imaginative forces manifest themselves and further the development of a cultural memory of the events of 1968. While many scholars acknowledge that "1968 —the actual event as well as the imagined connection—had a global quality"[12] research on the influence of this global quality on the cultural memory is still largely missing.[13] This study contends that this global transformation can be observed in fiction and examines the strategies deployed in order to represent these events as transnational events and to embed them in a cultural memory of the German student movement.

Through the spatial dimension, the cultural memory of 1968 that emerges from the literary texts contains a self-reflective and critical layer that transcends the function of an archive as a repository for memories and the past. 1968 memory novels written in German by authors with a migrant background anticipate an additional form of spatiality embedded in the literary text and hence take on a significant role in contributing to the public discourse and shaping discussions of Germany's future. The evocation of their place of origin in German language texts further highlights the transnational aspects of the cultural memory of 1968.[14] By playing with notions of origin, belonging, and historical appropriation, these texts broaden the definition of German culture in the twenty-first century. The construction of cultural memory of 1968 as transnational memory anticipates Germany's future and challenges a Germany that is slow in recognizing that it is, in fact, a country of migration.

1968 in the 1990s

Though long over, the 1960s and 1970s constitute a part of the German past that will not go away. Their meaning and importance gained renewed attention after 1989 when the unification of Germany created a need to write a revised history of and for the new country. After 1989, 1968 gained popularity both as an object of academic interest as well as an, albeit controversial, point of reference in the academic discourse. From a West German perspective, 1968 served as the central event that marked the arrival of the Federal Republic in the Western world, a move confirmed once more by the end of the German Democratic Republic (GDR) in 1989/90. Access to the files of the East German Ministry for State Security continues to have a profound impact on this rewriting of history.[15] The connections between West German terrorism and the GDR have become apparent, initiating new controversies about the influence the state in the East had exercised over internal affairs in the West.[16] For the GDR, both public discourse and academic research proclaimed and bemoaned the nonexistence of 1968. This presumed lack of protest in the 1960s marginalized the GDR by conveniently forgetting political protests in the now-gone state, initiating a second oppression of those who showed the courage to resist and protest in the GDR. Revisiting 1968 in the 1990s points to the problem of studying protest and opposition in Germany in general since the occurrence of protest in societies that are considered totalitarian, such as the GDR or the Third Reich, challenges narratives that assert that protest in these societies was impossible. Thus, the 1990s provided ideal conditions to remember and historicize 1968 as a controversial but, thankfully, past event.

After 1968, each anniversary was greeted by commemorations and publications, slowly shifting the attention from the 1960s student movement to 1968 as a symbolic marker of the period and as a discursive field of intense debates.[17] In 1998, the victory of a red-green coalition in the federal election in Germany coincided with the thirtieth anniversary of 1968. While the student movement had been commemorated in the old Federal Republic right from the start, marked by speeches, conferences, and book publications, this election provided a new opportunity to emphasize the significance of the movement.[18] Many elected and appointed officials of the new German parliament and government were former activists—the most prominent being Secretary of State Joschka Fischer, the second-highest elected official in the new cabinet. While those on the left in particular felt as if their former comrades had sold out, those condemning the movement and its "long march through the institutions" called for critical scrutiny of former deeds and misdeeds of the newly elected officials.[19] This reproachful interest even led to a plenary session that investigated Fischer's conduct during the 1970s in Frankfurt am Main, where he had participated in street protests that included violent clashes with the police.[20]

These attempts to denounce the student movement as a violent and fundamentally anti-democratic movement left their mark on academic research on the 1960s. Currently, many studies zero in on terrorism and the question of violence and its precursors, yet few studies concentrate on the student movement and the development of diverse social movements in its aftermath.[21] The 2001 terrorist attacks in the United States only fueled the focus on violence and prompted German commentators to compare and contrast terrorism in Germany in the 1970s and terrorism in the new millennium.[22]

This focus on terrorism tends to overshadow the 1960s student movement and, at times, even conflates the political activists and the terrorists by drawing direct causal relationships between the student movement and terrorism. However, the 1960s student movement needs to be studied in its own right and not solely as a precursor to the violent attempts to undermine the state and to threaten its existence. This is even more important after 1989. This year marks a global caesura that initiated a substantial rethinking in the following decade. This rethinking challenged the conventional understanding of political dichotomies such as left and right, peaceful and violent, East and West, democratic and totalitarian, and their representations in the cultural sphere. 1968 proves to be one concept that invites these kinds of investigations in particular since the former '68ers were eager to participate in the discourse.

While 1998 marked the ambivalently received zenith of power for the former '68ers, 2008, the year of the fortieth anniversary, heralds the aging of this generation. Parallel to the attempts to come to terms with the Nazi past by the generation who lived during the Third Reich, the participants in the events in the 1960s and 1970s are actively shaping their legacy. They dominate this discourse in an astonishing and seemingly unprecedented way.[23] This is documented in the numerous publications and media events that accompany and mark the anniversaries of 1968.[24] Increasingly, former activists comment critically on their own limitations of a self-reflective reassessment of 1968 without either categorically denouncing or nostalgically romanticizing the movement.[25]

Former political activists contribute to the discourse in the 1990s because their biographies and their ideas and ideals are at stake. They collect, analyze, and publish their recollections and convert their memories into history in order to maintain the significance of the movement and to control the meaning of 1968 for the future. Generally, they are either nostalgic or self-critical and critical of the movement.[26] And it is interesting to note that the pressure from those who reject and denounce the 1960s student movement does not necessarily originate from those who are born after the event or from those who were already opposed to it in the 1960s, but from former activists who reconsider their own involvement in the movement.[27]

Debates about 1968 and its significance have been elevated to a "dritte Vergangenheitsbewältigung" (a third instance of coming to terms with the past).[28] This development has noteworthy effects: as a historical event, the student movement gains the status of the Third Reich and the GDR because 1968 triggers controversies that are similar in scope and intensity to the ones triggered by the Third Reich and the GDR. This discourse transforms the student movement into an incident that has traumatic effects on individuals and political and legal implications in the realm of guilt and responsibility. Accomplishments, if any, are often ignored in this context. Furthermore, since the 1960s activists understood themselves as fighting against fascism and constituted the New Left (which did not align itself with the GDR or with the Old Left), the previous two instances of "Vergangenheitsbewältigung" are now addressed by coming to terms with the student movement. The 1960s gain a central position in the cultural memory of Germany, regardless of whether participants condemn, justify or elevate the movement. Settling scores with the 1960s student movement allows settling scores with both National Socialism and the GDR concurrently.

This third "Vergangenheitsbewältigung" also creates a parallel situation between the generation who lived during the Third Reich (and who also attempted to shape their legacy) and the '68ers. The attempt to work through the legacy of the 1960s can be linked to the notion of "normalization," a highly debated buzzword in the late 1990s. Viewed with suspicion in particular by the former '68ers, "normalization" was perceived as the "desire to play down the centrality of the Nazi past in order to mitigate German guilt and instil [sic] national pride."[29] While the red-green coalition sought to appropriate the term "normalization" to indicate that the Berlin Republic had incorporated and learned from the lesson of the Nazi past, the public debates surrounding "normalization" nevertheless emphasized the need to deal with the German twentieth century. Since the German student movement was marked by numerous attempts to come to terms with the Third Reich and the Holocaust, the former '68ers, after 1989, were motivated to emphasize the continued centrality of the legacy of the Third Reich.[30] At the same time they transformed their personal experiences of the 1960s and 1970s, and their memories thereof, into a generational experience that was broad enough, and thus worthy, to shape the unified historiography of the new state.

I understand my own work as one of the first contributions to the discourse of 1968 in the field of literary criticism that is written by someone who does not have a vested personal interest in this discourse.[31] While I am not a '68er, I am sympathetic to the goals and motivations of the 1960s student movement. At the heart of this study lies the conviction that utopian thinking and attempts to improve one's own living conditions and to support others in their struggle for freedom, equality, and justice are as important as ever and will never be outdated.

In one of the groundbreaking historical studies on the student movement and its comparative analysis across Europe, historian Ingrid Gilcher-Holtey claims that she could not have conducted an analysis of the student movement without the participation of the former activists.[32] I, too, appreciate and rely on my friends, teachers, colleagues, and all the writers who identify themselves as (former) '68ers. Without them, this study could not have been written. Conversely, I am also wary of what Gerard J. DeGroot calls an obfuscating and stupefying nostalgia when it comes to studying 1968. He suggests that "too many romantic myths and hagiography have been peddled as serious scholarship"[33] and I certainly hope that my study passes as serious scholarship despite the apparent affinity to its subject matter. This study neither condemns nor rescues the 1960s, if indeed they need to be rescued at all. Instead, I hope to contribute to the discourse of 1968 from the perspective of its literary representations and to advance ideas that do justice to the legacy of its social, political, and cultural struggles in the twenty-first century.

Narratives of 1968

1968 received, and continues to receive, overwhelming attention.[34] Academic discourse in various disciplines turns its attention to 1968 in order to understand and analyze the significance of the movement. As debates among historians show, narrating the 1960s student movement is often overshadowed by ideology and political frameworks of interpretations.[35] In turn, these ideological differences spur the interest in the discourse of 1968.[36] Thus, it is often not a question of whether to write about 1968, but how and what to write about it. DeGroot, for example, does not present a structured narrative, but an "impressionistic wandering through the landscape"[37] in order to account for the fact that the 1960s lacked a coherent order. In order to understand how the late 1960s contributed to the civilizing of Germany, historian Konrad Jarausch focuses "less on ideology and events than on the hopes and experiences of both its proponents and its detractors."[38] With respect to the public discourse, research suggests that the media played an outstanding role during and after the events.[39] The media instrumentalized the student movement while in turn the student activists attempted to use the media as a platform to express their views. Kathrin Fahlenbrach argues that the 1960s protest movement is the first social movement in Germany that systematically adapts its public protest to the conditions of mass media. She considers the movement as a revolt against and within the media.[40] This ambivalence continues to shape processes of remembering after 1989.[41] Former '68ers continue to use the media in order to commemorate 1968 and to shape the (self-)representation of 1968 in the media as a generational experience.

This attention suggests that the 1960s student movement was hardly trivial or inconsequential, and yet it also poses the question of why 1968 receives this privileged treatment over so many other events that shaped Germany, Europe, and the world in the twentieth century. Did 1968 gain this nearly undivided attention because, as Sabine von Dirke states, the student movement represented the first disruption of the relative harmony of the Adenauer era?[42] Or was it the sheer number of participants that caused 1968 to dominate the discourse in the 1990s? Or was it the powerful contradictions that marked the 1960s student movement? In the realm of fiction, for example, on the one hand literature was pronounced dead, and on the other hand this pronouncement led to intense debates over how to write and triggered an increased diversity of literary production.[43]

Neither of these factors can adequately explain the powerful position 1968 acquired. After all, the 1960s were not the only moment of protest in Germany after 1945; the student movement was by no means the largest protest movement; and, while literary trends in the 1960s were indeed innovative, the 1960s were not the first decade to witness attempts to introduce avant-garde art and to encourage a plurality of literary styles and topics. Rather, the importance that 1968 gained in the 1990s can be attributed to two factors which serve as the frame for this study: the emergence of an interdisciplinary discourse on 1968, and the transnational intersections of the 1960s student movements across the globe.

The emergence of an interdisciplinary and multifaceted discourse on 1968 advances our understanding of its political and cultural significance. This research often examines the question whether the movement is to be understood as cultural or political in nature.[44] In her foundational contribution to the study of the 1960s from a cultural perspective, Sabine von Dirke examines the sub- and counter-cultural history of West Germany from the 1950s through the mid 1980s. Her methodology draws on the work of the Birmingham Centre for Contemporary Cultural Studies in the 1970s, especially its appropriation of Antonio Gramsci's account of hegemony. Her analysis avoids the binary dichotomy of the political and the cultural which ultimately reinscribes the debate that took place already in the 1960s by carefully explicating their mutual interdependence. As "myth, code, and caesura,"[45] 1968 signifies social and political transformations since the movement challenged the very nature of contemporary political culture. Some understand the 1960s as a "Wendezeit" (time of change);[46] others consider 1968 as the "intellektuelle Staatsgründung" (intellectual founding) of the Federal Republic of Germany (FRG),[47] and Peter Reichel calls it the "zweite, innere Staatsgründung" (second "inner" founding) of the FRG.[48] This tremendous political significance attributed to the historical event explains why some call the public discourse about 1968 in the 1990s a "dritte Vergangenheitsbewältigung" (third coming to terms with the past).[49] If indeed political scientists and historians agreed that the 1960s student movement performed this tremendous political function for West Germany, it is not surprising that, at least in significance, it is placed right next to the Third Reich and the GDR.

Given the tension between those who claim that the 1960s were mostly a cultural revolution and those who argue to preserve the political core of the movement, this study suggests that literary representations are most suitable in reframing this question in order to arrive at a more complex understanding of the relation between the cultural and the political. This study asks how fiction shapes the memories of 1968 and serves as postmemories for those who did not experience the events. As such, fiction contributes to a more nuanced understanding of cultural memories of 1968. This study also analyzes how fiction written in Germany responds to the 1960s student movement by constructing a transnational cultural memory of the events. Recent research shifts the focus from the national student movements to the student movements that occurred across the globe in the 1960s.[50] Even though reasons why these protest movements emerged differed from country to country, participants understood themselves as part of a global community of protest. This research suggests that even when protests were local in origin, scope, and cause, they incorporated and responded to international and transnational forces.[51] These memory spaces determine which events are remembered and to which effect. In light of this research, this study asks how these imaginative forces of a transnational movement that already existed in the 1960s manifest themselves in the cultural memory of 1968 that emerged after 1989.

Fiction published in Germany representing the 1960s employs two strategies that contribute to the transnational memory of 1968. Particular locations, cities such as Paris and Prague, countries such as the U.S. and Turkey, and houses and homes, constitute a topography of memories that evoke the personal experiences of the narrators and trigger and influence the reassessment of these memories in the context of the 1990s. Secondly, authors with a migrant background use their contributions to the cultural memory of 1968 in order to negotiate their belonging to Germany and their country of origin and as such insert themselves into the literary renegotiations of German history in the twentieth century. These connections can be understood as preliminary signs of the globalizing dynamic that characterizes life in Germany in the twenty-first century.

Storytellers of 1968

Numerous obstacles stand in the way of an effective analysis of the significance of the 1960s student movement, ranging from the "emotional polarization of personal memories" to "the lack of clear criteria for judging the effects of long-term sociocultural changes on the more short-term alterations of values and behaviors."[52] Most of the previously mentioned scholars represent the 1960s student movement and its legacy with "the necessary analytical distance"[53] that creates a meaningful reference for studying a contested topic. Another group, and the one that this study focuses on, consists of the numerous former '68ers writing about 1968. At times, these participants seem to suggest that they are the only ones who are entitled to talk about the event since they are its eyewitnesses. Their personal stake in the events and their legacy seem to provide them with a privileged position from which to speak.[54]

In order to illustrate the complexities that the activists-turned-scholars and writers encounter in their work, a comparison is fruitful of how two of the most prolific and outspoken members of this group, Wolfgang Kraushaar and Gerd Koenen, problematize their own positions as narrators of the events that they witnessed and shaped in the 1960s and 1970s. This comparison unveils an exit for the cul-de-sac that the activist-turned-scholars find themselves in and provides a solution for the development of a better understanding and articulation of the relationship between historiography, memory, and fiction.

Political scientist Wolfgang Kraushaar begins his study *1968 als Mythos, Chiffre und Zäsur* by expounding the challenges which confront the narrators who are also the eyewitnesses and participants in the historical events that they talk and write about.[55] He concludes his discussion with a rather resigned outlook for the position and function of the academic historian, while emphasizing the unique and privileged position of fiction writers and artists who possess the necessary freedom to protect memories against the demands imposed by historicization.[56] In his 2008 study of 1968, Kraushaar acknowledges his own positionality which he describes as "Tangential-Achtundsechziger" (tangential 68er) and seems to be more optimistic with regards to the historian's ability to tell a meaningful story of 1968 even if he is "in einem ganz persönlichen Sinne befangen" (in a personal sense biased).[57]

Historian Gerd Koenen, former member of a so-called "K-Gruppe" (Communist splinter group) and now one of the most vocal critics of the student movement, also comments on the role of the historian-narrator. In a seemingly radical tradition, in *Das rote Jahrzehnt. Unsere kleine deutsche Kulturrevolution 1967–1977*, Koenen claims that it is impossible to write an academic, historical account of one's own life.[58] Instead he considers the literary form as the only adequate narrative in order to tell his story of 1968. Specifically, he suggests a hybrid genre consisting of the epos written from a narrative perspective that is marked by irony and that alludes to the picaresque tradition of the modern novel.[59] Koenen's suggestion is noteworthy because my analysis of 1968 memory novels reveals a hybrid genre that represents processes of remembering and forgetting as well as the heterogeneous nature of the cultural memory of 1968. This hybrid genre makes use of additional layers of distancing and reflection. Since most 1968 memory novels are written from the perspective of first-person narrators, they privilege the (auto)biographical construction and reconstruction of personal lives and historical events that allow for the contemplation of the accompanying process of remembering, albeit within a completely fictional framework.

Both Koenen and Kraushaar emphasize the privileged position of literary art for the purposes of recuperating, reconstructing, preserving, and inscribing memories. In *Shattered Past*, historians Jarausch and Michael Geyer also emphasize the "powerful role of narration in turning recollections of the past into history."[60] They suggest that novels by Uwe Johnson, Christa Wolf, and Alexander Kluge, among others, are "multi-layered and multi-focal epics of the making and unmaking of individuals and nations that do not resort to a comforting telos of redemption."[61] Jarausch and Geyer cite Uwe Johnson's *Jahrestage* as an example of how history might be written in order to account for and do justice to the complexities of twentieth century German history. They describe a narrative technique that is marked by a switching of space and a layering of time. In the novel, history is viewed as "a net thrown over unpredictable events to locate them in an unstable space and an uncertain time."[62] The historians' analysis of Johnson's *Jahrestage* suggests that storytelling in its fictional form would be the most adequate way to represent German history and memories thereof. Is it true that writers of fiction and fictional texts are in a privileged position in order to contribute to a cultural memory, and, as one of the most eminent contemporary German historian suggests, even to a history of 1968? And why are those who use their poetic imagination to write stories of a time period that is remembered for its political, social, and cultural upheaval in a more advantageous position than those who rely on archives?

If already historians suggest the ever closer connection between history and fiction in order to tell the story of the German twentieth century, it comes as no surprise then that, within the field of literary and cultural studies, numerous scholars also affirm the privileged position of art for storytelling and the significant contributions by specifically literary texts to the public discourse. As Stephen Brockmann argues convincingly, German literature plays a notable role in the public discourse in Germany in general and in the discourse on national identity in particular.[63] Thus, literary texts published after 1989 participate in ensuing memory debates and very often open up more reflective spaces which allow readers to ponder the effects of this boom. In her important study of exemplary generational novels, Friederike Eigler concludes that fiction takes on the dual role of preserving memories of family histories and aspects of the collective history and of examining the development, inscription, and appropriation of these memories via storytelling.[64] Other literary critics focus on related aspects of the intersections of fiction, history, and memory. Erin McGlothlin analyzes the legacy of survival and perpetration in what she calls second-generation Holocaust literature.[65] Caroline Schaumann puts into dialogue several autobiographical texts written in German by female authors who illuminate the complexities of family novels as an expression of memory and history.[66] As these studies reveal, a cultural memory that is constituted by literary texts serves the dual function of archive and of site of reflection.

My study differs from research conducted in history and the social sciences where the focus lies on empirical data and events, on social movements, their origins and structures, their (alternative) concepts of politics, and their effects on established political and social institutions. Instead, I hope to contribute to the discussion of memory fiction and its various manifestations as family, generational, and autobiographical novels that emerged in the 1990s and continue to dominate the literary market in Germany today. I am interested in further penetrating the cultural mediation of political events, specifically the representation of protest and dissent. I scrutinize the contributions that a cultural and aesthetic product, such as a novel, renders to the contemporary discourse on 1968. My readings emphasize the unique, and privileged, position of storytelling versus other forms of writing because it is not limited by the expectation of the factual. Nevertheless, I recognize the connection between fiction and historiography and understand the notion of cultural memory as a site of negotiation between the two. Jarausch and Geyer posit that "[t]he manifold contradictions between ruptures and continuities, fracturing and restoring community, are therefore a central feature of German history in the twentieth century."[67] Given that memories are never complete and never completely truthful constructions of the past, but reconstructions of a past as it is remembered from the present, I argue that "disrupted time" and "fractured spaces"[68] reveal themselves in the processes of remembering and forgetting and that these processes constitute the genre of 1968 memory novels. Thus, the notion of cultural memory has to be understood in its temporal and spatial dimension, as a way to excavate the numerous layers of remembering and forgetting in twentieth century Germany and as a process that transcends the spaces and sites of the German student movement. Space as a site of remembering, and movements that transgress, transcend, and traverse space, transform a seemingly homogenous notion of cultural memory of 1968 in Germany into a transnational memory of a global 1968 that is embedded in the Cold War, political and economic migration, and, more recently, the clash of civilizations.

My approach to the study of 1968 is embedded in the tradition of studying literary representations of the 1960s student movement in conjunction with historical, social, and political developments. Specifically, I am benefiting from several studies on the literary representations of the student movement that were published prior to my own work. Martin Huber provides a useful overview of texts by Peter Schneider, Uwe Timm, and Bernward Vesper and interprets them within their aesthetic as well as political parameters.[69] Alois Prinz narrates the student movement as a critique of academia and reconstructs the utopian revolutionary theory of the '68ers through the analysis of Uwe Timm's *Heißer Sommer*, Peter Schneider's *Lenz*, and Nicolas Born's *Die erdabgewandte Seite der Geschichte*.[70] Ingo Cornils contributes in several articles to an analysis of the representation of the student movement. In "Successful Failure?" Cornils presents an overview of the discussion of whether the student movement was a success or a failure.[71] Given the developments in the 1990s, he argues that the struggle is not over yet, in particular the struggle over the significance of the events. In "Long Memories: The German Student Movement in Recent Fiction," Cornils examines three contemporary novels in light of their contributions to the discourse on 1968.[72] He stresses that these novels assert the continuing relevance of the students' utopian dream. In "Writing the Revolution: the Literary Representation of the German Student Movement as Counter-Culture," Cornils suggests that it is the aesthetic representation that is most suitable to answer those questions raised by the 1960s student movement that still are unresolved today.[73]

In this study, I propose an innovative framework of analysis that avoids the stalemate confrontations of the past. From the first to the last chapter, I draw a trajectory from the cultural memory of the student movement as a third coming to terms with the past to the transnational dimension of this memory as a way to accept and advance the diversity within Germany today. Given the linguistic turn that suggests that language itself constitutes an action that deserves critical analysis, this study's focus on memory also draws attention to the symbolic representation of personal and collective experiences, to exclusions and silences in fictional accounts, and to the dialogic nature of novels. In order to bring these aspects to light, the readings of the literary texts make use of the notions of remembering, rereading, and revisiting in order to highlight the symbolic importance of the construction of cultural and transnational memories of 1968.

Cultural and Transnational Memory

This study places the literary discourse of 1968 in the context of memory studies. No other discourse in recent years has managed to create a more flourishing interdisciplinary context for academic research and artistic production. Yet scholars warn against the uncritical, quasi-religious use of memory as an attempt to overcome postmodern discontents with history and historiography. In light of this warning, I redefine the use of remembering and forgetting and the notion of individual and cultural memory in the context of 1968 by suspending the tension at the location of fictional storytelling.

The connection between remembering and storytelling is at the critical core of the contemporary discourse of 1968. Fiction tells stories and, as such, remembers, but it also points to instances of "forgetting." Since without (at least a certain amount of) forgetting there would be no remembering, storytelling entails acts of remembering and forgetting. Remembering facilitates storytelling and corresponds with the ethical and moral yearning for justice.[74] Forgetting creates silences and omissions in the text that are linguistically marked and thus force remembering.[75]

The word memory implies that the person who remembers refers to his or her own experiences in the past. Based on Maurice Halbwachs and his theory of social memory, this study examines the phenomenon of remembering 1968 as one of cultural memory, that is, a memory that carries meaning for a group.[76] Cultural memory negotiates between personal memories and remembering in the public sphere. The cultural memory of 1968 consists of memories of 1968 and of memories and postmemories of National Socialism and the Holocaust. Since the 1960s student movement in Germany was marked by the attempt to come to terms with the Third Reich, it is not surprising that the discourse on 1968 after 1989 also includes another debate of German guilt and responsibility. Literary texts reflect and participate in this trend as the wave of publications of 1968 memory novels demonstrates.

1968 memory novels construct a three-dimensional palimpsest of memories that can be unearthed in the way Walter Benjamin proposes in his short text "Ausgraben und Erinnern."[77] He emphasizes that it is impossible to ever finish dealing with the past, even after the death of the last eyewitness of a particular event. His approach recognizes the moral and ethical obligation to remember, since concluding the work of remembering would mean to truncate the past and to artificially separate the past from the present. He suggests that there is a continuously renewed responsibility to approach the past under changed and changing circumstances, symbolized by the steadily increasing number of layers that cover past events. This means that memory is not only a tool to explore the past, but also a medium through which we gain access to this past. Without memory, there would be no past. In this context, 1968 memory novels provide an opportunity to dissect those layers and to add yet another layer to this palimpsest which will be excavated by future generations.

As a temporal concept, memory refers to the past, the present, and the future. Jan and Aleida Assmann's theory of memory develops this idea further.[78] They understand personal memories, located in the "Kommunikationsgedächtnis" (the short term communicative memory of individuals), as feeding into both the "kulturelles Gedächtnis" (cultural memory) and the "kollektives Gedächtnis" (collective memory). However, they caution that this process requires the preservation of memories that are palatable in the specific political and cultural context in which they are remembered. If an individual's memories are not acceptable then these memories tend to be forgotten, oppressed, and silenced. Memories that are preserved are shaped by the present in which they are remembered and take on a public, and at times political, function within the collective memory and a mediated form within the cultural memory of a community. These two forms of memory, collective and cultural, determine which past is remembered and how the past is remembered in the future.

This temporal structure is symbolized by the different layers of Benjamin's palimpsest. In the discourse of 1968, these temporal layers refer to the 1990s, 1968, and the Third Reich. 1968 memory novels construct these different layers, and thus make it possible to reflect upon the construction of a cultural and transnational memory of 1968. They create a structure for the representation of these historical ruptures and thus situate events and their effects in the fictional space. The first layer consists of the narrators' memories of their involvement in the student movement. This layer triggers a reassessment of the movement and its function for Germany before and after the fall of the Berlin Wall. In the second layer, the narrators reevaluate their attitudes toward the Nazi past. In this layer, the narrators not only remember events that shaped their lives, they also seem to "remember" the Nazi past, which, if at all, they only experienced as very young children. Marianne Hirsch coined the term "postmemories" in order to define memories that are not based on one's own experiences, but on narration by others, whether oral transmission, in books, through visual depictions of the past, or any other form of cultural representation.[79] In light of the concept of postmemories, the narrators tell stories based on their own memories of the student movement (in particular of the ways they attempted to come to terms with the legacy of the Third Reich) and based on postmemories of the Nazi past. These memories and postmemories construct the temporal layers of the cultural memory of 1968. They create problematic fusions and confusions and their intersections point to the constructedness of not only postmemories, but also memories. Even though memories rest upon one's own experiences, they are still reconstructed from a present perspective. Postmemories are removed one step further since they are mediated by some form of cultural representation or by someone else's (personal) memories. Fiction reveals the construction and constructedness of these memories and postmemories and allows insights into the processes that shaped the discussion of the cultural memory of 1968 in Germany in the 1990s. In that sense, narrating 1968 in memory novels published in the 1990s creates a layer of postmemories for all those who did not witness the 1960s student movement or the Third Reich. The ensuing "memory contests"[80] can be read as, often displaced, discussions about the nation, national history, and (national) identity in Germany. They contribute to the cultural memory of 1968 and slowly transform it into a transnational memory of 1968.

1968 Memory Novels

This study analyzes the representation of the 1960s student movement in German fiction in order to understand the contributions of these texts to the memory contests that marked the 1990s. In line with Koenen, Kraushaar, and Jarausch's observations, it privileges fiction as a particularly suitable means to represent and remember 1968 and to shape its significance. Literary texts respond to social, political, and historical realities; however, fiction is generally not burdened by any expectations to represent the truth. Therefore, it can construct possible, and not necessarily historically true, representations of the 1960s. This creative freedom can be understood as an opportunity to emphasize the significance of the past and to foreshadow the future in the utopian sense of the not-any-more and the not-yet.[81] With this freedom, fiction plays an important role in the public discourse and in the construction of a cultural memory of 1968 in the 1990s for the purposes of a joint future of East and West Germany within a European and global network.

German literature and 1968 as a historical, political, and social event enjoy a complex relationship. Many German authors played key roles and engaged in a critical dialogue with participants of the student movement. In literary history, the year 1968 marks the proclaimed death of literature. Hans Magnus Enzensberger, editor of the literary journal *Kursbuch*—one of the key publications of the 1960s student movement—wrote a widely read polemic "Gemeinplätze, die neueste Literatur betreffend," boldly asserting the death of literature due to its inability to serve a political function in the struggles of the 1960s.[82] Although his claim initiated a heated public debate, it did not really put an end to the publication of fiction. In fact, in the same volume of the *Kursbuch* numerous literary texts and even poetry were published, which attest to the survival skills and adaptability of fiction writing. The emerging debate over the function of literature led to a rejuvenated discussion about aesthetic questions and possible topics of literary texts. Thus, literary productivity and publication activities continued even after the proclaimed death of literature. From these discussions emerged the first representations of the events of 1968 in German literature. In the immediate aftermath of 1968, texts such as *Heißer Sommer*, *Kerbels Flucht*, and *Lenz* dealt with the disillusionment of the '68ers.[83] Thirty years later, some of the same authors engage again with 1968, this time in order to establish a cultural memory of 1968.

Shifts in the representations of the 1960s student movement during the last four decades reflect the discourse of 1968 and participate in the construction of a generation of 1968. These representations shift from a self-centered melancholy about a seemingly failed revolution to more distanced, critical, and self-critical attempts to contextualize the German movement in East and West within the European and global discourse on 1968. While many of the texts at the center of this study take a more critical stance toward the student movement, they also mirror and crystallize frameworks and debates that first were formed in the 1960s. Therefore, representations in the 1990s also appropriate and advance developments of themes prevalent in the 1960s.

This study focuses on literary texts that are not only representations of social, political, and historical events, but that are also narratives that resonate within the literary realm. I examine how novels dealing with 1968, in particular novels and trilogies by Ulrike Kolb, Irmtraud Morgner, Emine Sevgi Özdamar, Bernhard Schlink, Peter Schneider, and Uwe Timm, engage in a fruitful and playful dialogue with conventions of literary genre and literary historiography, thus challenging traditional conceptualizations of art and raising once more the question of the relation between the political and the aesthetic. A close reading of genre, narrative perspective, and the representation of the other excavates, in Walter Benjamin's sense, the different layers of memory. These literary texts serve as archives of memories and they create postmemories that in turn contribute to the cultural memory of 1968. Even more importantly they let the silences, created by processes of forgetting, resonate within the literary space. In addition, these texts represent a plurality of memories since complementary and contradictory memories coexist in the literary text. They create a cultural memory of 1968 that resists homogeneity and encourages the kinds of memory contests that mark the 1990s.

This study assembles novels and trilogies that, if read together, create a significant contribution to the creation of a cultural and transnational memory of 1968. In terms of text selection, my study does not even attempt to do justice to the wave of fiction that documents the 1990s' interest in 1968; the sheer number of novels makes their in-depth analysis in one study impossible. The novels interpreted in this study do not provide exhaustive, but rather exemplary insights into the construction of the cultural memory of 1968. They are connected by shared motives and narrative elements and each text also contributes a unique feature to advance this study's argument that the memory contests after 1989 slowly lead to the development of a transnational cultural memory of 1968. Novels by Peter Schneider and Uwe Timm are faced with the readers' expectations of enabling a privileged access to the past because of the authors' personal memories since both Peter Schneider and Uwe Timm were politically active in the late 1960s and 1970s. Ulrike Kolb belongs to the same generation and her texts can also be read against her biography as at least an eyewitness of the 1960s student movement. Irmtraud Morgner's *Salman* trilogy underscores the significance of 1968 for East Germany. A rereading of her trilogy within the context of the memory contests of the 1990s underscores the importance of the inclusion of memories of the GDR in the cultural memory of unified Germany. The trilogy reminds us of the many transnational connections among the activists that span the European continent. Finally, contributions by authors with a migrant background such as Emine Sevgi Özdamar add their labor of imagination to the representation of historical events and insert themselves and their experiences into a German memory that, in the 1990s and beyond, can no longer be understood in the same homogenous and monolithic terms as before even though the language to describe this process still falls short of the actual current developments.

The first part of this study places the emphasis on the entanglement of temporal structures within the German memory discourse and argues that the creation of a cultural memory of 1968 contributes to the unified memory of the two former German states. The second part expands the structural scope of the notion of a cultural memory through a focus on space. The consideration of space as a site for the exploration of exile, migration, origins, and identities expands the notion of a cultural memory of 1968 and leads to the construction of a transnational cultural memory of 1968. Within this literary memory discourse created by the novels included in this study, considerations of time and space overlap, intersect, and transcend the geographical and linguistic space of one nation. I propose to read the transnational memory of 1968 as a site of the numerous attempts in Germany after 1945 to acknowledge, integrate, and accept those of non-German descent or background, or those who were not regarded as being German. Through their representations in contemporary novels and the novels they contribute to this discourse, the construction of the cultural memory of 1968 as a transnational memory offers a diverse group of people the opportunity to participate in negotiations of the German past for the future.

Chapter 1, "Remember? 1968 in German Fiction," deconstructs the complex processes of remembering and forgetting 1968 after 1989. I argue that novels about the 1960s student movement contribute to the construction of a cultural memory that takes on important functions for the public discourse in the unified country. This cultural memory emphasizes the pivotal role of 1968 as one of the most important steps in order to come to terms with the Nazi past and the Holocaust. My analysis shows that literary texts published after 1989 acknowledge that, while the students' engagement with the past was sincere, it was not free of its own fallacies, fallacies that are retrospectively addressed and acknowledged.

I compare novels published in the 1990s with texts published in the 1970s, following the height of the movement. This discussion anchors the genre of 1968 memory novels in the broader context of the genre of memory texts and family stories and discusses their relevance for the aesthetics of novel writing in Germany at the turn of the millennium. Through a close reading, three related themes that contribute to the emergence of a genre of 1968 memory novels surface: the relation between cultural memory, history, and historiography, the significance of individual memory in its socially and culturally shaped configurations, and the discursive entanglement of literature and memory.

Chapter 2, "Forget it? 1968 in East Germany," counters the claim that isolates 1968 as a West German phenomenon that did not occur or leave an impact in East Germany. Newer research suggests that even though comparable historical events were missing, the influence of different European student movements found fertile ground in East Germany and influenced long-term political, social, and aesthetic developments in the GDR.[84] I read East German literature as a seismograph not only of East German dissent, but also of ruptures in West Germany and Europe during the 1960s. The seeming absence of massive student protests in the East does not mean that the West German, European, and global political and social unrest did not affect East Germany's youth, artists, and intellectuals.

A rereading of Irmtraud Morgner's *Salman* trilogy demonstrates that East German discourses of protest and opposition of the time were firmly embedded within the East German/West German and European context. The protests were politically motivated and had long-lasting effects, leading to a reconsideration of the founding myths of the GDR, of dominant literary and aesthetic traditions, and, ultimately, to the opening of the Berlin Wall. Thus, the *Salman* trilogy is indeed an important contribution to the cultural memory of 1968. It traces the 1960s protests from Paris to Prague via Berlin and foreshadows their transnational dimensions.

Chapter 3, "Transatlantic Encounters between Germany and the United States as Intercultural Exchange and Generational Conflict," interprets the discourse on 1968 as a transatlantic phenomenon. These representations enable the analysis of the real and imagined ties between Germany and the United States and their importance during the 1960s and 1970s and for the emerging cultural memory of 1968 in the 1990s. While the United States has long been an important topos in German literature, the country now gains new significance as the site of the encounter of (former) '68ers and Jewish survivors.

Furthermore, 1968 memory novels explore the changing significance of the United States for the three post-Second World War generations of Germans in the twentieth century and also the ambivalent feelings of the members of the student movement toward the country that, more than any other, signifies the idea of life, liberty, and the pursuit of happiness. Activists in the 1960s looked to the United States for inspiration for the political struggle, but detested the country's government because of its alleged imperialist and even fascist tendencies, represented by the involvement in the Vietnam War.

Chapter 4, "Transnational Memories: 1968 and Turkish-German Authors," analyzes the representation of 1968 by Turkish-German author Emine Sevgi Özdamar. The contributions to the discourse of 1968 by novels written in German by Turkish-German writers have so far been mostly overlooked. I argue that these texts create a transnational moment that not only advances our understanding of the 1960s but that also poses new theoretical and methodological challenges in light of the continuous globalization of literature and literary studies.

Encompassing and expanding the concept of identity, transnationalism points to the importance of border crossing and cross-border-interaction while questioning the narrative of the nation-state. Özdamar's trilogy, in particular the third novel *Seltsame Sterne starren zur Erde*, challenges the attempt to homogenize the cultural memory of 1968 at the expense of those who have a hyphenated identity. Instead, the first-person narrator inserts herself and her Turkish background into this discourse and actively negotiates her identity between East and West Berlin and Turkey.

As this study contends, 1968 is not an isolated national event but is marked by worldwide occurrences of unrest, rebellion, and civil disobedience. 1968 connects individuals, groups, and discourses not on a national or official level but rather through channels that undercut, subvert, and contradict official policies and politics as represented by nation-states and their elected representatives. As such, I examine 1968 and its representations in the literary discourse in Germany as a transnational phenomenon and as a contribution to the larger discourse on globalization by taking a close look at the construction of a cultural memory of 1968 as a transnational memory. Intersecting transnationalism with processes of memory construction emphasizes this study's anchor in time and space. Through the analysis of origins, locations, and destinations, and the analysis of border crossing and travel, space intersects with the moment of 1968 and its layers of memories and postmemories. These intersections constitute the palimpsest of 1968 that the 1968 memory novels construct and analyze at the same time.

Notes

1. Walter Benjamin, "Der Erzähler," in *Gesammelte Schriften*. II.2., ed. Rolf Tiedemann and Hermann Schweppenhäuser (Frankfurt a.M.: Suhrkamp, 1977): 438–465, 443. "The storyteller takes what he tells from experience—his own or that reported by

others. And he in turn makes it the experience of those who are listening to his tale." Walter Benjamin, "The Storyteller," in *Selected Writings*, ed. Michael W. Jennings and Howard Eiland, trans. Edmund Jephcott, Howard Eiland, and others (Cambridge, London: The Belknap Press of Harvard University Press, 2002): 143–166, 146.
2. Wladimir Kaminer, *Schönhauser Allee* (München: Manhattan, 2001).
3. Ibid.: 30. Hermann Kinder, *Der Schleiftrog* (Zürich: Diogenes, 1977): 206.
4. Peter de Lorent, *Die Hexenjagd* (Köln: Weltkreis, 1987). The novel describes the effects of the 1972 Decree against Radicals on a young teacher and led to a lawsuit that de Lorent won. The other title alludes to Peter Schneider's publication *…schon bist Du ein Verfassungsfeind* (Berlin: Rotbuch Verlag, 1975) with the same topic.
5. Kaminer, *Schönhauser Allee*: 30
6. This study follows the convention of using "1968" as the discursive label for the events comprising the German student movement even though others point to the fact that the label 1968 does not really capture the German student movement: e.g., Peter Schneider: "Ich finde die Bezeichnung '68er-Bewegung' eigentlich falsch. Sie trifft zu für die europäische Bewegung, für Rom, Paris, nicht für Berlin. In meinen Augen hat die Studentenbewegung vom 2. Juni 1967 bis zum Attentat auf Dutschke, Ostern 68, gedauert. Der eigentliche Aufbruch hat 67 stattgefunden, die Ansätze liegen noch früher" (I disagree with the name 68-movement. This is only true for the European movements in Rome and Paris, but not Berlin. The German movement lasted from June 2, 1967 to the attack on Dutschke, Easter 1968). Quoted in Uwe Prell and Lothar Wilker, ed., *Die Freie Universität Berlin 1948–1968–1988. Ansichten und Einsichten* (Berlin: Berlin Verlag, 1989): 188.
7. Hodenberg and Siegfried conclude that the 1960s can only be understood from a long-term perspective in which the years 1967–1969 only concentrated and put into focus what had been going on in society throughout the long range of the student movement from the end of the 1950s to the late 1970s. Christina von Hodenberg and Detlef Siegfried, ed., *Wo "1968" liegt. Reform und Revolte in der Geschichte der Bundesrepublik* (Göttingen: Vandenhoeck & Ruprecht, 2006).
8. These events include the establishment of a central prosecutor's office in Ludwigsburg, the media coverage of the Eichmann trial in Jerusalem as well as other trials in Germany, the debate about extending the deadline for persecutions of Nazi crimes in the Bundestag, and the publication of fiction and a growing number of television documentaries and movies that dealt with the question of guilt and responsibility. For a more detailed analysis of this history, cf. Peter Reichel, *Vergangenheitsbewältigung in Deutschland. Die Auseinandersetzung mit der NS-Diktatur von 1945 bis heute* (München: Beck, 2001) and Hans Kundnani. *Utopia or Auschwitz. Germany's 1968 Generation and the Holocaust* (New York: Columbia University Press, 2009).
9. Numerous public debates (e.g., the so-called historians' quarrel in the 1980s, the publication of Daniel Jonah Goldhagen's study *Hitler's Willing Executioners: Ordinary Germans and the Holocaust* (New York: Knopf, 1996), and Martin Walser's acceptance speech after having been awarded the peace prize of the German Book Trade in 1998) document the renewed attempts to come to terms with the Nazi past. A series of articles in *Die Zeit* in the fall of 2003 demonstrates how the link between 1968 and the Holocaust was brought to the forefront. It is particularly noteworthy

that all contributors to this series use literary texts in order to illustrate their arguments of how approaches to the Nazi past are currently shifting: Achatz Müller, "Volk der Täter, Volk der Opfer," *Die Zeit* 44, 23 October 2003: 35; Bernd Ulrich, "Alle Deutschen werden Brüder," *Die Zeit* 45, 30 October 2003: 46; Nicolas Berg, "Eine deutsche Sehnsucht," *Die Zeit* 46, 6 November 2003: 38; Christian Staas, "Verteidigung der Gegenwart," *Die Zeit* 48, 20 November 2003: 38.

10. For a comparative analysis of these two events from a historical perspective, see Konrad Jarausch's essay "1968 and 1989: Caesuras, Comparisons, and Connections," in *1968: A World Transformed*, ed. Carole Fink, Philipp Gassert, and Detlef Junker (Cambridge: Cambridge University Press, 1998): 461–477.

11. Philipp Gassert and Martin Klimke, "1968: Memories and Legacies of a Global Revolt," *Bulletin of the German Historical Institute* Supplement 6 (2009): 5–24.

12. Ibid.: 7.

13. The volume *Transnational Moments of Change. Europe 1945, 1968, 1989*, ed. Gerd-Rainer Horn and Padraic Kenney (Lanham: Rowman and Littlefield, 2003) presents several essays that engage with a transnational methodology in order to analyze moments of change in European history. Another recent volume, *Memories of 1968: International Perspectives*, ed. Ingo Cornils and Sarah Waters (Oxford: Lang, 2010), engages the intersections between national boundaries and processes of remembering that transcend and transform these boundaries.

14. Martin Klimke, "Revisiting the Revolution: 1968 in Transnational Cultural Memory," in *Memories of 1968. International Perspectives*, ed. Ingo Cornils and Sarah Waters (Oxford: Lang, 2010): 25–48.

15. E.g., the revelation that Karl-Heinz Kurras, the West-Berlin policeman who shot and killed Benno Ohnesorg in June 1967, was a member of the SED and a Stasi spy, stirred new controversy over the interpretation of the 1960s student movement within the Cold War constellation of East and West Germany. Cf. Götz Aly, "Wir alle haben uns geirrt," *Die Zeit*, 28 May 2009; Josef Joffe, "Kurraskapaden," *Die Zeit*, 28 May 2009; and Bernd Ulrich, "Der 68-er-Komplex," *Die Zeit*, 28 May 2009.

16. Robert Allertz, *Die RAF und das MfS. Fakten und Fiktionen* (Berlin: edition ost, 2008).

17. Elizabeth Pfeifer argues that "the unresolved questions, the heated debates, and the lingering wounds of 1968 in essence created a discursive commemoration through contestation which kept 1968 alive in political culture." "1968 in German Political Culture, 1967–1993: From Experience to Myth," PhD diss. University of North Carolina, Chapel Hill, 1997: 17.

18. Compare the following select publications marking the tenth and twentieth anniversary of the student movement: Martin W. Lüdke, ed., *Literatur und Studentenbewegung. Eine Zwischenbilanz* (Opladen: Westdeutscher Verlag, 1977); Peter Mosler, *Was wir wollten, was wir wurden. Studentenrevolte, zehn Jahre danach* (Reinbek: Rowohlt, 1977); Frank Wolff and Eberhard Windaus, eds., *Studentenbewegung 1967–69. Protokolle und Materialien* (Frankfurt a.M.: Verlag Roter Stern, 1977); Rainer Bieling, *Die Tränen der Revolution. Die 68er zwanzig Jahre danach* (Berlin: Siedler, 1988); Daniel Cohn-Bendit and Reinhard Mohr, *1968. Die letzte Revolution, die noch nichts vom Ozonloch wußte* (Berlin: Wagenbach, 1988); Tobias Mündemann, *Die 68er … und was aus ihnen geworden ist* (München: W. Heyne Verlag, 1988); Karl

A. Otto, ed., *APO. Außerparlamentarische Opposition in Quellen und Dokumenten (1960–1970)* (Köln: Pahl-Rugenstein, 1989).
19. "Der lange Marsch durch die Institutionen" alludes to the Long March which allowed Mao to consolidate his power in China in 1934/35. The expression was first used by Rudi Dutschke in 1967 in order to unify and broaden the scope of the protests which were primarily carried by the students until then. Later, some used the phrase to describe the students' alleged attempts to infiltrate and undermine society as educators, journalists, and politicians. The election of a red-green coalition was seen as the ultimate success of this strategy. Others use the term in order to show how ideas that were crystallized by the 1960s student movement entered the mainstream of society, e.g., feminism and the ecological movement.
20. Compare the transcript of the session of the German parliament on 17 January 2001 (Deutscher Bundestag, Plenarprotokoll 14/142, Berlin, Mittwoch, den 17. Januar 2001) which includes the questioning of Joschka Fischer with regards to a potential meeting between him and the terrorist Carlos. Attempts to denounce Fischer are countered by, e.g., Paul Berman's *Power and the Idealists. Or, The Passion of Joschka Fischer* (Berkeley: Soft Skull Press, 2005). In Berman's reading, the young Fischer, the Baader-Meinhof Gang, and the revolutionary cells were merely the rancid afterbirth of the street protests. The student movement itself, he writes persuasively, grew into a vibrant European anti-totalitarian tradition. This conflict, like many others that constitute the discourse of 1968 (e.g. the controversy surrounding Felix Ensslin, son of former RAF member Gudrun Ensslin), entails a gender conflict and can be analyzed from a gender/feminist perspective. After all, it was journalist Bettina Röhl, Ulrike Meinhof's daughter, who publicized the photos that show Fischer as a young militant apparently throwing stones at the police in Frankfurt during the 1970s. Her attempt to denounce the 1960s and 1970s can be read as the (belated) rebellion by members of the third generation against their parents, the '68ers. This is framed as yet another family conflict that takes on political implications. Traditionally, these conflicts were represented as father-son conflicts, however, ever since the 1960s and 1970s, mother-daughter relationships have come under increased scrutiny. This scrutiny often reinforces the image of the ideal mother as one that sacrifices herself for her children. While this study does not employ an overarching feminist approach, gender serves as a critical category whenever appropriate. This focus on gender reveals a much more nuanced image of the accomplishments as well as the failures of the 1960s student movement.
21. Willi Winkler describes the RAF as the direct and logical continuation of the student movement in *Die Geschichte der RAF* (Berlin: Rowohlt, 2007). Sara Hakemi traces a similar development in her study *Anschlag und Spektakel. Flugblätter der Kommune I, Erklärungen von Ensslin/Bader und der frühen RAF* (Bochum: Posth Verlag, 2008). See also Susanne Kailitz, *Von den Worten zu den Waffen? Frankfurter Schule, Studentenbewegung, RAF und die Gewaltfrage* (Wiesbaden: VS Verlag für Sozialwissenschaften, 2007). Within the field of literary criticism, Ingo Cornils and Monika Shafi are the notable and important exceptions to this trend that seems to support attempts to silence, and at times even criminalize, the German student movement at all levels.
22. Peter Schneider, "Rächer wollen sie sein," *Die Zeit* 11, 8 March 2007: 11.

23. See Geoff Eley's comments about this phenomenon at his luncheon address at the annual meeting of the German Studies Association, 4 October 2008 in St. Paul, Minnesota: "Telling Stories about Sixty-Eight: Troublemaking, Political Passions, and Enabling Democracy," *German Studies Association Newsletter* XXXIII.2 (Winter 2008/09): 39–50.
24. See the biographies and autobiographies of Inga Buhmann, Daniel Cohn-Bendit, Rudi Dutschke, Ulrich Enzensberger, Birgit Hogefeld, Dieter Kunzelmann, Till Meyer, Peter Mosler, Richard David Precht, Astrid Proll, and Margrit Schiller. For on overview of fictional representations, see chapter 1.
25. Already in 1988, Sylvia Bovenschen commented critically on the discourse and refers to it as "Erinnerungsakrobatik" (memory acrobatics): "Wir Achtundsechziger erinnern uns an 68. […] Es handelt sich um ein Ereignis in unserer Biographie, das zum historischen Datum zu werden scheint. Es handelt sich um ein historisches Datum, in das unsere Biographie, unsere biographische Ereignisgeschichte geflochten ist. […] Je nachdem, wie sich die öffentliche Meinung zu diesem Datum verhält, kann es unter der Hand zu einem Makel oder zu einem Ruhmesblatt auch unserer eigenen einzelnen Existenz werden. […] Wir sind die Generation, die ihr Erbe selber verschlingt, wir versuchen, alle Beurteilungsvarianten arbeitsteilig selber zu liefern, um den Spielraum für Außeninterpretationen klein zu halten. Erst haben einige das Ereignis romantisiert und als sie damit allen anderen auf die Nerven gingen, haben andere es bejammert, als niemand mehr das Gejammer ertragen konnte, haben wieder andere es denunziert. Im Moment sind wir in der Phase, ich gehöre dazu, der Selbstironisierung. Eine weitere, mehr oder weniger langweilige Methode, das Ereignis zu bewachen" (We '68ers remember 1968. The event in our biography changes into a historical date. It can turn into a flaw or an accomplishment in our biography, depending on public opinion. We are the generation who devours our own heritage by attempting to provide every possible interpretation of the event ourselves. First we romanticized, then we complained, and then we denounced the event. Currently, we are in a phase of self-irony, another more or less boring method to guard the event). Interview available at Glasnost, an archive of alternative news sources <http://www.glasnost.de/hist/apo/apo886.html.> (accessed 7 July 2009).
26. Klaus Harprecht points to a third group, namely those who experienced the 1960s as students and who are now part of the "establishment" they fought against. Nevertheless, they decorate their homes with life-size photos of Fidel Castro or the exclusive Berlin China Club with a massive portrait of Mao: "Freilich drängt sich die Frage auf, ob die Gründer des sündhaft teuren Etablissements und die handverlesenen Mitglieder in ihren Studententagen einst selbst mit Mao-Transparenten wie die Besessenen durch die Gassen hopsten, das rote Büchlein der Revolution schwenkend, und ob sie in den Zeiten der lärmenden Hysterie davon träumten, in Kuba oder Nicaragua Zuckerrohr zu schneiden, der United Fruit Company, dem US-Imperialismus und der CIA mit der roten Machete auf den Leib zu rücken" (The question arises whether the founders and members of the exclusive private club in their student days participated in the street protests of the 1960s with the red book in hands, dreaming to join the farmers in Cuba and Nicaragua in order to threaten U.S. imperialism with the red machete). Klaus Harprecht, "Große Vorsitzende, grell

geschminkt. Warum Che Guevara, Mao Tse-tung und Fidel Castro im Westen noch immer wie Götzen verehrt werden," *Die Zeit* 39, 21 September 2006: 22.
27. E.g., the most recent autobiographical accounts by Peter Schneider, *Rebellion und Wahn. Mein '68* (Köln: Kiepenheuer & Witsch, 2008) and Götz Aly, *Unser Kampf. 1968—ein irritierter Blick zurück* (Frankfurt a.M.: S. Fischer, 2008).
28. Cf. the contributions by Jochen Bölsche, Ulrich Greiner, and Josef Joffe in 2001 when the public discourse focused on the personal conduct of its elected officials in the past, in particular on Joschka Fischer, but also Jürgen Trittin: "Der mit vergilbten Zitaten geführte Streit über die Staatsfeinde von einst, die sich heute als Staatsmänner präsentieren, hat den Deutschen plötzlich und unerwartet eine dritte große Debatte über die Bewältigung ihrer Vergangenheit beschert. Diesmal geht es nicht um die Nazi- oder die Stasi-Zeit, sondern, delikaterweise, um die Vergangenheit jener, die sich vor einem Dritteljahrhundert selbst als Antifaschisten und teils als Kommunisten verstanden und die Generation ihrer Eltern pauschal mit einem 'Nazi-Kontinuitätsverdacht' [Fischer] überzogen haben" (The debate centered around old arguments about those who were once considered to be enemies of the state and who now present themselves as statesmen. This discourse initiated a third debate about the German past. However, this time it is neither the Nazi nor the Stasi past that is at stake, but the past of those who understood themselves as antifascists and, at least in part, as communists and who accused their parents of continued involvement with fascism even after the end of the Third Reich). Jochen Bölsche, "Die verlorene Ehre der Apo," *Der Spiegel* 5, 29 January 2001: 68–85. Similarly Joffe: "Es läuft das Drama 'Dritte Vergangenheitsbewältigung'. […] Aber nicht ums Aufrechnen geht es, den billigsten rhetorischen Trick, sondern um die Inszenierung postmoderner Politik. […] Doch wäre dieser Bissen nicht so appetitlich angerichtet ohne die Große Regieanweisung postideologischer Politik. Und die besagt, um einen verqueren Slogan der 68er-Generation aufzugreifen, dass das Persönliche tatsächlich zum Politischen geworden ist. Die Biographie eines jeglichen Politikers lauert als Anklageschrift und Drehbuch im Untergrund. […] Wir leben in einer Welt, in der Jenny Elvers und Boris Becker die Quote machen, in der die Inszenierung das Instrument, das Mediale der eigentliche Machtkampf ist" (They give the play "Third Coming to Terms with the Past." This play is a staging of postmodern and post ideological politics. The personal is indeed the political. The biography of each politician can be scrutinized and is available for attack. In a world of reality TV, it is the quota of the staging that has the real power). Josef Joffe, "Politik im Container," *Die Zeit* 5, 25 January 2001. Also Ulrich Greiner, "Wahrheit ist die beste Verteidigung. Joschka Fischer, die Achtundsechziger und die dritte deutsche Vergangenheitsbewältigung," *Die Zeit* 3, 11 January 2001.
29. Stuart Taberner, "Introduction: German Literature in the Age of Globalisation," in *German Literature in the Age of Globalisation*, ed. Stuart Taberner (Birmingham: Birmingham University Press, 2004): 1–24, 6.
30. The '68ers were, however, by no means the first ones to "deal" with the Holocaust. In "Wende um 360 Grad? Nationalsozialismus und Judenvernichtung in der 'zweiten Gründungsphase' der Bundesrepublik," in *Wo "1968" liegt. Reform und Revolte in der Geschichte der Bundesrepublik,* ed. Christina von Hodenberg and Detlef Siegfried (Göttingen: Vandenhoeck & Ruprecht, 2006): 15-47, Wilfried Mausbach offers a

careful and in-depth analysis of the different stages of the German engagement with the past which can be traced back to the generation of 1945. Mausbach concludes that while the '68ers contributed to the "Vergangenheitsbewältigung" they also decelerated it by radicalizing it to the point that perpetrators and victims became anonymous and seemingly merged.

31. William Collins Donahue discusses teaching the 1960s student movement at American colleges and universities. He argues that those teaching it often have a specific political investment and suggests to not conceal this investment, and instead to use it as a teachable moment. "Elusive '68: The Challenge to Pedagogy," *Die Unterrichtspraxis/Teaching German* 41.2 (Fall 2008): 113–123.
32. Ingrid Gilcher-Holtey, *Die 68er Bewegung: Deutschland, Westeuropa, USA* (München: Beck, 2001).
33. Cf. Gerard J. DeGroot, ed., *Student Protest: The Sixties and After* (London, New York: Longman, 1998): X.
34. Cf. Albrecht von Lucke, *68 oder ein neues Biedermeier. Der Kampf um die Deutungsmacht* (Berlin: Wagenbach, 2008) for a (polemical) overview of the viewpoints that shape the discourse.
35. Cf. Edgar Wolfrum's analysis in which he interprets the ongoing interest in '1968' as a political fight in order to shape history for current and future purposes. "1968" in der gegenwärtigen deutschen Geschichtspolitik," *Aus Politik und Zeitgeschichte (B 22-23/2001)* <http://www.bpb.de/apuz/26243/1968-in-der-gegenwaertigen-deutschen-geschichtspolitik> (accessed 26 June 2012).
36. Research is facilitated by the publication of guides to archives, e.g., Thomas P. Becker and Ute Schröder, ed., *Die Studentenproteste der 60er Jahre. Archivführer-Chronik-Bibliographie* (Köln: Böhlau, 2000); and Philipp Gassert and Pavel A. Richter, *1968 in West Germany: A Guide to Resources and Literature of the Extra-Parliamentarian Opposition (*Washington DC: German Historical Institute, 1998).
37. Gerard. J. DeGroot, *The Sixties Unplugged. A Kaleidoscopic History of a Disorderly Decade* (Cambridge: Harvard University Press, 2008): 3.
38. Konrad Jarausch, *After Hitler. Recivilizing Germans, 1945–1995* (Oxford: Oxford University Press, 2006): 158.
39. Cf. Todd Gitlin, T*he Whole World is Watching: Mass Media in the Making and Unmaking of the New Left* (Berkeley: University of California Press, 1980).
40. Kathrin Fahlenbrach, *Protest-Inszenierungen. Visuelle Kommunikation und kollektive Identitäten in Protestbewegungen* (Wiesbaden: Westdeutscher Verlag, 2002).
41. Cf. Ullrich Fichtner, Thomas Kleine-Brockhoff, Roland Kirbach, Nils Minkmar, and Stefan Willeke, "'Springer will Rot-Grün stürzen.' Ein Medienkonzern entdeckt sein Feindbild wieder: Die 68er," *Die Zeit* 6, 1 February 2001.
42. Sabine von Dirke, *"All Power to the Imagination!" The West German Counterculture from the Student Movement to the Greens* (Lincoln: University of Nebraska Press, 1997).
43. Roman Luckscheiter, *Der postmoderne Impuls: Die Krise der Literatur um 1968 und ihre Überwindung* (Berlin: Duncker & Humblot, 2001).
44. For a general overview of the notion of countercultural movements see Steve Giles and Maike Oergel, ed., *Counter-Cultures in Germany and Central Europe. From Sturm and Drang to Baader-Meinhof* (Oxford: Lang, 2003). The volume Between

Marx and Coca-Cola: Youth Cultures in Changing European Societies, 1960–1980, edited by Axel Schildt and Detlef Siegfried (Oxford: Oxford University Press, 2005), examines the emergence of youth cultures in the 1960s and 1970s and their impact.

45. Wolfgang Kraushaar, *1968 als Mythos, Chiffre und Zäsur* (Hamburg: Hamburger Edition, 2000).
46. Matthias Frese et al., ed., *Demokratisierung und gesellschaftlicher Aufbruch. Die sechziger Jahre als Wendezeit der Bundesrepublik* (Paderborn: Ferdinand Schöningh, 2003).
47. Clemens Albrecht, Guenter C. Behrmann, Michael Bock, Harald Homann, and Friedrich H. Tenbruck, *Die intellektuelle Gründung der Bundesrepublik. Eine Wirkungsgeschichte der Frankfurter Schule.* (Frankfurt a.M.: Campus, 1999): 20.
48. Peter Reichel, *Vergangenheitsbewältigung in Deutschland*: 125.
49. Ibid.
50. The following studies focus on the global scope of 1968: Carole Fink, Philipp Gassert, and Detlef Junker, ed., *1968: A World Transformed* (Cambridge: Cambridge University Press, 1998); George Katsiaficas, *The Imagination of the New Left: A Global Analysis of 1968* (Boston: South End Press, 1987); and Jeremi Suri, *Power and Protest: Global Revolution and the Power of Détente* (Cambridge: Harvard University Press, 2003). There are several comparative studies with a more specific focus, e.g., a transatlantic comparison: Belinda Davis, Wilfried Mausbach, Martin Klimke, and Carla MacDougall, ed., *Changing the World, Changing Oneself: Political Protest and Collective Identities in 1960s/70s West Germany and the U.S.* (New York: Berghahn, 2010); Martin Klimke, *The Other Alliance: Student Protest in West Germany and the United States in the Global Sixties* (Princeton: Princeton University Press, 2010); Arthur Marwick, *The 1960s. Cultural Revolution in Britain, France, Italy, and the United States, 1958–1974* (Oxford: Oxford University Press, 1998); and Michael A. Schmidtke, *Der Aufbruch der jungen Intelligenz. Die 68er Jahre in der Bundesrepublik und den USA* (Frankfurt a.M.: Campus, 2003). Some study violence and terrorism in a comparative fashion, e.g., Jeremy Varon, *Bringing the War Home: The Weather Underground, the Red Army Faction, and Revolutionary Violence in the 1960s and 1970s* (Berkeley: University of California Press, 2004). Some studies focus on Europe, e.g., Schildt and Siegfried, *Between Marx and Coca-Cola*; and Martin Klimke and Joachim Scharloth, ed., *1968 in Europe: A History of Protest and Activism, 1956–1977* (New York: Berghahn, 2008). Some focus on specific cultural influences and transfers, e.g., Sebastian Gehrig, Barbara Mittler, and Felix Wemheuer, ed., *Kulturrevolution als Vorbild? Maoismen im deutschsprachigen Raum* (Frankfurt a.M.: Lang, 2008).
51. Timothy Brown argues that "the global finds expression in the local in a particularly profound way in divided Germany." In: "1968 East and West: Divided Germany as a Case Study in Transnational History," *The American Historical Review* 114.1 (2009): 69–96, 70.
52. Konrad Jarausch, *After Hitler*: 157.
53. Ibid.
54. Cf. DeGroot, *The Sixties Unplugged*.
55. "Beim Thema 1968 wird, wie bei jedem anderen historischen Ereignis auch, die Frage nach der Erzählerrolle, ihrer Angemessenheit oder auch Unangemessenheit, aufgeworfen. Geschichte schreiben heißt, ungeachtet aller legitimen Kritik an der

bloß narrativ ausgerichteten Optik vieler Historiker, vor allem zu erzählen. Insofern besteht die vorentscheidende Frage darin, welche Rolle ein Autor als Erzähler einnimmt und welche Qualität ihr im Hinblick auf die Erzählkunst beigemessen werden kann" (The topic 1968 like any other historical event poses the question of the role of the narrator, its appropriateness and inappropriateness. Despite all legitimate criticism of the historian who only focuses on the narrative, to write history means to tell a story. Hence, one of the first questions is which role the author as narrator plays and how this role shapes the quality of the narration). Kraushaar, *1968 als Mythos, Chiffre und Zäsur*: 12.

56. "Vielleicht besitzt nur ein Schriftsteller oder Künstler die Freiheit, die notwendig ist, seine Erinnerungen, in denen die Imagination offenbar lebendig geblieben ist, vor dem immer aufdringlicher werdenden Zugriff der Historisierung zu schützen" (Perhaps only a writer or artist possesses the necessary freedom to protect their memories which ensure a vivid imagination against the ever more demanding historicization of the past). Kraushaar, *1968 als Mythos, Chiffre und Zäsur*. 52.

57. Kraushaar, Wolfgang, *Achtundsechzig. Eine Bilanz* (Berlin: Propyläen, 2008): 49.

58. "Sich zum Historiker der eigenen Lebensgeschichte zu machen, wenn man selbst Akteur gewesen ist, ist ein zweifelhaftes, wenn nicht unmögliches Unternehmen. Das vorliegende Buch ist denn auch keine wissenschaftliche Darstellung, sondern ein aus Texten, Szenen, Berichten und Erinnerungen gemischtes Bild jenes eigentümlichen roten Jahrzehnts" (To become the historian of one's life, especially after having been a political activist, is a doubtful, if not impossible undertaking. The present book is not an academic treatment but an image compiled from texts, scenes, reports, and memories from this strange red decade). Gerd Koenen, *Das rote Jahrzehnt. Unsere kleine deutsche Kulturrevolution 1967–77* (Köln: Kiepenheuer & Witsch, 2001): 9.

59. "Von allen Erklärungsnotständen abgesehen, in die man sich als Don Quichotte seiner alten, ex-revolutionären Adelstitel bringt – die Epopöe des roten Jahrzehnts läßt sich, wie jene des edlen Ritters, weithin nur aus einer Position der Anteil nehmenden Ironie noch erzählen" (Disregarding all pressures stemming from being the Don Quixote of ex-revolutionaries, the epopee of the red decade can only be narrated from the perspective of empathic irony). Koenen, *Das rote Jahrzehnt. Unsere kleine deutsche Kulturrevolution 1967–77*: 500.

60. Konrad Jarausch and Michael Geyer, *Shattered Past. Reconstructing German Histories* (Princeton: Princeton University Press, 2002): 30.

61. Ibid.: 32–33.

62. Ibid.: 357–358.

63. Stephen Brockmann, *Literature and German Reunification* (Cambridge: Cambridge University Press, 1999).

64. Friederike Eigler, *Gedächtnis und Geschichte in Generationenromanen seit der Wende* (Berlin: Erich Schmidt, 2005).

65. Erin McGlothlin, *Second-Generation Holocaust Literature. Legacies of Survival and Perpetration* (Rochester, NY: Camden House, 2006).

66. Caroline Schaumann, *Memory Matters. Generational Responses to Germany's Nazi Past in Recent Women's Literature* (Berlin: Walter de Gruyter, 2008).

67. Jarausch and Geyer, *Shattered Past*: 12.

68. Ibid.: 356–357.
69. Martin Huber, *Politisierung der Literatur–Ästhetisierung der Politik* (Bern: Lang, 1992).
70. Alois Prinz, *Der poetische Mensch im Schatten der Utopie. Zur politisch-weltanschaulichen Idee der 68'er Studentenbewegung und deren Auswirkung auf die Literatur* (Würzburg: Königshausen & Neumann, 1990).
71. Ingo Cornils, "Successful Failure? The Impact of the German Student Movement on the Federal Republic of Germany," in *Recasting German Identity. Culture, Politics, and Literature in the Berlin Republic*, ed. Stuart Taberner and Frank Finlay (Rochester, NY: Camden House, 2002): 106–122.
72. Ingo Cornils, "Long Memories: The German Student Movement in Recent Fiction," *German Life and Letters* 56.1 (2003): 89–101.
73. Ingo Cornils, "Writing the Revolution: the Literary Representation of the German Student Movement as Counter-Culture," in *Counter-Cultures in Germany and Central Europe*, ed. Steve Giles and Maike Oergel (Bern: Lang, 2003): 295–314.
74. See Harald Weinrich, *Lethe. Kunst und Kritik des Vergessens* (München: Beck, 1997) for an extensive discussion of forgetting, including Friedrich Nietzsche as one of the best-known proponents of forgetting.
75. See Umberto Eco, "An *Art Oblivionalis*? Forget It!" *Publication of the Modern Language Association of America* 103 (1988): 254–261.
76. Maurice Halbwachs, *The Collective Memory*, trans. Francis J. Ditter, Jr. and Vida Yazdi Ditter (New York: Harper & Row, 1980).
77. Walter Benjamin, "Ausgraben und Erinnern," in *Gesammelte Schriften* IV.1, ed. Tillman Rexroth (Frankfurt a.M.: Suhrkamp, 1972): 400f. His contemporary Sigmund Freud also employs the metaphor of the archeologist when talking about the task of remembering. He describes the work of the analyst as follows: "Seine Arbeit der Konstruktion oder, wenn man es so lieber hört, der Rekonstruktion, zeigt eine weitgehende Übereinstimmung mit der des Archäologen, der eine zerstörte und verschüttete Wohnstätte oder ein Bauwerk der Vergangenheit ausgräbt" (When the patient attempts to remember the forgotten or repressed, it is the task of the analyst to reconstruct the forgotten or repressed event out of the traces that the event left). "Konstruktionen in der Analyse," in *Gesammelte Werke 16* (Frankfurt a.M.: S. Fischer, 1950): 41–56, 45. Both Benjamin's cultural and Freud's psychoanalytical approaches point to the fact that personal memories depend upon those who participate in the process of remembering and on the locations and layers where the memories, or traces thereof, are stored and preserved.
78. Aleida and Jan Assmann, "Das Gestern im Heute. Medien und soziales Gedächtnis," *Studienbegleitbrief zur Studieneinheit 11 des Funkkollegs Medien und Kommunikation* (Weinheim: Beltz, 1991); and Aleida Assmann, *Erinnerungsräume. Formen und Wandlungen des kulturellen Gedächtnisses* (München: Beck, 1999). The Assmanns' theory is very useful, yet it lacks a component to study the dynamic nature that is inherent in memory. Its fleeting, evolving, and contested nature cannot simply be contained by the Assmanns' rather static understanding of cultural memory as an archive that preserves. In addition to memory as an archive, current research explores memory as a site of negotiations and conflicts.

79. Marianne Hirsch, *Family Frames: Photography, Narrative, and Postmemory* (Cambridge: Harvard University Press, 1997). Since Hirsch develops the concept of postmemory in order to talk about survivors of the Holocaust and their children, I adapt and use the concept with the understanding that the trauma experienced by those persecuted by the Nazis and their children defies comparison with the perpetrators' experiences on the German side. The experiences by both of these groups constitute a shared yet ultimately separating and incompatible history. In consideration of James Young, who is reluctant to "apply individual psychoneurotic jargon to the memory of national groups … individuals cannot share another's memory any more than they can share another's cortex" [*The Texture of Memory: Holocaust Memorials and Meaning* (New Haven, London: Yale University Press, 1993): xi] I am cautious not to conflate individual psychological phenomenon onto imaginary collectives. However, as Harald Welzer in his important research on the passing on of memories and their construction within family histories shows, individual memories are indeed developed within and framed by a cultural context that leads to a shared cultural memory. Harald Welzer, Sabine Moller, and Karoline Tschuggnall, *"Opa war kein Nazi." Nationalsozialismus und Holocaust im Familiengedächtnis* (Frankfurt a.M.: S. Fischer, 2002).
80. Anne Fuchs, *Phantoms of War in Contemporary German Literature, Film and Discourse: The Politics of Memory* (New York: Palgrave Macmillan, 2008): 3.
81. Cf. Ernst Bloch, *Das Prinzip Hoffnung* (Frankfurt a.M.: Suhrkamp, [1938–1947] 1959).
82. Hans Magnus Enzensberger, "Gemeinplätze, die Neueste Literatur betreffend," *Kursbuch* 15 (1968): 187–197.
83. Peter Schneider, *Lenz* (Berlin: Rotbuch, 1973); Uwe Timm, *Heißer Sommer* (München: Bertelsmann, 1974); and Uwe Timm, *Kerbels Flucht* (München: Verlag Autoren-Edition, 1980).
84. Timothy Brown, "1968 East and West."

Chapter 1

Remember? 1968 in German Fiction

> Aufgearbeitet wäre die Vergangenheit erst dann,
> wenn die Ursachen des Vergangenen beseitigt wären.
> Theodor W. Adorno[1]

After 1989, 1968 memory novels intervene with the attempts to write a homogenizing history of unified Germany by remembering moments of protest and rebellion that challenged and disrupted, at least temporarily, the usual workings of society. These novels inaugurate more reflective spaces in order to remember 1968 and its impact on unified Germany, and they revisit the 1960s' discourse about the legacy of the Third Reich. These texts combine self-reflexivity and introspection with a moral and ethical obligation to remember and hence contribute to the culture of memory that shaped the 1990s in unified Germany.

The Discourse of the Holocaust

The discourse of the Holocaust consists of publications, conferences, political and legal interventions, films, art, architecture, museums, and exhibitions. This discourse documents the continuous engagement with the Third Reich, the Holocaust, and the Second World War after 1945. Those who participate in this discourse attempt to interpret and evaluate the historical events within ever evolving contexts. Additionally, since 1989 one can observe the trend to evaluate the way in which the legacy of the Third Reich has been dealt with since 1945. This is reflected in the title of the first major exhibit dealing with the Holocaust in Germany, *Holocaust. Der nationalsozialistische Völkermord und die Motive seiner Erinnerung* (The Holocaust. The National Socialist Genocide and the Motifs of its Memory), which indicates that the history and the historicization and memorialization of the Holocaust are all equally important.[2]

While debates about the Holocaust and its legacy continue, talking or not talking about the Holocaust in Germany is never an easy conversation or a simple silence. Utterances are always scrutinized with respect to their explicit and implicit meanings, and their interpretations are frequently informed by the positionalities of those who are speaking and listening.[3] Cultural, particularly literary, representations address these problems in a variety of ways. In *Fünfzig Jahre danach. Zur Nachgeschichte des Nationalsozialismus*, Birgit Erdle and Sigrid Weigel argue that the difference between perpetrators and victims manifests itself in the way silence is expressed within speech, often as a loud or eloquent silence.[4] Ernestine Schlant observes similar literary strategies in her monograph *The Language of Silence* and concludes that most West German fiction after 1945 attempts to silence memories in one way or the other.[5] Thus, she perpetuates the conclusions that the activists in the 1960s drew, namely that the parents' generation was not only collectively guilty of the Holocaust, but that this generation after 1945, also collectively concealed their guilt and responsibility by keeping silent about the Third Reich and their involvement in these events.

At first sight, the notion of collective guilt renders the suggestion obsolete that the Holocaust only happened because of Hitler and his supporters. Instead, the notion of a collective guilt holds everybody accountable who lived in Germany during the Third Reich. Ultimately, however, the notion of collective guilt creates a convenient myth that enables the individual to deflect personal responsibility and guilt and to hide in the collective. Furthermore, the students either did not hear or did not understand the silence about the Holocaust that resonated in the 1950s and early 1960s as a speaking silence. Numerous studies in recent years point to the fact that the 1950s, beginning with the immediate postwar period, was marked by attempts to talk about the Holocaust, even if these attempts did not follow the criteria of the appropriate way of talking about the Holocaust proposed by the student activists in the 1960s.

In stark contrast to assertions of a complete silence in Germany regarding the Third Reich and the Holocaust, the many attempts of coming to terms with the past ("Vergangenheitsbewältigung") since 1945 form complex relationships, trigger academic controversies, inspire aesthetic representations, and receive public attention. The term "Vergangenheitsbewältigung" can only be translated uncomfortably into English and can be understood in two ways. First it is used to describe and analyze what has happened in Germany since 1945 in order to deal with the Third Reich in an attempt to find closure and lay the past to rest. Second it also contains a normative meaning emphasizing the moral-ethical obligation to deal with the Third Reich, even if it creates discomfort for the individual and dissonance among the public.[6] In *Utopia or Auschwitz: Germany's 1968 Generation and the Holocaust*, Hans Kundnani reaches the conclusion that "the 1968 generation both intensified Germany's engagement with the Nazi past and drew a line under it."[7] In *Phantoms of War in Contemporary German Literature, Film and Discourse: The Politics of Memory*, Anne Fuchs juxtaposes the "old paradigm of 'Vergangenheitsbewältigung'" (overcoming the past) with the concept of "memory contests" that emphasizes a pluralistic memory culture that does not embrace a normative understanding of the past. Instead, it puts forth the idea that individuals and groups tell different and even competing stories of their pasts in order to forge their sense of identity.[8] In her discussion, it is not completely clear whether the paradigm of memory contests replaces the attempt of "Vergangenheitsbewältigung" or whether it simply describes and analyzes more adequately the contemporary discourse of the German past as marked by, at times fierce, memory contests. The notion of memory contests is useful for the interpretation of fiction since it does not charge the literary text with a normative approach to dealing with the Holocaust, which then often leads to a normative aesthetic of how to write about the Holocaust. In this sense, fiction gains a critical role within these memory contests as another means to challenge conventional approaches to history, identity, and the formation of cultural memory.

Fictional texts offer fertile grounds for memory contests. Embedded in a rich tradition that began with Plato, writers and their literary works are simultaneously confronted with accusations of fabricating only lies while, at the same time, they are threatened with expulsion from the community because of these potentially powerful and damaging lies. While the assertion of fabricating lies would render writers and their texts irrelevant, Plato nevertheless deems it necessary to expel them from the ideal polis. This contradiction confirms the persuasive power of fictional texts that extends beyond the realm of the aesthetic to all areas of life. The focus on memory contests supports the assumption that fiction acquires as equally important a status when it comes to constructing and preserving memories as any study in the field of history or any text for that matter. Beyond that, fiction outlines different plausible narratives that invite the play with complementary and even contradictory memories and mark the silences that cloud the discourse on the Holocaust.

In the second half of the twentieth century, the question of representation took on a new dimension with a focus on representability. After 1945, authors and critics challenged the ability of fiction to adequately represent human experiences. In light of the tremendous suffering brought by the Holocaust and the Second World War, fiction was charged with expectations of addressing the moral and ethical challenges individuals, artists, and society as a whole faced. Despite Adorno's verdict that "nach Auschwitz ein Gedicht zu schreiben, ist barbarisch" (to write a poem after Auschwitz is barbaric),[9] that was interpreted, or rather misinterpreted as Klaus Hofmann argues, as either the inability to write fiction after the Holocaust or as the ban to write after and/or about the Holocaust, a myriad of literary texts represent the Holocaust.[10] 1968 memory novels focus on the memories of the "Aufstand gegen die Nazi-Generation" (rebellion against the Nazi-generation)[11] which enables the reader to revisit the memories of the 1960s and the memories and postmemories of the Third Reich and its legacy.

1968 in German Fiction

A growing number of literary texts engages with the German student movement in the 1960s, a testimony to renewed interest in the era.[12] In contrast to the first wave of literary texts about the student movement, published already in the 1970s, the representation of 1968 in the 1990s changed, in particular in those texts written by former activists and participants.[13] Whereas the novels that appeared in the 1970s provide a seemingly unmediated and therefore apparently authentic insight into the experiences of the students, novels published after 1989 contribute to the construction of a cultural memory of the 1960s and of the generation of 1968. These contemporary representations shift from a self-centered melancholy about a seemingly failed revolution to a more critical and self-critical remembering and forgetting. While the first group of texts foreshadows the *New Subjectivity* of the 1970s, the latter takes a more reflective approach and firmly embeds the fictional narrative into the discourse on cultural memory.[14] While the texts published in the 1970s document the intergenerational struggle as a family conflict between parents and their children, texts from the 1990s also narrate the intragenerational struggle among the former activists and participants of the student movement who attempt to shape the significance of the movement according to their own, at times divergent, interpretations of the 1960s and 1970s. While the notion of generational conflict as a conflict between different generations is a common place, those writers who are former activists seem to propagate an intragenerational conflict as a conflict among those who define themselves or are defined as '68ers, a conflict that not only erupted already in 1968 and its aftermath, but one that erupts regularly at each anniversary, most recently in 2008 at the fortieth anniversary of 1968.[15]

Describing the literary scene in Germany in the 1990s, Jörg Magenau points to the proliferating and accelerating declarations of generations after 1989. Magenau explains this increase as a function of literary productivity that is understood as an act of self-expression and self-understanding.

> War vor 1989 eigentlich nur die Generation der Achtundsechziger bekannt, die damals allerdings noch schlicht 'Studentenbewegung' hieß, so wurden in den Neunzigern nacheinander die Neunundachtziger, die Achtundsiebziger, die Generation X, Y und Z, sowie die Generationen 'Ost', 'Berlin' und schließlich mit dem Titel des Bestsellers von Florian Illies, die *Generation Golf* aus der Taufe gehoben.[16]

I argue that the discursive shift from 1960s student movement to the generation of 1968 should not be understood as a departure from previous representations but rather as a productive and purposeful continuation and appropriation of the discourse of 1968. In the 1990s, texts by former '68ers are not so much interested in creating a story about the events, but rather in creating a memory of the generation in its multitude of meanings. Representing the memories of the 1960s as a generational experience guarantees the privileged status of the 1960s for the purposes of contemporary history and fiction writing because the discourse on generations defines and structures cultural trends and historical developments after 1989. Magenau points to a discursive shift that has important implications for the legacy of 1968: whereas the reference "1960s student movement" summarizes the experiences of those who participated in the events in 1967 and 1968 and its aftermath, the designation "generation of 1968" indicates the attempt in the 1990s to reinterpret the 1960s in order to define a group with collective experiences and substantial political, social, and cultural clout and to make a contribution to the construction of cultural memory in Germany.[17]

From Student Movement to the Generation of 1968: Generational Conflicts in German Novels from the 1970s and 1990s

Two authors, Peter Schneider and Uwe Timm—often considered representative members of the generation of 1968—both wrote novels in the immediate aftermath of the student movement, *Lenz* (1973) and *Heißer Sommer* (1974). Thirty years later, both also engage in (self-)reflective discussions of these events in their respective novels *Eduards Heimkehr* (1999) and *Rot* (2001). A comparative reading of all four texts highlights the differences in representation between the novels published in the 1970s and those published in the 1990s and emphasizes the representational shift from student movement to a generation of 1968. These representational shifts contribute to the construction of a cultural memory of 1968 that is less concerned with a working through the experiences the activists made during the 1960s and 1970s than with the construction and selection of memories for the purposes of remembering 1968 in unified Germany. Three issues will serve as the anchor points of this comparison: the narrative perspective, the representation of the other, and the embeddings of the texts in the tradition of literary history and historical discourse in general.

The comparative reading of the four novels, *Lenz*, *Heißer Sommer*, *Eduards Heimkehr* and *Rot*, sheds light on the generational memory that shapes the discourse on 1968. Whereas the student movement is often described as a youth movement carried out by young people addressing young people in order to change the status quo, the discourse on the generation of 1968 reveals aging memories of the formerly young generation that, in turn, is challenged by today's young generation. Instead of understanding a generation as a developmental stage that young people naturally pass through, the generation of 1968 is understood here as a generational cohort—that is a group of people whose experiences in their youth continue to unify them throughout their lives. Analyzing the discourse on 1968 from a generational perspective calls for the exploration of the relationship between culture and nature since the generational paradigm embodies both the fact that one is born within a specific generation in a particular location and the fact that a generation is culturally and socially determined.[18] This tension is reflected in the construction of the cultural memory of this generation as memories that are suspended between one's own experiences and postmemories, between the local and the global, and the inscription of self and other into a discourse that reshapes Germany and broadens the concept of German identity.

My approach utilizes the concept of the generation and furthers our understanding of it as both a descriptor of literary and historical processes and an analytical category. In the selected novels, German history after 1945 is rewritten as a history of generations whereby the second generation, the generation of 1968, is wedged between the first generation that lived through the Third Reich and the third generation that is currently shaping an increasingly global and globalized world. As these four novels reveal, the former activists persuasively present themselves as the generation that dealt with the Nazi past, pushed for democratization, and avoided the pitfalls of globalized and seemingly limitless capitalism. In the following, my reading presents a comparative reading of *Lenz* and *Heißer Sommer* followed by a comparative analysis of *Eduards Heimkehr* and *Rot*. In a final step I outline how the four novels read together support the attempt to move beyond the student movement in order to construct the cultural memory of a generation of 1968.

The Student Movement in *Lenz* and *Heißer Sommer*

Bestsellers at the time of their first publication, *Lenz* and *Heißer Sommer* subsequently found their place in literary history.[19] Karl-Heinrich Götze claims that these novels, when read together, shape the image of the 1960s student movement more than any other representation.[20] Their reception by literary critics in the 1970s and 1980s emphasizes the rupture between the tradition of canonical German literature and the aesthetic, theoretical, and political debates that were in part initiated by the 1960s student movement and that came to define it.[21] These debates focused on the nexus between writing and political activism, the feasibility of revolutionary change, and the question of how art and literature contribute to initiating and implementing this change. My analysis shifts focus and places *Lenz* and *Heißer Sommer* in the context of the cultural memory of the generation of 1968, a memory that emerged in the 1990s in conjunction with the publication of an increasing number of fictional texts dealing with the 1960s and 1970s. Rereading texts published in the 1970s through the vantage point of the 1990s reveals that already texts like *Lenz* and *Heißer Sommer* oscillate between creating narratives of the student movement and foreshadowing the formation of the generation of 1968 that serves as a basis for memory construction.

Timm's novel *Heißer Sommer* inscribes the memories of the 1960s student movement into the tradition of the Bildungsroman. The novel takes place in two of the urban centers of the movement in Germany, Munich and Hamburg. The narrator follows the main character Ullrich Krause, who is at a dead end in his studies. Krause experiments with the sexual freedom the 1960s bring and also with the various strands of left politics, including the German student organization SDS, a hippie commune, and the communist party. Realizing the false promises of the New Left in its various manifestations, Krause graduates and begins working as a teacher at a vocational school in order to support the working class. Whereas Krause seems to find his calling at the end of *Heißer Sommer*, Schneider's story *Lenz* debates whether it is possible to find individual happiness without changing society as a whole, or without at least working toward that change. With this focus, *Lenz* contributes to the fiction that is known in literary history as *New Subjectivity*. The novel introduces the main character Lenz awakening from a nightmare that leaves him staring angrily at a poster of Karl Marx above his bed, confronting the image with the question: "Were you ever happy?"[22] This opening indicates the main character's ambivalent feelings towards the waning student movement; it is not the quest for political change, but the search for a fulfilled, "happy" life that occupies Lenz. In the end, Lenz escapes from his aimless life in Berlin to Italy, joins the fight of the Italian left, and regains his sense of self. After being expelled from Italy due to his political activism, he decides to return to Berlin. Asked what he plans to do there, he answers: "Dableiben" (Stay).[23] While this ending has been interpreted as a positive outlook for the future, the open end does not reveal what Lenz will do next and whether he will be able to give his life some meaning.

Rereading these texts confirms the perception of the student movement as one carried out by young people enrolled at universities, mostly in the urban centers of Germany, who, dissatisfied with conventional politics, pushed for a liberalization and democratization of the Federal Republic. Both omniscient narrators in *Lenz* and *Heißer Sommer* remember the disillusionment of their protagonists in the aftermath of 1968 without any irony. The main characters are not so much interested in the political and societal implications of their experiences; rather, they focus on the exploration of their own feelings with respect to their immediate and personal environment in the aftermath of the 1960s student movement.

This narcissistic focus causes the problematic representation of and difficult engagement with the other. While it was one of the declared goals of the student movement to take into account the positions of those who were not part of mainstream society and to show solidarity with those who were oppressed and underprivileged, its participants ultimately failed to realize this goal. This is exemplified in their problematic relationships with their parents, in the failure to account for and to live with the diversity within the movement, and in their pursuit of romantic relationships and sexual fulfillment.

The family conflicts between the protagonists and their parents are an important part of the generational conflict that activists in the 1960s experienced. In their representations in the 1970s, the narrators emphasize that this struggle occurs on the outside, as an external conflict, since the protagonists' internal responses or the parents' emotions are not revealed. These tensions can be read as an answer to the proclamation of a society without fathers.[24] Krause and Lenz challenge their parents because they take on the generational attitude of their peers and attempt to impress members of the opposite sex by either disengaging from their parents and in doing so emphasizing their independence or by provoking a conflict to be able to disassociate from unwanted family obligations. *Lenz* and *Heißer Sommer* understand the attempts to disengage as a generational conflict since the students contend with the parents' real or assumed involvement with the Third Reich. However, instead of confronting their own parents and dealing with this problem face-to-face, the students reproach the parents collectively. While the parents are understood as a collective so as to avoid individual and familial interaction, the students' understanding of themselves as a generation is foreshadowed. In the aftermath of the movement, Krause and Lenz insist on their individuality, not realizing the inherent contradictions and fallacies of this approach.[25]

In *Lenz* and *Heißer Sommer*, both protagonists are incapable of dealing with the heterogeneous character of the student movement. They feel disenfranchised from the movement notwithstanding and even because of this diversity. Despite the many different opportunities in bringing about the change that all the activists call for, Krause and Lenz do not align themselves with any group. The very diversity of the movement incurred a lack of agreement over which kind of change to initiate and how to achieve it. This discord led to a weakening of the student movement and, ultimately, its dissolution in numerous groups that worked on change independently of each other. Indeed, despite their common ground in the student movement, these groups even (mis-)understood each other as ideological enemies. The tendency to emphasize the heterogeneity of the movement increases radically in the novels published in the 1990s, becoming one of its positive traits and as such underscoring the notion of a generation of 1968 whose diversity is celebrated.

The troubling representations of romantic relationships contribute to the sheer insignificance of the other in *Lenz* and *Heißer Sommer*. Romantic relationships are marked by silence and a lack of communication and trust. In *Heißer Sommer*, Krause impregnates his girlfriend, and then accepts responsibility for the unwanted pregnancy by paying for an abortion, still illegal in Germany at the end of the 1960s.[26] While still together with his girlfriend, he has random sexual encounters that confirm the general liberalization of sexual mores beginning in the 1960s with the introduction of the birth control pill.[27] Yet these encounters remain unfulfilling, and the gender relations and the emotional side of these encounters are not further explored. Schneider's Lenz longs for intimacy with a woman identified as L. with whom he has had a relationship and who now rejects him. The representations of these relationships emphasize that, while the discourse on gender relations and sexuality was very much alive in the 1960s, this discourse neither guaranteed nor fulfilled the desire for mutually beneficial and emotionally nurturing romantic relationships. The discourse remained abstract and did not touch on the lived experiences of men and women, in particular because feminist claims were not taken seriously within the student movement. This is symbolized by Helke Sander's, by now legendary, throwing of a tomato at the SDS meeting in Frankfurt in 1968 that ultimately led to the split between the students and the feminists.[28]

The interrelationship between representation, literary history, and historical discourse and their inherent political significance contribute to the novels oscillating between forming narratives of the student movement and foreshadowing the formation of a generation of 1968. This interrelation correlates with the 1960s' claim that the personal is political insofar as fiction allows the exploration of possible worlds and thus contains a utopian potential. Both novels emphasize the importance of a generational approach within the context of youth rebellion. At the same time, as the numerous public debates in the 1990s demonstrate, fiction written in German and authors in their roles as intellectuals are taken very seriously as seismographs of historical and political developments. Thus, *Lenz* and *Heißer Sommer* can be read as a contribution to the political debates that took place in the 1960s and both novels are important factions in the construction of the cultural memory of 1968 in the 1990s.

In the 1960s and 1970s, the question of revolutionary change soon came to involve the discussion of the legitimate use of violence. Schneider's *Lenz* frames the question of violence within the German literary tradition. Schneider not only references Georg Büchner's *Lenz* (1839) by name, but also incorporates direct quotes from Büchner's text.[29] Schneider seems to agree with Büchner's position that while violence is sometimes necessary as a form of counter-violence against the state and against oppressive leaders, the time to use violence has to be right in order to actually achieve revolutionary change. Clearly, neither Büchner nor Schneider was convinced that their respective historical situations warranted the use of violence. And yet even though activists and social groups answered the question of violence and its legitimacy in the aftermath of the student movement, albeit with different results, novels published in the 1990s continue to struggle with its legitimacy in the political struggle and the legacy of the use of violence in history, ranging from the Third Reich to the Red Army Fraction to the GDR.

Timm's *Heißer Sommer* does not seem to address the question of violence, at least not explicitly. Timm employs the genre of the Bildungsroman in order to embed the novel within the literary tradition and to discuss the all-important question of education and its significance for the individual as well as society. Following the tradition of the Bildungsroman, a genre most explicitly concerned with youth and its education within the tradition of the Enlightenment, Timm creates an interesting tension between the form of his novel and the goal of the student movement. In the 1960s, political activists denounced traditional, formal education and exposed an educational tradition that did not aim to liberate the individual but that had a disciplinary function in order to coerce individuals to conform to societal norms. The students initiated educational reform on all levels, from early childhood education to attempts to liberalize the university system and to form new communities of learning for disadvantaged young people in the care of the state. The novel evokes the notion of structural violence that is a violence that is embedded in society and its structures.[30] Yet, instead of building on the tension he creates between the genre and the story itself, Timm follows the genre convention in a rather predictable fashion. Everything that Krause experiences serves to bring him one step closer to the goal of uniting him with the working class. Since Timm was a member of the Communist Party, and as such belongs to the Old Left, he refutes claims by the New Left and by numerous groups advocating alternative lifestyles. He represents Krause as a lost sheep that undergoes a dialectic of education in order to ultimately join and support the Old Left. At the end of the novel, Krause combines his political engagement with his studies in order to work as a teacher.[31]

Considering the unforgiving nature of the German state that prevented many of those who participated in the student movement from joining its pay roll, it is highly doubtful whether Krause would have been allowed to become a teacher in the end.[32] In this case, Timm's literary imagination glosses over the historical reality of the "Radikalenerlaß" (the 1972 Decree against Radicals) and the far-reaching authority with which the state punished the activists in the aftermath of their protests. With his trust in traditional education, mirrored in the genre of the Bildungsroman, Timm inscribes his text into the German literary tradition and is able to explore the interrelation of fictional representation, literary history, and the political significance of his novel. Like Peter Schneider's *Lenz*, *Heißer Sommer* can be read as a text that narrates the 1960s student movement and foreshadows the construction of a generation of 1968 as a cultural memory of the events in the 1960s.

The comparative reading of *Heißer Sommer* and *Lenz*, focused on narrative perspective, the treatment of the other, and the relation between representation, literary tradition, and historical discourse, has shown that these novels oscillate between creating narratives of the student movement and foreshadowing the formation of a generation of 1968, the latter in particular when rereading these novels through the lens of those novels about 1968 that were published in the 1990s. The texts actively inscribe themselves in the German literary tradition as well as in the public discourse on the 1960s student movement. However, their focus on the activists' experiences as personal and their attempts to find individual solutions for those who feel disillusioned by the outcome of the protests limit and undermine the broader significance of the 1960s. These broader implications become apparent in the attempts to consciously and strategically define a generation of 1968 in the 1990s, in particular by adding previously silent voices and by adding self-reflective layers of remembering via the narrative perspective.

From the 1960s Student Movement to the Generation of 1968

Monika Shafi's assessment that there is a "relative lack of 1968 novels"[33] is contradicted by the ongoing literary interest in the 1960s and 1970s. Other critics, Ingo Cornils among them, devote much attention to the literary representation of 1968. In his essay "Romantic Relapse," a response to the thirtieth anniversary of 1968, Cornils provides an overview of the reception of the literature about the student movement.[34] This reception ranges from outright contempt for a literature that seemed to betray the political goals of the movement, to a cautious reevaluation of its literary value, to the claim that all literature published after 1968 has to be read in light of the political, social, and historical change that occurred in the late 1960s and 1970s. The sheer number of texts and their comparability in content and form enable us to speak about an emerging genre of novels about the generation of 1968. Authors, narrators, and literary figures engage in the poetic labor of remembering and forgetting and of telling, writing, and performing biographies, autobiographies, stories, and history. Fictional texts in the 1990s embrace the notion of a generation of 1968 and utilize it to emphasize the historical significance of the 1960s student movement that reaches far beyond personal experiences and shapes the national history and the cultural memory of Germany. In this kind of poetic labor, *Eduards Heimkehr* and *Rot* turn their attention to the contested legacy of the 1960s and 1970s and self-reflectively and self-consciously create layers of memory that recognize the importance of a continuous engagement with the past and its shifting significance, depending on the context in which we remember and forget.

Eduards Heimkehr and *Rot* differ from *Lenz* and *Heißer Sommer* and develop some themes already present in these texts further. Novels published in the 1990s introduce a first-person narrator whereas *Lenz* and *Heißer Sommer* are written from the perspective of a third-person narrator. This contrast coincides with the narrative shift from the events themselves to the formation of a cultural memory that is based on self-conscious remembering and storytelling by the former activists. With respect to the representation of the other, the novels from the 1990s attempt to let the silence speak and to fill the voids that the texts from the 1970s created. Read in conjunction with the intersections of narration and history, fiction from the 1990s places a particular emphasis on the inclusion of all those voices that were previously missing. Thus, these texts not only contribute to the cultural memory of 1968 but they also view the legacy of the Third Reich and the Holocaust through the process of self-critically remembering the 1960s student movement.

In *Eduards Heimkehr* and *Rot*, individual memories meet and compete over the most convincing interpretation of the historic events, returning to the seemingly unfinished project of the 1960s student movement whose goal was to radically transform society. This memory contest reinforces the notion that history is a process that needs to be accompanied by remembering through storytelling. Whereas in *Lenz* and *Heißer Sommer* each figure stood for something and exemplified one of the political, theoretical, and cultural positions that shaped the student movement, in *Rot* and *Eduards Heimkehr* the authors create characters that develop and change over time. The first-person narrators reconstruct and understand their own biographies and those of the many individuals that participated in the movement, inspired by the utopian hope for equality, freedom, and worldwide peace. As memory novels, both texts blur genre boundaries by drawing on elements of novels, autobiographies, and historiographies in order to create meaningful stories about a past that resists overarching interpretations.

Situated in the 1990s in Berlin, Timm's novel *Rot* recounts Germany's twentieth-century history from the perspective of a former '68er.[35] On his way to meet his lover Iris, the protagonist and first-person narrator Thomas Linde is hit by a car. As he lies dying,[36] Linde reflects on his own life, which he intersects with the life stories of his family, his former political friends, his former wife, Iris and her friends, and those for whom he held eulogies. A secular eulogist skilled in remembering and forgetting, Linde addresses the imagined audience of his own eulogy and interrupts his storytelling to ponder the art and aesthetics of storytelling as a contribution to a cultural memory.[37] Linde's comments dissolve the linearity, causality, and rationality of the narration that loses coherence as the narrator drifts in and out of consciousness. The end of the novel coincides with the narrator's death.

Linde recounts his family's story as a struggle between his father and himself. Having never reconciled with his father, Linde still harbors resentment toward him and only now reevaluates his own approach toward National Socialism, the main point of contention between his father and him. For the first time, Linde admits the limitations of his own generation which blamed the parents' generation collectively for the rise of National Socialism. Linde's introspection is spurred by his confrontations with members of the younger generation, among them Iris, her husband Ben, and their friend Nilgyn, the daughter of Turkish guest workers who arrived in Germany in the 1950s. Because of these encounters, Linde is forced to acknowledge that the '68ers' attempts to come to terms with National Socialism by depositing the guilt on the parents and by claiming victim status due to their parents' fascist way of raising children had its own limitations. This approach toward the past can only be understood as yet another attempt to come to terms with the legacy of National Socialism and the Holocaust. The work of engaging with the past is an ongoing process that does not end or find closure with one particular effort. These encounters symbolically represent encounters between the second and third generations that demonstrate the way the next generation deals with the legacy of the Third Reich. Whereas Iris criticizes Linde's failure to deal with his parents and to engage with the Holocaust survivors personally, Ben, Iris' husband, represents those members of his generation who want to conclude the seemingly endless debates about the legacy of the Third Reich and the Holocaust because they feel that the past should be the past. Nilgyn, on the other hand, claims that many former '68ers came to betray the leftist cause. A dentist and a member of the Communist party, Nilgyn treats illegal immigrants for free in order to practice her political convictions. Her character hints at the fact that not only those who are German by blood and family relations but also those who migrated to Germany after 1945 are affected by Germany's history. Their stories are an important aspect of the memory contests that take place in the 1990s and their contributions to the cultural memory of 1968 are discussed in chapter four of this study. Iris, Ben, and Nilgyn are three representatives of unified Germany that stand for the diversity that informs memory contests in the 1990s.

In addition to remembering his own family and being confronted about his particular contribution to dealing with National Socialism by the next generation, Linde remembers his former friends and acquaintances, most importantly Aschenberger, whom Linde eulogizes as per Aschenberger's request in his last will. Linde remembers him as the most radicalized member of the commune who suffered the most severe consequences after having professionalized the protest attitude of the student movement and joined one of the many leftist groups that developed in the 1970s.[38] In reflecting on Aschenberger's life, Linde recalls how another student in their commune spied on Aschenberger and betrayed him to the West German secret service. Subsequently, Aschenberger was tried and sentenced under the 1972 Decree against Radicals and could not become a teacher. At this point the self-reflective and self-critical narrative leaves the reader in the dark: Linde claims not to know who worked as an informant and only mentions the devastating effects on Aschenberger in passing.[39] This omission can be read as a continuation of the silence that clouds historical events that continue to make their participants or eye witnesses feel uncomfortable. Even the reflective and self-reflective narrative of a memory novel written from the first person perspective continues to construct silences that surround events that need to be rescued from oblivion.

Linde's deliberations on Aschenberger's life remind the reader of the political significance of work and how work, having work, and access to certain professions and positions continues to be ideologically shaped. Both Linde and Aschenberger worked in professions that engage with the past and rework it from the present perspective. Whereas Linde as a eulogist is interested in the function of individual remembering and forgetting, Aschenberger devoted his life time to the reconstruction of history and German historiography. In the tradition of the history workshop movement whose aim is to promote a history from below, a history of everyday life, or simply a people's history, Aschenberger offered alternative guided tours through Berlin. These tours highlighted the history of the left and of the oppressed, murdered, and disadvantaged in an attempt to give them a voice in the historical process.

However, working as an alternative tour guide in Berlin was not Aschenberger's only occupation. When Linde takes a closer look at Aschenberger's apartment he notices materials, most notably explosives that seem to indicate that Aschenberger intended to blow up the Victory Column in Berlin, which he perceived as a symbol for Prussian and German militarism.[40] While the reader is left to wonder whether this was really Aschenberger's intention or whether this plan only exists in Linde's fantasy, this development makes clear that the 1970s still cast a long shadow and that the question whether it is legitimate to use violence in the political struggle has not yet been answered to everyone's satisfaction. Was Aschenberger naïve enough to believe that the destruction of a monument could erase a history of militarism and its legacy? Or did he intend to raise awareness with regard to this history by destroying its monument? Did he intend to recreate this space after the destruction of the monument in order to change the significance of the site as a site of mourning for all those who suffered under militarism? The text does not answer these questions, but the text responds to the memory contests of the 1990s by illustrating the complexities of remembering ruptures and dissonances in commemorative practices. The juxtaposition of Linde and Aschenberger with respect to the use of violence in the political struggle serves as a reminder that the generation of 1968 is much more diverse than the current public discourse that tends to either criminalize or downplay the 1960s student movement acknowledges.

Whereas the novels published in the 1970s were told from the perspective of the third-person narrator, *Rot* is told from the perspective of a first-person narrator and *Eduards Heimkehr* from an omniscient third-person narrator. This shift forces the introspection of the protagonist and emphasizes their willingness to engage critically and self-critically with the 1960s student movement and their memories thereof. The first-person narrative in *Rot* shifts between the limited perspective of the literary character and the retrospective position of the narrator who can comment on the experiences of his former self. Within this constellation, the reader is tempted to think of the narrator as having the last word. Yet unreliable first-person narrators are not uncommon since they do not necessarily tell the whole story. These narrators create silences and omissions in the story that need to be interpreted in order to get a fuller picture of past events and the diverse viewpoints of their significance for the present. One of these omissions is the fact that Iris, Linde's lover, is pregnant with their child. Linde only alludes to this pregnancy in passing since the thought of becoming a father raises ambivalent feelings in him.[41] He is neither sure he wants a child nor does he want the pregnancy to reveal his relationship with Iris. He is afraid of the responses by Iris's husband and friends, all of whom apparently suspect nothing. This example demonstrates that the shift to a first-person narrator allows more nuanced insights into the protagonist since he reveals his emotions and inner thoughts. Furthermore, the first-person perspective engages, or is forced to engage, with the other in a much more substantive way, as Linde's interactions with former activists and members of the next generation reveal.

In *Eduards Heimkehr*, Peter Schneider tells the story of Eduard Hoffmann, an apparently matured version of Lenz, who returns to his native Berlin after having spent most of his working life as a scientist at Stanford University. The story is told from the perspective of a third-person narrator who is intimately familiar with Eduard's emotions, thus allowing the reader insights into the character that create the illusion of a first-person narrative. At the same time, the narrator emphasizes those characters that serve as the other in the novel who allow the construction of a generation of 1968 as a heterogeneous and historically significant group. While *Lenz* centered on Lenz alone, *Eduards Heimkehr* is more interested in the relations among the different characters who each play an important role for shaping our understanding of the generation of 1968.

The fall of the Berlin Wall creates two opportunities for Eduard: He receives an offer to conduct research at a leading German science institute and he inherits an apartment building from his deceased grandfather. Both his future workplace and the apartment building are located in the former East Berlin. Upon his arrival in Berlin, he feels confused in the newly unified city and misses the clear line of demarcation the Wall once presented.[42] Furthermore, he is faced with unanticipated difficulties. At work, he experiences the East–West conflict, which jeopardizes his research project. And squatters threaten his claim to his inheritance by publicly declaring that his grandfather illegally gained ownership of the apartment building during the Third Reich, taking advantage of the previous Jewish owner. The third-person narrator creates a reflective and self-reflective story which is marked by distance and irony towards his protagonist Eduard Hoffmann, who rather naively stumbles into three of the biggest hornet's nests of twentieth-century Germany: the attempts to come to terms with unification, with the 1960s student movement, and with the Third Reich.[43]

Historical guilt is negotiated within the realm of economic obligations and debt.[44] When Eduard learns about his inheritance he is not concerned with questions of the legitimacy of ownership per se. Only the squatters, belonging to the third generation, challenge his right of ownership by rhetorically linking the anarchist claim "ownership is theft" with the crime of anti-Semitic plunder during the Third Reich. As such, they represent the next step in the succession of generational conflict as the struggle of young people against the older generation. This conflict takes on a particularly ironic significance since the squatters target Eduard, who used to be a political activist engaged in similar generational struggles and who still defines himself in light of these experiences. Thus, the '68ers and the next generation are unified by their respective struggles against the older generation. Both conduct their struggles by using the media, in particular television, to publicize their claims. However, the two generations are separated by the fact that the second generation adhered to a political ideology whereas the squatters do not have a clear political orientation. They use seemingly familiar countercultural rhetoric; however, their claims are inconsistent and self-contradictory and their behavior is explosive, unruly, and prone to violence. When Eduard watches one of their demonstrations against speculation in the real estate market on TV, he is confused whether he only imagines the revolution or whether the squatters' protest is a simulacrum or simply a game.[45]

In *Eduards Heimkehr*, houses and apartments gain significance as homes and as shelters of family histories. They serve as archives, monuments, and memorials and they serve as sites that preserve, trigger, and obscure memories. Homes also function as reminders of forgetting and, for the squatters, they are contested spaces which allow them to manifest their protest and their political convictions. In the 1970s, Lenz experiences the urban environment as an oppressive reality without being able to express his discomfort in a communicable way and without adding any historical significance to his emotions. In the 1990s, however, this dominance of the city, the spatial dimension of cultural memory, is undermined in three ways: the renegotiation of the space of East Berlin, the opportunity to build on lots that had been vacant since 1945, and the attempt to build a new Berlin in a way that acknowledges the Nazi past while at the same time providing closure for this past. Thus, Eduard's experiences are framed within a historical and political discourse that shapes the emerging generation of 1968.

The young Eduard, like Lenz, is not concerned with German history per se. The student movement treated the Third Reich as a manifestation of fascism. As such, it was approached from the perspective of class struggle and explained with various communist, Marxist, Maoist, and anarchist models. However, the older Eduard, now the member of an emerging generation of 1968, is confronted with the recognition that these explanations are not adequate to explain and account for National Socialism. Eduard is forced to learn more about his family history and thus to acknowledge that inner soul searching and generational posturing are not sufficient. The individual cannot arbitrarily cut and evade family ties, since one's own life, one's family, and historical processes are intertwined and create history. While the texts from the 1970s represent the activists' disillusionment which led to their retreat from the public, texts in the 1990s emphasize the need to actively engage with one's personal environment in order to shape the public discourse. Eduard slowly learns to understand that the student activists inadvertently contributed to the concept of collective guilt which made it easy for individuals to blame society as a whole rather than asking oneself uncomfortable questions about one's own involvement and responsibility.

Within the temporal paradigm of the novel, the Holocaust serves as the point of reference and the "site of origin."[46] Eduard had thought that his involvement with the 1960s student movement and his marriage to the daughter of Holocaust survivors had sufficiently accounted for his critical relationship with the Third Reich and its legacy. Looking back on his life after 1989, Eduard emphasizes the problematic aspects of his engagement with the past, an engagement that was marked by silences in order to forget and obliterate the past. Eduard reflects on his generation's inability and unwillingness to engage in a direct dialogue with their parents. Instead, the students assumed that their parents' generation bore a collective guilt for the Holocaust. The students displaced the historical victims of National Socialism by posing as victims of the perceived fascist structures in West Germany. They claimed that these fascist structures were perpetuated through conventional family structures and traditional education. Thus, the students abused, at least rhetorically, the position of the victim and survivor since the victims and survivors of the Holocaust and National Socialism did not find their space within this discourse about fascism in the 1960s. After 1989, when Eduard attempts to claim his inheritance, he is forced to engage with his family history on a more personal level, rather than hiding behind claims of collective guilt as he did in the 1960s. Thus, the 1960s' claim that the personal is the political gains new significance in the 1990s. The personal needs to be recognized and examined within the sphere of the personal as well as the sphere of the public. Like an archeologist, Eduard excavates documents in order to illuminate his family's history during the Third Reich. This paper trail leads him to a survivor of the Holocaust who seems to be an important source of information for Eduard. By traveling to Florida to meet with this survivor, Eduard complements his postmemories with the survivor's memories.[47] This representation stresses the ongoing responsibility of the second and third generation for a past that will not go away. Revisiting 1968 emphasizes that without the dialogue with the survivors and their descendants and an engagement with their experiences, memories, and postmemories, the discussion of the Nazi past will remain incomplete. (This aspect of the cultural memory of 1968 will be discussed in detail in chapter 3.) The recognition of the importance of the past and the ongoing responsibility for the past and for engaging with the past contributes to the formation of the generation of 1968. This insight differentiates the representation of the 1960s student movement as an event and of the generation of 1968 that shapes the cultural memory of 1968 in Germany in the 1990s.

The complexities of the past are mirrored in Eduard's own marriage to the daughter of Holocaust survivors. Their relationship is strained because, as Eduard believes, his wife is not able to experience sexual pleasure or, even more troubling to him, he is not able to fulfill her sexual desires. Eduard attempts to explain her sexual frustration with reference to Wilhelm Reich, who claimed that in order to fully liberate sexual experiences, one had to also liberate oneself from other repressive feelings. The students in the 1960s read Reich in light of the legacy of the Third Reich and the Holocaust. However, Eduard's wife Jenny is not interested in this psychopolitical explanation.[48] Jenny's refusal to participate in this conversation creates an interesting tension to, and serves as a critique of, the assertions by male activists regarding the state of their libido in the 1960s. In 1966, Dieter Kunzelmann famously declared that he had an orgasm problem that deserved the attention of society.[49] These and other equally narcissistic claims were brought forward in order to challenge society and to exemplify the notion that the personal is indeed political. Jenny suggests that this claim, despite its liberating intentions, entails a normative expectation, in this case, the expectation that sexual activity, and orgasm in particular, is at the heart of human desire. She refuses to conflate the personal and the political or to see them as opposites and thus personifies the true radical. She resists the appropriation by any ideological discourse that adheres to disciplinary and normative powers and explanations. Instead, she insists on finding a practical, experimental, and imaginative solution to their (perceived) sexual problems that focuses on individual experience and joint pleasure.[50]

In *Rot* and *Eduards Heimkehr*, the representations of relationships and their conflicts can be read as the attempt to redefine the symbolic significance of love. These relationships shed light on German history in the twentieth century and, with respect to the Third Reich, connect generational and gender experiences and historical-political categories such as perpetrator, victim, and bystander.[51] Romantic relationships serve as a connection between the memories of 1968 and the postmemories of the Third Reich and the Holocaust. This literary strategy sheds light on one of the most important aspects of the student movement, namely the complicated entanglement of political and sexual revolution and its repercussions for the constitution of the generation of 1968 in the 1990s. For some critics, 1968 is marked by the attempts to liberalize sexuality, attempts that were ultimately not successful, as the novels of the 1970s, *Lenz* and *Heißer Sommer*, document. Both Lenz and Krause encounter the limits of free sexuality as a discursive rather than a physical act and as one that needs to be paired with a politically correct consciousness. Thus, the '68ers linked repressive morality to National Socialism and declared the unity of sexual and political liberation as an act of resistance, albeit belated, against National Socialism.

In her work on sexuality in Germany in the twentieth century, Dagmar Herzog points to the fallacies of this thinking and shows that the students in fact responded to the restrictions of the 1950s rather than the sexual mores in the Third Reich, which were regulated by far more contradictory policies set up by the Nazis as a system of racist and anti-Semitic rewards and prohibitions of sexual activity.[52] Even though the student movement in the 1960s seemed to have addressed both issues sufficiently, forty years later guilt and shame and their repercussions still play a decisive role in the attempts to come to terms with the past. Their relationship with each other and with historical events and personal experiences seems to defy rational explanations and contributes to the silence surrounding the Jewish persecution by the Nazis and sexual taboos. This silence manifests itself in the narratives of the 1990s. In *Rot* and *Eduards Heimkehr*, couples hide their secrets from each other, engage in illicit love affairs, and continuously search for sexual satisfaction; however, rarely do they discuss their relationships openly. Thus, despite the attempts for both general and sexual liberation in the 1960s, not much seem to have changed in the 1990s. Liberalization, be it general or sexual, cannot simply be celebrated as one of the accomplishments of the 1960s student movement; instead, the construction of a generation of 1968 necessitates an in-depth discussion of the implications of love for the personal and for the public sphere.

The intersection between the personal and the public, represented in these memory novels in the configuration of romantic relationships, continues to play a significant role in the 1990s. *Rot* portrays the love relationship between a former '68er and a woman from the third generation. Whenever Thomas Linde feels that Iris only engages in a relationship with him to receive history lessons from the gentler version of her own father, the relationship seems to take on an incestuous character. In the end, Iris is pregnant with Linde's child. In contrast to Krause's girlfriend in *Heißer Sommer,* Iris decides to keep the child even though neither her husband Ben nor Linde are committed to having children.[53] Linde not only serves as a father figure for Iris, but he also becomes the father of her child, thus functioning symbolically as a grandfather for the unborn child. This situation points to the intersections of genealogy, generation, and generational conflict which mark the formation of the generation of 1968.

In an ironic twist at the end of *Eduards Heimkehr*, Schneider also provides an outlook onto the next generation and their way of handling the generational conflict. Throughout the novel, the squatters, representing part of the third generation, allude to moments of protest and attempts of revolutionary change in Germany in the last three centuries and appropriate these moments for their own purposes. However, due to the squatters' eclecticism and only fragmentary knowledge of history, they are also the ones who misrepresent Eduard's grandfather. The squatters suggest—wrongly, as it turns out—that he had obtained the house illegally and illegitimately. Furthermore, their protest ends once they have the opportunity to purchase the apartment complex. The day they sign the deed of sale is marked as their return to mainstream society: they cover the table with a white table cloth, roll out the carpets, and offer coffee and homemade cake to Eduard.[54] One couple is expecting their first child and plans a wedding. Their future as conforming participants in a Western capitalist democracy is foreshadowed. Just like the chain of short-lived and failed revolutions in Germany, the revolutionary attitude expressed by this generation is only an adolescent phase which the individual outgrows. This forms a stark contrast to the representation of the generation of 1968, who, after all, does not define its protest in the 1960s as an adolescent phase, but rather as a formative experience. The development from the 1960s student movement to the generation of 1968 in the 1990s emphasizes that the '68ers are unified and defined by the experiences in their youth. These experiences led to the development of attitudes and values that continue to shape their thinking and their way of life.

1968 Memory Novels

My comparative reading of four novels, *Lenz, Heißer Sommer, Eduards Heimkehr,* and *Rot*, suggests that in these texts by former activists, a shift occurs from an intergenerational struggle, mostly represented as conflicts between parents and their children, to an intragenerational struggle among former activists and participants of the student movement who attempt to shape the significance of the generation of 1968 according to their own, at times divergent, interpretations of the 1960s and 1970s. Texts by younger authors such as Sophie Dannenberg, Zoë Jenny, and Alexa Hennig von Lange, who also engage in the representation of the 1960s and 1970s, contribute the next layer to this cultural memory of 1968 that emerges from generational conflicts. In contrast to *Eduards Heimkehr* and *Rot*, however, these texts focus again on the intergenerational struggles between the children of the '68ers and their parents, continuing the notion of rebellion of the younger generation against the older that was prevalent in the novels in the 1970s, represented in this chapter by *Lenz* and *Heißer Sommer*.[55]

In all four novels, *Lenz*, *Heißer Sommer*, *Eduards Heimkehr*, and *Rot*, the focus on intragenerational struggles initiates a discussion of the changed self-perceptions and self-understandings of the former '68ers. The differences between the first-person narrators in the novels in the 1990s and their youthful former selves, described in texts in the 1970s, lead to a nearly schizophrenic split in those individuals that constitute the generation of 1968. Peter Schneider's newest text, an autobiographical account of 1968 that intersects the recollections of the author, who celebrated his seventieth birthday in 2010, with the diary entries of the twenty-year-old student, points to this psychological condition in its title, *Rebellion und Wahn. Mein '68* (Rebellion and Delusion. My '68).[56] The title suggests that the author reclaims the generational experiences as personal experiences, thus assuming agency and responsibility while at the same time indicating the delusions that caused and excused some of the youthful follies of the rebellion.

All four novels question homogenizing notions of German identity as based on blood relations and critique the many ways Germans and Germany in the twentieth century have attempted to come to terms with the Nazi past. The novels published in the 1970s chronicle the disillusionment with the attempts to break completely with the past and with the apparent failure of the movement to achieve a complete liberation of the individual and society. In contrast, the two novels published in the 1990s, *Eduards Heimkehr* and *Rot*, reconsider the ways in which the activists of the student movement sought to distance themselves from their parents' generation by collectively blaming them for the rise of the Nazis and the Holocaust. Written from the perspective of former '68ers, these novels acknowledge the ongoing need to engage with the German past and ask uncomfortable but necessary questions regarding the individual's responsibility in light of or despite their generational membership.

In her analysis of constructions of the generation of 1968 in literary texts, Susanne Komfort-Hein polemically asks whether the tendency to celebrate the anniversaries of 1968, always accompanied by countless events and publications highlighting the accomplishments of the generation of 1968, in fact annihilates their accomplishments which, after all, consisted in a rebellion against a society that now celebrates them and thus attempts to subsume 1968 into the mainstream.[57] In light of the continuous literary interest in 1968 I would like to shift the focus of this polemic and suggest that "the generation of 1968" in fact owes its existence to the novels, films, and events that narrate, perform, and memorialize the 1960s student movement. Literary texts published in the 1990s are credited for participating in ensuing memory debates and very often open up more reflective spaces which allow readers to ponder the effects of this boom.

Literary texts and other narratives position 1968 as one of the central events for West Germany that shapes the historiography of unified Germany after 1989. The shift from 1960s student movement to a generation of 1968 occurs in order to allow more people to identify with the historical moment and its memorialization. At the same time, the shift signals that 1968 is no longer understood as a political but rather a cultural movement, a turn away from the original intent of some of its participants, yet one that ensures broad-based support. The shift from texts focusing on individual experiences published in the 1970s to memory novels narrating generational experiences published in the 1990s could indicate the seemingly self-serving attempt to disguise the obsession with oneself by promoting the notion of a "generation of 1968," a notion that transforms the individual into the exemplary, as Magenau polemically observes with reference to German novels of the 1990s.[58] Furthermore, the attempt to secure the privileged position of the West German movement in the cultural memory of 1968 takes place at the expense of corresponding events in the GDR and their repercussions in fiction published in the GDR. The next chapter provides a rereading of Irmtraud Morgner's *Salman* trilogy in order to create a cultural memory of 1968 for unified Germany that reflects its divided history between 1949 and 1989 and recognizes and inscribes events on both sides of the Berlin Wall.

Notes

1. To have come to terms with the past would require eliminating the reasons for this past first. Theodor W. Adorno, "Was bedeutet: Aufarbeitung der Vergangenheit?" in *Gesammelte Schriften* 10.2, ed. Rolf Tiedemann (Frankfurt a.M.: Suhrkamp, 1986): 555–572, 572.
2. The exhibit was organized by the German Historical Museum in Berlin in 2002. Given the focus of the exhibit on the memorial aspects of this history, it is surprising that the attempts made by the 1960s student movement to come to terms with the past were not recognized, with the exception of a cursory remark concerning Bernward Vesper's *Die Reise*. (Frankfurt a.M.: Zweitausendeins, 1977).
3. It is a commonplace to acknowledge the importance of subject positions within the Holocaust discourse even though Dominick LaCapra cautions that "[t]he notion of subject-position is only a beginning, not an end point, in analysis and argument." He continues: "One's own identity does not allow [to] enact one's positionality, or to benefit from the unearned authority one's background may at times furnish." In: *History, Theory, Trauma: Representing the Holocaust* (Ithaca: Cornell UP, 1994): 46.
4. Birgit Erdle and Sigrid Weigel, ed., *Fünfzig Jahre danach. Zur Nachgeschichte des Nationalsozialismus* (Zürich: vdf, 1996).

5. Ernestine Schlant, *The Language of Silence: West German Literature and the Holocaust* (New York: Routledge, 1999).
6. For a history of the term and its significance, see Werner Bergmann, "Kommunikationslatenz und Vergangenheitsbewältigung," in *Vergangenheitsbewältigung am Ende des 20. Jahrhunderts*, ed. Helmut König, Michael Kohlstruck, and Andreas Wöll (Opladen: Westdeutscher Verlag, 1998): 393–408; Peter Dudek, "'Vergangenheitsbewältigung'. Zur Problematik eines umstrittenen Begriffs," *Aus Politik und Zeitgeschichte B 1-2* (3 January 1992): 44–53; Helmut Fleischer, "Mit der Vergangenheit umgehen. Prolegomena zu einer Analytik des Geschichtsbewußtseins," in *Vergangenheitsbewältigung am Ende des 20. Jahrhunderts*, ed. Helmut König, Michael Kohlstruck, and Andreas Wöll (Opladen,: Westdeutscher Verlag, 1998): 409–432; Grete Klingenstein, "Über Herkunft und Verwendung des Wortes 'Vergangenheitsbewältigung,'" *Geschichte und Gegenwart* 4 (1988): 301–312; Helmut König, "Von der Diktatur zur Demokratie oder Was ist Vergangenheitsbewältigung," in *Vergangenheitsbewältigung am Ende des 20. Jahrhunderts*, ed. Helmut König, Michael Kohlstruck, and Andreas Wöll (Opladen: Westdeutscher Verlag, 1998): 371–392; Michael Kohlstruck, *Zwischen Erinnerung und Geschichte. Der Nationalsozialismus und die jungen Deutschen*, (Berlin: Metropol, 1997); and Bernhard Schlink, "Die Bewältigung von Vergangenheit durch Recht," in *Vergangenheitsbewältigung am Ende des 20. Jahrhunderts*, ed. Helmut König, Michael Kohlstruck, and Andreas Wöll (Opladen: Westdeutscher Verlag, 1998): 433–450. Since this study is based on the premise that the Nazi past can never and should never be forgotten, I do not discuss any revisionist stances toward the Holocaust, even though I recognize their existence and the importance of dealing with them politically.
7. Hans Kundnani, *Utopia or Auschwitz. Germany's 1968 Generation and the Holocaust* (New York: Columbia University Press, 2009): 308.
8. Anne Fuchs, *Phantoms of War in Contemporary German Literature, Film and Discourse: The Politics of Memory* (New York: Palgrave Macmillan, 2008): 3.
9. Theodor W. Adorno, "Kulturkritik und Gesellschaft," in *Gesammelte Schriften* 10.1, ed. Rolf Tiedemann (Frankfurt a.M.: Suhrkamp, 1986): 11–30, 30.
10. Klaus Hofmann, "Poetry after Auschwitz—Adorno's Dictum," *German Life and Letters* 58.2 (2005): 182–94.
11. Flyer distributed at a demonstration in Berlin 1967. Reprinted in Ulrich Ott and Friedrich Pfäfflin, ed., *Protest! Literatur um 1968* (Marbach: Deutsche Schillergesellschaft, 1998): 43.
12. Among them: Bernd Cailloux, *Das Geschäftsjahr 1968/69* (Frankfurt a.M.: Suhrkamp, 2005); Sophie Dannenberg, *Das bleiche Herz der Revolution* (München: Deutsche Verlagsanstalt, 2004); Friedrich Christian Delius, *Amerikahaus und der Tanz um die Frauen* (Reinbek: Rowohlt, 1997) and *Mein Jahr als Mörder* (Berlin: Berlin Verlag, 2004); Wilhelm Genazino, *Eine Frau, eine Wohnung, ein Roman* (München: Hanser, 2003); Jürgen Kehrer, *Das Kappenstein-Projekt* (Dortmund: Grafit, 1997); Ulrike Kolb, *Frühstück mit Max* (Stuttgart: Klett-Cotta, 2000); Georg Meier, *Alle waren in Woodstock, außer mir und den Beatles* (Berlin: Dittrich, 2008); Rainer Merkel, *Das Gefühl am Morgen* (Frankfurt a.M.: S. Fischer, 2005); Klaus Modick, *Der Flügel* (Frankfurt: S. Fischer, 1994); Sten Nadolny, *Selim oder die Gabe der Rede* (Frankfurt a.M.: Piper, 1990); Emine Sevgi Özdamar, *Seltsame Sterne*

starren zur Erde (Köln: Kiepenheuer & Witsch, 2003); Robert Schindel, *Gebürtig. Roman* (Frankfurt a.M.: Suhrkamp, 1992); Bernhard Schlink, *Der Vorleser* (Zürich: Diogenes, 1995); Elke Schmitter, *Leichte Verfehlungen* (Berlin: Berlin Verlag, 2002); Peter Schneider, *Skylla* (Berlin: Rowohlt, 2005); Leander Scholz, *Das Rosenfest* (München: Hanser, 2001); Gerhard Seyfried, *Der schwarze Stern der Tupamaros* (Berlin: Eichborn, 2006); Franz Maria Sonner, *Als die Beatles Rudi Dutschke erschossen* (München: Kunstmann, 1996), and *Die Bibliothek des Attentäters* (München: Kunstmann, 2001); Ingrid Strobl, *Ende der Nacht* (Berlin: Orlanda, 2005); Uwe Timm, *Der Freund und der Fremde* (Köln: Kiepenheuer & Witsch, 2005); Stephan Wackwitz, *Neue Menschen. Bildungsroman* (Frankfurt a.M.: S. Fischer, 2005); Heipe Weiss, *Fuchstanz. Roman* (Frankfurt: Dipa-Verlag, 1996); Ulrich Woelk, *Rückspiel* (Frankfurt a.M.: S. Fischer, 1993) and *Die letzte Vorstellung* (Hamburg: Hoffmann & Campe, 2002).

13. I differentiate between literature *of* the movement, that is, texts by authors that base their writing on the political goals and theoretical and aesthetic debates that mark the 1960s and 1970s, and *about* the movement, that is, texts that represent the events without necessarily attempting to align theory and aesthetic or narrative structures.
14. In addition to the two novels discussed in this chapter, *Heißer Sommer* and Lenz, the following texts, dealing with the student movement, were published immediately following the student movement: Nicolas Born, *Die erdabgewandte Seite der Geschichte* (Reinbek: Rowohlt, 1976); Rolf Dieter Brinkmann, *Keiner weiß mehr* (Köln: Kiepenheuer & Witsch, 1968); and Peter Renz, *Vorläufige Beruhigung* (Hamburg: Hoffmann und Campe, 1980).
15. E.g. the controversy surrounding the publication of Götz Aly's *Unser Kampf. 1968 —ein irritierter Blick zurück* (Frankfurt a.M.: S. Fischer, 2008) most notably in reviews in *Die Tageszeitung*, 25 February 2008 by Jan Feddersen, *Die Zeit* 9, 20 February 2008 by Axel Schildt, *Süddeutsche Zeitung*, 19 February 2008 by Franziska Augstein, and *Frankfurter Rundschau*, 16 February 2008 by Harry Nutt.
16. "The '68ers were the last ones to experience a generational conflict that sharpened the sense of generational belonging (as opposed to other factors such as place of birth or residence or a shared sense of consumerism)." Jörg Magenau, "Literatur als Selbstverständigungsmedium einer Generation," *Zeitschrift für Literaturwissenschaft und Linguistik* 124 (2001): 56–64, 59.
17. This shift is also reflected in the research dealing with 1968. Earlier publications tend to reference the student movement, e.g., Martin W. Lüdke, *Literatur und Studentenbewegung. Eine Zwischenbilanz* (Opladen: Westdeutscher Verlag, 1977) and Lothar Baier, Wilfried Gottschalck, Reimut Reiche, Thomas Schmid, Joscha Schmierer, Barbara Sichtermann, and Adriano Sofri, *Die Früchte der Revolte. Über die Veränderung der politischen Kultur durch die Studentenbewegung* (Berlin: Wagenbach, 1988), whereas contemporary publications reference 1968, the 1960s, and, increasingly, the generational aspect of the movement, e.g., Aly, *Unser Kampf* and Monika Shafi, "Talkin' 'Bout My Generation: Memories of 1968 in Recent German Novels," *German Life and Letters* 59.2 (2006): 201–216.
18. Sigrid Weigel, *Genea-Logik. Generation, Tradition und Evolution zwischen Kultur- und Naturwissenschaften* (München: Wilhelm Fink Verlag, 2006).

19. Lenz sold over 100,000 copies by 1980, and *Heißer Sommer* more than 50,000 copies, according to Michael Buselmeier, "Peter Schneider," in *Kritisches Lexikon zur deutschsprachigen Gegenwartsliteratur*, ed. Heinz Ludwig Arnold (München: Edition Text und Kritik, 1978–): 1–12.
20. The relevance of fiction about the 1960s student movement and, in turn, the relevance of the movement for aesthetics and literary history is evident in many German literary histories where the historical caesura of 1968 serves as an important mark that structures literary history, e.g., Wolfgang Beutin, ed., *Deutsche Literaturgeschichte. Von den Anfängen bis zur Gegenwart*, 7th ed. (Stuttgart: Metzler, 2008) and Klaus Briegleb and Sigrid Weigel, ed,. *Gegenwartsliteratur seit 1968. Hansers Sozialgeschichte der deutschen Literatur 12* (München: Hanser, 1992): 21–72.
21. Cf. essays by Michael Buselmeier, "Nach der Revolte. Die literarische Verarbeitung der Studentenbewegung," in *Literatur und Studentenbewegung. Eine Zwischenbilanz*, ed. Martin W. Lüdke (Opladen: Westdeutscher Verlag, 1977): 158–185; Karl-Heinz Götze, "Gedächtnis. Romane über die Studentenbewegung," *Das Argument* 127 (1981): 367–382; Klaus Hartung, "Die Repression wird zum Milieu. Die Beredsamkeit linker Literatur," *Literaturmagazin* 11 (1979): 52–79; and Rolf Hosfeld and Helmut Peitsch, "'Weil uns diese Aktionen innerlich verändern, sind sie politisch.' Bemerkungen zu vier Romanen über die Studentenbewegung," *Basis. Jahrbuch für deutsche Gegenwartsliteratur* 8 (1978): 92–126.
22. Peter Schneider, *Lenz* (Berlin: Rotbuch, 1973): 5.
23. Ibid.: 90.
24. Compare the highly influential publications by Alexander and Margarete Mitscherlich, among them *Auf dem Weg zur vaterlosen Gesellschaft. Ideen zur Sozialpsychologie* (München: Piper, 1963). Novels that belong to the so-called "Väterliteratur" include: Peter Härtling, *Nachgetragene Liebe* (Darmstadt: Luchterhand, 1980); Christoph Meckel, *Suchbild. Über meinen Vater* (Düsseldorf: Claassen, 1980); Ruth Rehmann, *Der Mann auf der Kanzel. Fragen an einen Vater* (München: Hanser, 1979); and Brigitte Schwaiger, *Lange Abwesenheit* (Wien, Hamburg: Zsolnay, 1980).
25. Albrecht von Lucke, who provides an excellent overview of the different players and their positions within the layered discourse on 1968, argues that the '68ers did not want to be perceived as a generation since they feared that their protest could be misunderstood as a youth revolt instead of a (political) world revolution. *68 oder ein neues Biedermeier. Der Kampf um die Deutungsmacht* (Berlin: Wagenbach, 2008).
26. Uwe Timm, *Heißer Sommer*: 59, 65.
27. Ibid.: 49–57, 65–69.
28. See Halina Bendkowski. *Wie weit flog die Tomate? Eine 68erinnen-Gala der Reflexion* (Berlin: Heinrich-Böll-Stiftung, 1999).
29. Georg Büchner, *Lenz* (Stuttgart: Reclam, 1957).
30. For a more detailed discussion of structural violence see Johan Galtung, "Violence, Peace, and Peace Research," *Journal of Peace Research* 6 (1969): 167–191.
31. See Buselmeier who argues that Timm, due to his own membership in the Communist Party, attempts to represent the student movement only as the chaotic and disorienting precursor to the true engagement in the proletarian movement. Hosfeld and Peitsch make a similar argument when he claims that Timm focuses heavily on the anti-authoritarian tendencies of the movement at the expense of its political impetus.

32. Compare with the experiences by Peter Schneider documented in ... *schon bist du ein Verfassungsfeind* (Berlin: Rotbuch Verlag, 1975).
33. Shafi, "Talkin' 'Bout My Generation: Memories of 1968 in Recent German Novels:" 213.
34. Ingo Cornils, "Romantic Relapse? The Literary Representation of the German Student Movement," in *German Studies Towards the Millenium. Selected Papers from the Conference of University Teachers of German, University of Keele, September 1999*, ed. Christopher Hall and David Rock (New York: Lang, 2000): 107–123.
35. Timm's novel has been analyzed from a variety of perspectives and contexts. For an overview, see the collection of essays *"(Un-)Erfüllte Wirklichkeit." Neue Studien zu Uwe Timms Werk*, ed. Ingo Cornils and Frank Finlay (Würzburg: Königshausen & Neumann, 2006). Timm's novel also contributes to the discourse on Berlin in the literary imagination, cf. Katharina Gerstenberger, *Writing the New Berlin: The German Capital in Post-Wall Literature* (Rochester, NY: Camden House, 2008).
36. The scene evokes the car accident in Wim Wender's film *Der Himmel über Berlin* (1987), embedding the novel in a tradition of Berlin texts that narrate the city throughout the twentieth century.
37. Eulogies are placed in the tradition of funeral biography, a practice that in the sixteenth century was popularized by early Lutheran preachers who recognized the genre to belong to the ceremonial discourse of traditional rhetoric while at the same time recognizing an individual's Christian life. Cf. Cornelia Niekus-Moore, *Patterned Lives: The Lutheran Funeral Biography in Early Modern Germany* (Wiesbaden: Harrassowitz, 2006).
38. This development is documented in other narratives, most notably in Gerd Koenen's account *Das rote Jahrzehnt. Unsere kleine deutsche Kulturrevolution 1967–77* (Köln: Kiepenheuer & Witsch, 2001) and in Stephan Wackwitz' novel *Neue Menschen* (Frankfurt a.M.: S. Fischer, 2005). Both remember a time in which they considered it most important to support the cause of their respective leftist group with all means, an attitude which they now evaluate very critically.
39. Timm, *Rot*: 323–328.
40. Ibid.: 103, 424–426.
41. Ibid.: 35, 174.
42. Schneider, *Eduards Heimkehr*, 23–28.
43. Others analyze different aspects of the novel: Carol Anne Costabile-Heming reads the novel in the context of post-1989 Berlin narratives ["Tracing History through Berlin's Topography: Historical Memories and Post-1989 Berlin Narratives," *German Life and Letters* 58.3 (2005): 344–356]; Paul Michael Lützeler focuses on the representation of the literary space Berlin in the trilogy that Schneider wrote in the 1980s and 1990s, *Der Mauerspringer, Paarungen*, and *Eduards Heimkehr* ["'Postmetropolis': Peter Schneiders Berlin-Trilogie," *Gegenwartsliteratur* 4 (2005): 91–110]; and Siegfried Mews analyzes Schneider's contribution to the ongoing attempt to come to terms with the German past. ["The Desire to Achieve 'Normalcy'—Peter Schneider's Post-Wall Berlin Novel Eduard's Homecoming," *Studies in Twentieth and Twenty First-Century Literature* 28.1 (2004): 258–285].
44. Cf. Sigrid Weigel, "Shylocks Wiederkehr. Die Verwandlung von Schuld in Schulden oder: Zum symbolischen Tausch der Wiedergutmachung," in *Fünfzig Jahre danach*.

Zur Nachgeschichte des Nationalsozialismus, ed. Birgit Erdle and Sigrid Weigel (Zürich: vdf, 1996): 165–192.
45. Schneider, *Lenz*: 288.
46. Sigrid Weigel, "'Generation' as a Symbolic Form: On the Genealogical Discourse of Memory since 1945," *Germanic Review* 77.4 (2002): 264–278, 264.
47. Schneider, *Eduards Heimkehr*: 355–367.
48. Ibid.: 244f.
49. Quoted in Richard McCormick, *Politics of the Self: Feminism and the Postmodern in West German Literature and Film* (Princeton: Princeton University Press, 1991): 32. Cf. Uta G. Poiger, *Jazz, Rock, and Rebels: Cold War Politics and American Culture in a Divided Germany.* (Berkeley: University of California Press, 2000): 219f. for a more extensive discussion of the so-called "orgasm problem."
50. Schneider, *Eduards Heimkehr*, 244f.
51. This is a prominent pattern in German literature, evident already in earlier literature that attempts to come to terms with the Nazi past, e.g., in the novels *Wo warst du, Adam?* by Heinrich Böll (Opladen: Friedrich Middelhauve, 1951) and *Die Rote* by Alfred Andersch (Olten/Freiburg: Walter, 1960). Both transpose the historical perpetrator-victim position onto the romantic and gender relationships.
52. Dagmar Herzog, *Sex after Fascism: Memory and Morality in Twentieth-Century Germany* (Princeton: Princeton University Press, 2005).
53. Timm, *Rot*: 302.
54. Schneider, *Eduards Heimkehr*: 385–387.
55. Cf. Sophie Dannenberg, *Das bleiche Herz* (München: Deutsche Verlags-Anstalt, 2004); Alexa Hennig von Lange, *Peace* (Köln: DuMont, 2009); and Zoë Jenny, *Das Blütenstaubzimmer* (Frankfurt a.M.: Frankfurter Verlagsanstalt, 1997).
56. Peter Schneider, *Rebellion und Wahn. Mein '68.* (Köln: Kiepenheuer & Witsch, 2008).
57. Susanne Komfort-Hein, "'1968': Literarische Konstruktionen einer Generation," in *GeNarrationen. Variationen zum Verhältnis von Generation und Geschlecht*, ed. Eveline Kilian and Susanne Komfort-Hein (Tübingen: Attempto, 1999): 191–215.
58. Jörg Magenau, "Literatur als Selbstverständigungsmedium einer Generation:" 56–64.

Chapter 2

Forget it? 1968 in East Germany

IN PRAG IST PARISER KOMMUNE

In Prag ist Pariser Kommune, sie lebt noch!
Die Revolution macht sich wieder frei
Marx selber und Lenin und Rosa und Trotzki
stehen den Kommunisten bei

Der Kommunismus hält wieder im Arme
die Freiheit und macht ihr ein Kind, das lacht,
das Leben wird ohne Büroelephanten
von Ausbeutung frei und Despotenmacht

Die Pharisäer, die fetten, sie zittern
und wittern die Wahrheit. Es kommt schon der Tag
Am Grunde der Moldau wandern die Steine
Es liegen vier Kaiser begraben in Prag

Wir atmen wieder, Genossen. Wir lachen
die faule Trägheit raus aus der Brust
Mensch, wir sind stärker als Ratten und Drachen!
Und hatten's vergessen und immer gewußt

Wolf Biermann[1]

Numerous attempts, some explicit, others implicit, relegate 1968 in the GDR into oblivion. Those who acknowledge the existence of East German '68ers tend to focus on very few and prominent participants, like Florian Havemann, at the expense of those who remain anonymous in their protest.[2] Havemann asserts, however, that there were other "Ost-68er" (East '68ers).[3] Among this small group of roughly two hundred people, he counts Thomas Brasch, Katharina Thalbach, Nina Hagen, Barbara Honigmann, Toni Krahl, Reinhard Stangl, Hans Scheib, and Thomas Heise. Havemann emphasizes that activists in East and West shared many concerns during the 1960s. These concerns included political questions and extended to the social and cultural structures of life, such as gender relations, education, the arts, and the relation between the individual and society. He concludes: "68 ging es um den ganzen Menschen, und also mußte jeder einzelne von uns alles sein. Kein Wunder, daß bei all diesen so ins Grundsätzliche gehenden Bemühungen erst einmal wenig herausgekommen ist—erst einmal, denn es ist ja dann, wie sich im Verlaufe der folgenden Jahre erwies, sehr, sehr viel herausgekommen" (68 dealt with the whole person, and therefore, everybody had to be everything at first. It is not surprising that this radical effort did not produce much at first—at first, because after some years it became clear that a lot had changed).[4] In addition to the similarities between East and West '68ers, Havemann also describes the differences, most importantly the response by the GDR to activities that were considered illegal in the East, but perfectly acceptable in the West. He recounts that fifteen copies of a pamphlet that he had not yet distributed landed him in prison whereas in the West political pamphlets were widely distributed, yet hardly read. Another important difference between East and West '68ers was their treatment of the fascist past, specifically the ways in which they engaged with the parents' generation. After all, the parents' generation in the East could not be collectively accused of having been Nazi perpetrators since many of them chose to live in the GDR, returning as victims of the Third Reich with the goal of developing a socialist state in an anti-fascist tradition. The generational conflict that marked the youth movement in the West, namely the accusations of their parents' involvement in the Third Reich, was missing in the East. Dorothee Wierling argues that "GDR parents in the 1960s were not challenged by questions about their attitude and activities in Nazi Germany, but were regarded as victims of the Nazi regime and spared any critical doubts."[5] Instead, the generational conflict that marked the GDR was triggered by the sons and daughters of the leaders of the GDR who constituted a prominent and probably the largest group of protestors. According to Havemann, their rebellion was directed against their parents' beliefs that the GDR was indeed the "better" Germany. Their protests in the late 1960s foreshadow the end of the socialist GDR.

Author and playwright Thomas Brasch also describes his generation's experiences with 1968. His stories "Vor den Vätern sterben die Söhne" show the disillusionment of the young generation with the lack of freedom in the GDR. "Sie wollen unseren Blick auf die angeblich großen Dinge lenken, damit wir unsere eigenen Erfahrungen nicht ernst nehmen. Wir dürfen auf die Barrikaden gehen, wenn es um Musik geht oder um Frisuren oder um Hosen. Das schadet keinem" (They want to steer us toward worthy causes, so that we do not value our own experiences. We are allowed to protest as long as the protest addresses the mundane such as music, hair styles, or trousers).[6] These struggles show the ideological differences between the older and the younger generation and point to the fact that, just as in the West, the political extended to the cultural and personal realm, such as lifestyle and personal tastes. Brasch's text documents that the awareness of the East '68ers was not limited to the events on both sides of the Wall, but extended to global events. In order to escape the politically charged atmosphere in the capital of the GDR, three of the protagonists of one of his stories take a vacation at the Baltic Sea. When they hear about an American folk blues festival in the Friedrichsstadtpalast (Frederick City Palace, a centrally located venue for performances in the center of Berlin dating back to the late nineteenth century) they decide to return to East Berlin in order to see the musicians of the American Civil Rights movements, e.g., Big Bill Broonzy, Charlie Parker, Otis Rush, Sleepy John Estes, Yank Rachel, Big Joe Turner, Jack Myers, and Pete Williams. Brasch's protagonists also watch movies about the revolution, e.g., the movie *The Strawberry Statement*, showing that media consumption was part of the youth revolt on both sides of the Wall. In this particular instance, film production in the West was yet another way to popularize the protestors' ideology whereas the opportunity to watch a movie in East Berlin that was produced in the West represented an opportunity to develop and express dissent with the regime in East Berlin. The last message from one of the protagonists who was killed when he attempted to cross the Berlin Wall illegally is a pessimistic outlook on the European attempt to participate in the global revolutionary uprisings: "Sie [Europa] will ihre Jugend wieder, deshalb sucht sie Liebschaften mit den jungen Revolutionen der anderen Kontinente, aber es wird keine Liebe daraus, denn die starken Stöße aus Südamerika, Afrika und Asien beantwortet der Körper Europas mit einem müden Zucken" (Europe wants its children, that's the reason Europe is looking for romance with the young revolutions of other continents; however, these romantic advances do not turn into love, instead, the tired European body answers the strong pushes from South America, Africa, and Asia with a tired twitch).[7] Ultimately, the 1960s student movements on both sides of the Berlin Wall did not lead to radical changes in either German state. While retrospectively the movements are widely credited with furthering democratization in the West and with laying the groundwork for the fall of the Wall, the harsh and disproportionate responses by both states that affected many protestors adversely are less widely acknowledged and discussed.

Both Brasch and Havemann were among those who suffered severe consequences for protesting against the Russian invasion of Prague in 1968.[8] After they received the news about the invasion they wrote and distributed pamphlets in Berlin. Both were arrested and received harsh prison sentences, Havemann stayed in prison for more than two years. In 1971, he fled East Germany; Brasch followed in 1978. Even though there were no mass demonstrations in the GDR, the events that shaped 1968 took place on both sides of the Berlin Wall and caused ruptures in individual biographies. These ruptures still ripple through the cultural memory of 1968 since they cannot be readily appropriated into one coherent narrative.

This study's attempt to understand the experiences of East Germans as contributions to the cultural memory of 1968 also facilitates our understanding of gender as one of the important characteristics that structures this memory. As my previous discussions showed, the relation between the 1960s student movement and the women's movement is underexplored and not much attention has been paid to the gendered aspects of the social movements that emerged in the late 1960s and 1970s, which is all the more surprising since the advancement of women is universally credited as one of the accomplishments of 1968. Reading East Germany in this context shows how East German women in particular contribute to raising the awareness of 1968 in the GDR. After the fall of the Berlin Wall, author Barbara Köhler describes memories of her youth: "Wir spielten Himmel und Hölle es war das Jahr Achtundsechzig [sic] als unser Held vom Himmel stürtzte [sic]. Gagarin starb. In jenem Sommer, zwischen Nachrichten von Barrikaden und Panzern, muß unsere Kindheit verlorengegangen sein" (We played heaven and hell; it was the year 1968 when our hero fell from the sky. Gagarin died. In that summer, among news of barricades and tanks, our childhood must have been lost).[9] Barbara Köhler's memories highlight the significance of 1968 as a time of coming of age when the innocence of childhood fantasies ended and were replaced with news of protest and violence. In her essay "A la recherché de la révolution perdue. Ein innerdeutscher Monolog," she provides numerous examples that attest to the awareness of East German youth of the global protests that occurred in 1968. She also recounts watching the film *The Strawberry Statement* about the student revolution in the United States several times, emphasizing her sadness at not being in the picture, at not being able to fully participate in this movement. Köhler connects the increasing radicalization in West Germany that led to the emergence of terrorism to the exodus in East Germany that occurred in the wake of the Prague Spring. "Ich erinnere mich an das Jahr Sechsundsiebzig, an den Tod Ulrike Meinhofs, die Ausweisung Wolf Biermanns, an das Jahr Siebenundsiebzig, Mogadischu und Stammheim" (I remember the year 1976, the death of Ulrike Meinhof, the expulsion of Wolf Biermann, and the year 1977, Mogadishu and Stammheim).[10] In her memories, the events that took place in the late 1960s and 1970s are understood as global events that eventually led to the fall of the Berlin Wall even though the end of the GDR was not yet in sight in 1968.

More than twenty years after German unification in 1990, an event that marked the official end of the existence of the GDR, the challenges of writing a history for the unified Germany remain. In recent years, attempts have been made to address these challenges. In a 2011 forum on H-Net, "Integrating Post-1945 History," Konrad Jarausch calls for an integrated German history that avoids the "risk of producing a self-congratulatory 'victors' history' which reinforces the Western dominance of the unification process and fuels Eastern resentment."[11] The 2008 conference "Das Jahr 1968 aus der Perspektive der Gesellschaften Mittel-, Ost- und Südosteuropas" (The Year 1968 from the Perspective of Societies in Middle, East, and South East Europe) reflects a new beginning in the research on 1968 in the GDR and Eastern Europe.[12] Speakers included former activists such as Havemann who reflected on his experiences in East Germany in the 1960s, in particular his incarceration after protesting against the invasion in Prague by placing a Czech flag outside his parents' apartment.[13] Other speakers, namely historians, weighed the successes and failures of the East German '68ers. While Marc-Dietrich Ohse argues that they had only limited influence among the opposition in the GDR, Bernd Gehrke supports Havemann's claim of the relevance of 1968 in both states.[14] Analyzing newly accessible documents, Gehrke shows how widespread the support for the Prague Spring in the GDR was. Consequently, he defines 1968 as a key year in GDR history—similar to the numerous attempts to mark 1968 as a key year in the West. Gehrke's research offers the opportunity to reconsider the question whether 1968 indeed also happened in the GDR. Previous scholarship simply and categorically negated this question in order to maintain a line of argument that pointed to distinct differences in the development of the two German states. With respect to 1968, this juxtaposition posited that the GDR was a completely totalitarian state that did not permit any opposition whereas the FRG permitted and enabled protests as a way to further democratization and Westernization. However, in light of attempts to write a historiography for Germany that reflects the history of both German states between 1945 and 1990 this argument needs to be analyzed in terms of its ideological motivation since it does not adequately reflect the complexities of German history in both states during the 1960s and 1970s. No matter how hard party officials tried, the GDR was not an isolated and self-contained society. Cultural meaning circulated and cultural transfer and exchange happened, albeit in the context of the restrictions of the Berlin Wall and the Cold War. Hence, the history of the GDR needs to be studied within the context of broader concepts, such as the history and cultural memory of global social movements in the second half of the twentieth century. Actions by individuals, and here I am including artistic productivity and production, cannot be simply attributed to the extreme poles of conformity and resistance, but instead need to be understood as a process of negotiation. Ina Merkel describes this process as a creative one in which the participants "create or reproduce the social structures, and within these structures, they fashion their very own lives."[15] Wierling takes the attempt to integrate the 1960s into a joint history of East and West in a different direction by asserting that "the GDR youth of the 1960s became part of the West—despite the Wall, and in a very specific way that differed from West Germany."[16] While Wierling talks about youth consumption of material goods and popular culture, her interpretation is applicable to cultural production and the exchange of ideas in order to advance political and social goals by those social movements that emerged in the 1960s. This frame of cultural production and exchange as a process of negotiation enables the study of 1968 in the GDR and places 1968 in the East within a German, European, and global context.

In literary studies, most of the research on 1968 conducted thus far has focused on the West German movement and on literary production and aesthetic debates in the West. The inconclusive evidence of whether 1968 in fact happened or not in the GDR seems to be reinforced when one considers the public response by prominent GDR intellectuals and writers to the Prague

Spring. Christa Wolf, for example, wrote on 4 September 1968 in the official party newspaper of the Socialist Unity Party of Germany (SED) *Neues Deutschland* (New Germany) that all contradictions marking this century could only be solved by socialism and that the Czechoslovak Socialist Republic (ČSSR) could only survive in close cooperation with Moscow.[17] With this opinion, Wolf was not alone. While not exactly supporting it, other East German intellectuals and writers who did not belong to the younger generation also either legitimized or at least did not publicly criticize the invasion of Prague.[18] This generational constellation creates a parallel to the West where the fault lines, whether one was in favor or against the 1960s protest, in most cases ran along generational lines. At the same time, *Nachdenken über Christa T.* (The Quest for Christa T.), published in 1968, documents Wolf's thought processes initiating a critical distancing from the GDR and its regime. Thus, the 1960s not only were marked by generational differences, but also by the increasingly self-critical and critical engagement of those who had supported the founding and existence of the GDR as a socialist alternative to the West. Against the backdrop of the Berlin Wall and the various global protest movements, this situation created ambiguity as a space for negotiation of meaning and reflected the cultural transfer that challenged the isolation of the GDR and the insurmountability of the Wall as a protection against Western influences. Given these shifting frameworks of interpretation, it is thus not surprising that the topic of 1968 in the GDR caused considerable difficulties and was ultimately largely omitted from public and academic discourse before 1989.

However, the fall of the Berlin Wall and the end of the Cold War offers the opportunity to revisit this history.[19] Since hardly any attention has been paid to the connection between 1968 and cultural production in the GDR this chapter seeks to fill a considerable gap by contextualizing texts written in the GDR in the 1960s and 1970s within the discourse on 1968 in its East German, West German, European, and global dimensions. The overall argument of this study rests on the premise that the 1990s, as a period of rapid transformation, also initiated a significant reshaping of the cultural memory of 1968 and witnessed the emergence of the genre of the 1968 memory novel. Thus, the act of rereading texts published in the GDR in the 1970s through the lens of the discourse on 1968 and its various layers of memory is understood here as an act of remembering. Rereading GDR fiction and connecting it with the various discourses of remembering in the 1990s constitutes an act against forgetting. This process of rereading permeates the border of time that was created in 1989 and 1990. Even after the official end of the East German state, its literature survives. Its rereading creates postmemories that are memories negotiated and transmitted via cultural representations that are central to the cultural memory of 1968.

Cultural production in East Germany serves as a sign not only of East German dissent, but also of ruptures taking place in West Germany, Europe, and the world. Films such as *Die Legende von Paul und Paula* and *Spur der Steine*, plays such as *Die neuen Leiden des jungen W.* and fiction such as Plenzdorff's novel with the same title, Irmtraud Morgner's *Salman* trilogy, Heiner Müller's dramatic work, Lutz Rathenow's poetry, the emergence of bands playing Rock' n Roll and jazz music, and in general, the rapid development of a youth culture coexisting with the official youth organizations in the GDR document that both the physical and ideological borders between East and West during the 1960s were much more permeable than often assumed and allowed the kind of cultural transfer that contributes so significantly to the emergence of a vibrant and heterogeneous cultural memory of 1968.[20]

After 1989: Rereading GDR Literature of the 1960s and 1970s

In the 1990s, many scholars of GDR literature admitted self-critically that before 1989 they had read this literature not in light of its literary or aesthetic accomplishments, but rather exclusively as an expression of an exotic, yet fascinating, experiment called "GDR." Sociopolitical interpretations prevailed over most other theories or methodologies.[21] This approach overlooks the inherent political implications of storytelling, in particular through its narrative form and perspective, and therefore also misses the opportunity to examine the specific literary and aesthetic qualities of fictional texts. In addition, these interpretations were confined to an East–West dichotomy whereby the West and its literature set the benchmark for literary production in German. And while these debates attempt to come to terms with the GDR and its aftermath, they do little to free fiction from the grip of ideological reception which uses and abuses literary texts in order to confirm, advance, or contradict political convictions.

In the revised edition of his literary history of the GDR, the eminent critic of GDR literature, Wolfgang Emmerich, challenges his own approach to GDR literature in the original edition published in 1981. In the revised version, he calls for a productive rereading of GDR literature that transcends its traditional frameworks of interpretation and sheds new light on a literature that was written in the now long-gone state.[22] Before 1989, GDR literature from the 1960s and 1970s offered readers in the West the opportunity to anchor their own political and cultural convictions within these texts and thus, to argue either in support or against them. Rereading these same texts in the 1990s offers the opportunity to anchor the 1960s student movement in a cultural memory of the generation of 1968.

Considering that research on the literary representations of the student movement in West Germany is only slowly developing, it is not surprising that the same topic with respect to literature written in the GDR has not yet found any research interest. Emmerich outlines some areas that deserve further attention. He points to concerns developing in the GDR in the 1960s and 1970s which could be linked to developments in the West, among them increasing feelings of objectification and alienation, a growing skepticism regarding the optimistic belief in technology and in unlimited economic growth, and concerns about the continuing inequality between the sexes. These concerns can be attributed partially to developments within the GDR, yet they can also be attributed to the access to information about protest movements in other countries; e.g., news about the Prague Spring and the student protests in Paris and other Western countries. These transnational exchanges served as an important factor that spurred discontent among younger people in the GDR. Thus, the state did not only have to respond to Marxist criticism from within, e.g., by Rudolf Bahro, Wolf Biermann, Volker Braun, and Robert Havemann, but also to criticism from members of the next generation who were part of countercultural movements which were comparable to their Western counterparts, e.g., the antinuclear, the peace, and the women's movements.[23]

As my research shows, these tensions also found an entry into the literary realm. Some literary representations of the 1960s student movements acknowledge the impact of 1968 in East Germany, in particular the influence that student movements from across the globe exercised over the mostly young protestors in East Berlin and elsewhere in the GDR. Among those authors in the GDR who participated in and contributed to the literary discourse in the 1960s and 1970s, Irmtraud Morgner deserves special attention. I present a rereading of Irmtraud Morgner's *Salman* trilogy consisting of the novels *Leben und Abenteuer der Trobadora Beatriz nach Zeugnissen ihrer Spielfrau Laura. Roman in dreizehn Büchern und sieben Intermezzos* (The Life and Adventures of Trobadora Beatrice as Chronicled by Her Minstrel Laura), first published in 1974 (in West Germany in 1976, an English translation appeared in 2000), and its sequel *Amanda. Ein Hexenroman* (Amanda. A Witch's Tale), published in 1983. Morgner's untimely death in May 1990 at the age of 57 meant that the planned third volume *Die cherubinischen Wandersfrauen: ein apokrypher Salmanroman* (The Angelic Errant Women: An Apocryphal Salmannovel) did not reach its final form. It was edited as a fragment under the title *Das heroische Testament: Roman in Fragmenten* (The Heroic Testament. A Novel in Fragments) by Rudolf Bussmann in 1998.[24] Rereading Irmtraud Morgner's trilogy allows us to understand the continued cultural significance of East German fiction. Even though this literature lost the country in which it was conceived and written, it still resonates in its cultural space. At the same time, the literary significance of Morgner's trilogy was at no point, neither before nor after 1989, restricted to and by experiences in the GDR. Instead, its plot is characterized by transnational movements across the physical wall and the many ideological barriers that marked the Cold War. Morgner's narrative emphasizes the need for aesthetic collaboration and as such is characterized by a process of negotiation among the figures who claim ownership of the texts. In addition, the trilogy can be contextualized as a cultural memory within a context of protest and rebellion that emerged in the 1960s and 1970s around the globe.

Helen Bridge's study *Women's Writing and Historiography in the GDR* aims to illuminate the complex intertwinement between discourses of literature, literary criticism, and history in the GDR.[25] While all operated within the boundaries of official state policy, Bridge shows how fiction from the 1970s onward was more successful than historiography in challenging the ideological party lines of Marxist socialism. Bridge's study emphasizes that the women's movements on both sides of the Berlin Wall serve as important markers of similarity in both states, sharing a discursive field and comparable concerns. At a recent conference, Ute Kätzel argued that even though East German women did not employ the same forms of protest that characterized the women's movement in the West, due to the different political environments in East and West Germany, they nevertheless shared the conviction that the personal is the political.[26] In addition, Kätzel maintains that feminist East '68ers made important contributions to the opposition movements in 1989, and, as such, have a very different legacy than the West German women's movement. Given this research, the close rereading of Morgner's trilogy advances another aspect of the entanglement of 1968 in both Germanys and the memories of women and of the women's movement of the 1960s and 1970s.

The current cultural memory of 1968 mostly omits a gender-specific discussion of the movement and its legacy.[27] This apparent gender blindness is surprising given the fact that the origins of the student and the feminist movement are closely linked. And yet, maybe the gender-blind discourse in the 1990s simply perpetuates and as such points to the unfinished business of the 1960s. After all, while the emergence of the (second wave) feminist movement is closely linked to the student movement, the two groups soon split and went their own ways because even though the student movement was seeking the liberation of all, it was not willing to reflect on the inequalities caused by gender. Contributions interested in the specific roles played by men and women during the 1960s and in the gender-specific aspects of the two decades often treat the women's movement as a separate entity disconnected from the other social movements of the time. In fact, while some read the SDS congress in 1968 in Frankfurt am Main as the event that marks the separation of the student and the women's movement and as such read the birth of second wave feminism literally out of the student movement, others create more distance between the two movements. Alice Schwarzer declares 1971, the year the German magazine *Stern* publicly presented women's confessions of having had an abortion, as the birth of the German feminist movement.[28] These interpretations reflect the contested legacy of the women's movement that continues to function as a dividing force, even among women in unified Germany. These divisions within West Germany also raise the question of the relation to the women's movement in East Germany. Even though Morgner refused to call herself a feminist, her work certainly suggests that she is interested in gender equality, women's work, and women's political participation. As such, I propose to understand her trilogy as a gendered intervention into the discourse on 1968. The inclusion of Morgner's fiction into the cultural memory of 1968 thus emphasizes the significance of gender for the shaping of a cultural memory of 1968.

At its first publication in 1974 (East) and 1976 (West) respectively, Morgner's novel *Leben und Abenteuer der Trobadora Beatriz nach Zeugnissen ihrer Spielfrau Laura* was widely read and received a lot of attention in the media and in academia. While the East emphasized Morgner's engagement with socialist humanism, in the West the novel was introduced as the "Bibel einer aktuellen Frauenemanzipation in der DDR" (Bible for the contemporary women's movement in the GDR)[29] and "eine Art *Dr. Faustus* für Feministinnen" (a kind of *Doctor Faustus* for feminists).[30] This reception, however, ultimately limited the reading of Morgner's work to two dominant frameworks: as GDR literature, to a sociopolitical context, and as a text written by a female author, to the context of women's literature. While we cannot undo history, we can reread literary texts and include the so-called "GDR literature" and the so-called "women's literature" in the discourse on the student movement, one of the prevalent discourses emerging after and due to the fall of the Berlin Wall. Against all voices that claim that with the end of the GDR any engagement with its literature is superfluous, my aim is to anchor GDR literature in the shared memories and history of unified Germany, a history that, in the 1990s, was negotiated and determined through the lens of the discourse on 1968.

In light of the extensive research on Morgner's work it is impossible to give a complete and detailed overview of its reception.[31] In recent years, fewer sociohistorically oriented and more theoretically diverse readings of Morgner's texts have begun to appear. In these new contexts, only a few voices address Morgner's interest in the 1960s, among them, most notably, Agnès Cardinal, Beth Linklater, and Siegrund Wildner. Agnès Cardinal hints at the influence of the Western student movement on Morgner's trilogy by opening her essay with a rather impressionistic, yet enlightening imagined walk, passing the sites of uproar in Paris in the 1960s.[32] Wildner examines the influence of Ernst Bloch's concept of "utopia" on Morgner's work. She claims that Morgner's representation of utopia marks the concept as a dialectic process, as a concrete utopia, as "Möglichkeitsdenken" (a thinking of possibilities), and as an aesthetic experiment—concepts that manifest themselves as contradictions, ruptures, divergences, and discontinuities in Morgner's novels.[33] Wildner's study sheds light on one of the critical categories and one of the most influential thinkers of the 1960s in both East and West, however, without explicitly linking these contexts to 1968.

Beth Linklater examines Morgner's literature in the context of sexuality and love and places it within feminist traditions of the 1970s. She argues that "the juxtaposing of theoretical writings by Western critical theorists and fiction by Eastern women can offer new perspectives upon both sets of texts. The convergence between Morgner's work and Western critical theories allows this prose to be read from a position which is not bound to terms of reference dependent upon concepts of East German cultural politics."[34] Linklater makes productive use of theories developed or rediscovered in reference to 1968 and applies them to East German texts that, if not explicitly, seem to anticipate, make use of, and advance these theoretical developments in their narratives.

Following these scholars' attempts to leave limiting frameworks of interpretation behind, I propose to reread Morgner's trilogy as an important addition to the cultural memory of 1968, a cultural memory that transcends national borders and embraces the notion of a transnational cultural memory of 1968. Since Morgner's novels do not only speak about the GDR, the state in which they were written and published, they can be analyzed as contributions to global conversations and actions that raised awareness of poverty, social and racial injustice, and gender inequality, and initiated social change. Morgner addresses a variety of relevant themes, among them the Cold War, the Vietnam War, feminism, and the Civil Rights movement. These themes link the trilogy directly to concerns raised by the protest movements in the 1960s and 1970s on both sides of the Wall.[35]

Between Paris and Prague via Berlin

In *Leben und Abenteuer der Trobadora Beatriz nach Zeugnissen ihrer Spielfrau Laura*, Morgner places the representation of the 1960s prominently at the beginning and the end of the novel. This narrative positioning emphasizes the central role the 1960s student movement plays within Morgner's trilogy, a text so rich in material and form that it continues to resist all overarching and conclusive interpretations. Morgner constructs her story around the fantastic legend of Beatriz de Dia, reportedly one of the few female troubadours in the thirteenth century who are recognized as the first female composers of secular music in the Western world. Beatriz awakens after a near eight-hundred-year-long sleep in France in 1968, just in time to experience the student movement before she moves on to enter the GDR, a country that is referred to as "ein Ort des Wunderbaren" (a place of miracles) in the first and last sentence of the novel. In the introduction, the reader also encounters the character of Laura whose mundane life as a citizen of the GDR and as a struggling working single mother is briefly narrated. After Beatriz enters the GDR the two women meet and Beatriz hires her as minstrel. In a harmonious fusion of opposites Laura develops into Beatriz's other half until the two women are nearly indistinguishable towards the end of the novel.

Developing the vision of a Faustian voyage beyond the confinements of the GDR, Beatriz adds the magical dimension of the imagination that Laura lacks in her life. While Laura goes about her daily chores in Berlin, Beatriz travels around the world, experiments with various sexual relationships, and converses with mystical and legendary figures of classical and Nordic origin. Since Beatriz refuses to write the travel novel whose rights Laura has already sold in order to earn money, Laura starts writing. Finally, Beatriz returns to the GDR. As she is becoming more and more domestic, Laura enters into a conventional, albeit progressive marriage with Benno. Together, the three celebrate the election victory of the left in France in 1973 which they interpret as the beginning of a utopian state in the West. However, their optimism is only short-lived. The next day, Beatriz has a deadly accident while cleaning the windows of their apartment in a high-rise in East Berlin. This scene marks the end of the first novel of the trilogy.

In *Leben und Abenteuer der Trobadora Beatriz nach Zeugnissen ihrer Spielfrau Laura*, Beatriz's ability to fly over state borders undermines the authority of the totalitarian state in the East to impose travel restrictions on its citizens and creates transnational connections with protestors in other countries that challenge the isolation of the population in the GDR. The cosmopolitan nature of youth culture transcends state borders. In the 1960s, travel and imagined travel were an important means to escape any confinement and foreshadow a borderless Europe that became reality with the Schengen agreement signed in 1985 for people in the West and, after the fall of the Berlin Wall, for all people in central Europe.[36] Beatriz's ability to travel transforms East Berlin into the site where the student movements on both sides of the Iron Curtain encounter each other and their impact is negotiated. In the novel, the Berlin Wall takes on a peculiar double meaning:

> On the one hand, the Wall meant shutting out the Western world; but on the other hand, it also meant precisely the opposite, namely permanent virtual transgressions of the border. The emigration of people, experiences, goods, and ideas determined life in the GDR in a decisive manner. Because of the Wall, those objects, people, ideas, metaphors, plots, and so on that did manage to cross it attained a very special meaning.[37]

Through Beatriz's travel, the center of the protests in the East, Prague, is connected with one of the centers in the West, Paris, and both encounter each other in East Berlin, Beatriz's home.

Beatriz's travel also challenges the West and its claim that life in the West was more desirable and desired than life in the East. The fact that Beatriz travels from Paris to East Berlin (in the first part of the trilogy) serves as an ironic juxtaposition to all those who waited, often for many years, to be able to leave the GDR to go to the West. Furthermore, the fact that Beatriz travels freely throughout the world forms a stark contrast to Laura, the GDR citizen who only hears about other places from Beatriz. Beatriz's travels connect her with the 1960s students in the West, since traveling and the encounter with others were crucial parts of the experiences that spurred the emergence of student movements worldwide. Given the narrative suspension of the plot between Paris and Prague via East

Berlin, *Leben und Abenteuer der Trobadora Beatriz nach Zeugnissen ihrer Spielfrau Laura* emphasizes that the 1960s student movement was indeed a German–German, European, and global event.

Paris

In the first three of what are altogether thirteen books that comprise the first novel, Morgner introduces the geographic space of Paris at the historical juncture of the events in May 1968. Paris as the site of rebellion and a particularly vocal student movement takes on a symbolic meaning. As French students were successful in organizing workers and others on the left in order to call for radical political change Paris is especially suited to make visible the continued significance of the 1960s student movement. Hence, Beatriz travels from the south of France to Paris looking for her sister-in-law called the beautiful Melusine. Melusine is supposed to assist Beatriz as she reintegrates into contemporary life and to assign her tasks that advance the goal of creating a matriarchy. On her journey, Beatriz learns about the student movement in Paris from the media and she is increasingly optimistic that change indeed is happening and that the utopia envisioned by the protestors can be transformed into reality. Specifically, she hopes for the realization of equality for women and for the successful search for a man to love.

However, optimism and utopian expectation do not prevail for long on Beatriz's journey to Paris since one of the first scenes described is an act of sexual violence. When Beatriz hitchhikes to Paris, the driver rapes her while the radio is reporting on unrest among students in Paris and the violent responses by the police. Thus, the first mention of the student movement is not represented as a hopeful sign of a complete and peaceful liberation and fulfillment of the individual. Instead, the movement is exposed to police violence and the violence reported by the radio is accompanied by a physical act of violent sexual exploitation by a man against a woman.[38] The text equates the power held by the state with the gendered power structures between the sexes. This equation was also popular among West German feminists who equated the brutality of the Nazis with their parents' education whereby the fathers in particular were seen as authoritarian and repressive figures. Thus the gendered representations of the 1960s student movement point to the similarities between East and West and the shared moments in particular of the feminist movement in both countries. At the same time, it is these gendered representations that most clearly call into question the persuasiveness of these arguments. In the 1990s, we observe the trend either to demonize those who brought forth these arguments, or to pledge continued support for these claims that were subsumed under the umbrella claim that the personal is the political. The literary representations of these debates of binary opposites shed light on their potentially normative function and disciplinary nature and suggest other ways of transcending the ideological stalemate between these positions.

As recent research shows, the media took on a particularly important and new role for the student activists in the 1960s. While the students used the media in order to publicize their claims, they were also haunted by the media's power to influence public opinion. Despite her position as a secular singer and public performer, Morgner's troubadour is not able to analyze the signs of the twentieth century, in particular the information conveyed by media outlets. I read this failure as a commentary on the kinds of information the media makes accessible and as a critical juxtaposition of information marketed by the media and stories told by the literary imagination.[39] After the rape, Beatriz finds shelter with a group of construction workers. In a parallel construction to the rape scene, the workers expect her to have sexual intercourse with them. Female sexuality is treated as a commodity, exemplifying yet another instance of exploitation in the capitalist market place, since the workers agree to replace her torn dress in return. This scene confirms once more the observation that true liberation from all exploitation has to include gender equality. Beatriz stays with them and they ask her to listen to the radio and to provide them with up-to-date information on the political developments in Paris since they consider joining the political fight. Only slowly and with great difficulty is Beatriz able to recount the details of the news reports, and she never gains full understanding and interpretative command of their contents.[40] While this could be interpreted as a serious handicap for her joining any political organization, it also points to her particular position as a troubadour that is not marked by short-term interests but by a creative faculty that relies on historical knowledge and cultural heritage that transcend the stream of daily information provided by modern media outlets. Beatriz's position offers an advantage over those who see the utopia that the 1960s outline only as an unobtainable goal. For Beatriz, despite all the violence and exploitation she experiences, the possibilities for utopia are real, and her hope takes on fantastic dimensions that can only be satisfied in the aesthetic realm of fiction.

Melusine expects Beatriz to use her art as a tool in the political struggle. Melusine gives her the order to go directly to Paris and to support the workers' revolutionary efforts with her art by singing revolutionary songs: "Melde Dich also sofort nach Deiner Ankunft beim Streikkomitee der Renault Werke und der ORTF. Wenn Du die Poesie der Straße verwendest, werden Deine Lieder bald in aller Munde sein."[41] ("Report to the strike committee of the Renault plant and to Radio ORTF as soon as you arrive. If you use the poetry of the street, your songs will soon be on everyone's lips.")[42] Melusine also includes a list of "authentic slogans," that are being used in the political fight, among them "Seid Realisten, verlangt das Unmögliche; Der Traum ist Wirklichkeit; Die Poesie ist auf der Straße."[43] ("Be realists, demand the impossible. Dreams are reality. The poetry is on the street.")[44] She suggests that Beatriz uses them as a basis for her own compositions. This narrative development highlights the importance of art and of the individual's artistic engagement for the political struggle. At the same time, it questions traditional enlightened notions of art as high culture and of the work of art as an individual, creative, and original expression. Melusine emphasizes the revolutionary purpose of Beatriz's art. She describes Beatriz's art as a combination of individual and communal aspects. Since her art relies on and incorporates previous creative expressions, and is embedded in a political and social context of meaning-making, it mirrors the provocative and aesthetic/playful creativity of the students during the 1960s in the tradition of surrealism and situationism. This tradition points to the fruitful and longstanding relationship between the political and the aesthetic. This relationship defies any representational model that approaches the literary text as if it simply reproduced historical reality and thus can be interpreted as a historical document, without acknowledgement of its aesthetic tradition and form. Beatriz advances her understanding of her own art by contextualizing it with contemporaneous developments during the 1960s student movement.

Beatriz continues her journey to Paris which is marked by misunderstandings. She encounters a group of people who dress like her, an eclectic style best described as shaggy chic. "Weshalb ihr zunächst die ausgefransten Säume in die Augen fielen. Hosensäume, Rocksäume. Die Röcke waren auch bodenlang. Und nicht nur lumpig, sondern auch schmutzig."[45] ("Which is why she first noticed the frayed hems. Pants hems. Skirt hems. The skirts reached the grounds too. And they were not just ragged, but also dirty.")[46] Since she is not familiar with the drastically changing lifestyle, including the dress style that the students introduce in the 1960s, she mistakes them for other troubadours who have awaken from their sleep and plan to join the revolution. She is particularly pleased to see a sign of apparently decreasing gender trouble between the sexes since the group consists of both men and women. "Jedoch zweifelte sie keinen Augenblick, daß auch sie zu ehemaligen Schläferinnen gehörten. Die Trobadora war keine Ausnahme! Viele waren ihrem Beispiel gefolgt! Sogar Männer! Von dieser unverhofften, zu den schönsten Aussichten berechtigenden Offenbarung hingerissen, eilte Beatriz auf die Lumpigen zu und umarmte alle."[47] ("Yet she didn't doubt for a moment that these garments belonged to ex-sleepers too. So the trobadora was not an exception! Many had followed her example! Men too! Enraptured by this unexpected revelation that seemed to be grounds for the most favorable prospects, Beatrice hastened to the rag wearers and embraced them all.")[48] While Beatriz expresses euphoria which ironically is even described in terms of a religious experience as a revelation, the hippies keep their cool, leaving her with some drugs which Beatriz mistakes for sugar and consumes.[49] This scene represents yet another confusion of the authentic and the symbolic. Whereas Beatriz deciphers appearances at face value and shares her immediate emotional responses freely, the younger generation relies on drugs in order to expand their horizons, spur their imagination, and make their dreams come true, at least as long as the effect of the drugs last.

When Beatriz looks for overnight shelter, she approaches a building thinking that it still is the cloister that it was during the Middle Ages. However, the space is now used as a museum. The significance of the cloister as a space providing shelter and education is now preserved in the museum as a site exhibiting the cultural heritage. This changed function of the site further emphasizes the transcendental homelessness of people in the twentieth century and their need and hope for renewed utopian expectations. After drug consumption and a long journey, Beatriz is rather disheveled. When she attempts to tell her story to the museum director he mistakes her for a student who suffers from what he considers the traumatic events of Paris. As a member of the educated, liberal elite he frames the political events within the psychological notion of trauma. Displaying his sympathy, he takes her in, and together with his wife they watch the events in Paris unfold on the TV screen.[50] This provides yet another instance to document the importance of the media. At the same time, the museum director stands in for those who supported the uprisings ideologically but who would not join the actual movement. Even in France, where solidarity between the students and the workers was much stronger than elsewhere, the left did not unify in order to realize radical political change.

When the troubadour finally reaches Paris, the height of the student movement has already passed. Just like the other participants, Beatriz is confronted with the disappointment about the failure of the student movement and the decision which of the emerging groups that hope to continue the struggle to join. Temporarily, she moves into an apartment rented by four students, two of whom have already left for their summer vacations: "Und wo soll ich singen? fragte Beatriz. Die Studenten lachten bitter. Begriffen nicht, wie ein politischer Mensch den Wahlsieg der Reaktion verschlafen konnte."[51] ("'And where am I to sing?' asked Beatrice. The students laughed bitterly. Couldn't understand how a political person could sleep through the reactionaries' election victory.")[52] In order to support herself Beatriz works as a prostitute and soon marries one of her customers. Living under the disguise of the wife of the small business owner, she joins the political fight by conducting terrorist attacks in Paris. Furthermore, she falls in love with Alain, a socialist who takes on the task of educating Beatriz. As soon as she discovers that Alain is already married, a doppelganger is created. The other Alain, a member of the commune "Roter Mai" (Red May) counters these educational efforts. From him, she learns the following: "Ein Revolutionär verachtet jede Lehrmeinung und verzichtet auf alle Wissenschaft von der Welt. Er überläßt sie künftigen Geschlechtern. Er kennt nur eine einzige Wissenschaft: die Zerstörung. ... Es gibt für ihn nur einen einzigen Genuß, einen einzigen Trost, eine Belobigung und Befriedigung: den Erfolg der Revolution."[53] ("A revolutionary despises every doctrine and renounces every science in the world. He leaves that up to future generations. He knows only one science, that of destruction. ... For him, there is only one single pleasure, one single consolation, one commendation and satisfaction: the success of the revolution.")[54] While Beatriz enjoys having sex with Alain and other members of the commune she continues reading Marx and begins to learn German, since the first Alain insists on reading Marx and Engels in the original.[55]

This plot development indicates that Morgner was acutely aware of the tensions surrounding the intersections between political and personal fulfillment. These tensions intensified after the disappointing ending of May 1968 in Paris. After the height of the student movement in May 1968 solidarity among the protestors vanished and instead numerous political fractions emerged. All of them proposed different approaches in order to continue the political fight. Some decided to return to the mainstream and to change society from within, others joined various Marxist, Marxist-Leninist, Maoist, and Trotskyite organizations, and others decided to go underground and to fight against the state with violence. Emerging terrorism led to discussions whether violence was a legitimate means in the political struggle. Beatriz embodies these historical developments. Since she arrived too late to support the students by singing, she learned to build and throw bombs, privileging destructive and terrorist activities over a poetic engagement with the world in order to achieve radical change. While she enjoys the sexual freedom and the countercultural lifestyle in the commune and conducts terrorist attacks, she is secretly in love with the socialist Alain who follows the rather conventional path, albeit on the left, since he is married, works hard in order to educate himself, and teaches her. Morgner's familiarity with these tensions within the 1960s student movement and subsequent developments reveals the text's goal to align utopianism and radical politics, even if only in the literary realm.

The text suggests that Beatriz's art is a potentially powerful tool in the political struggle; however, Beatriz arrives too late in order to support the students with her art. Since the text attributes great importance to language, it criticizes the language use of the 1960s student movement as inadequate. Despite some catchy and witty slogans, the protestors were not able to develop a language that represents the utopian hopes and dreams of the students and foreshadows a utopian reality becoming reality. Hence, Beatriz expresses her disappointment with the movement's language use. While the activists searched for new ways to express themselves and to radically alter the relationship between the self and the world, this search did not manifest itself in an adequate language. Rather, language remained a tool in the hands of those of power, whether they were representatives of the state and other authorities or leaders of the 1960s student movement. The language the students used also failed to adequately represent experiences and could not overcome the real or imagined abyss between the representational mode of language use and the seemingly authentic immediacy of their experiences. This lack of progress when it comes to language and its use is blamed for the failure to introduce the desired utopia. During a nightly flight on Melusine's back who appears in the shape of a dragon, Beatriz comments on the disagreement between the two women: "Beatriz erinnerte der Sprachstil von Melusine an gewisse Debatten der Kommunemitglieder in Paris. Auch war die Rückenpanzerung so scharf, daß Beatriz bald unter Sitzbeschwerden litt, weshalb sie die Schönheiten, die ein nächtlicher Flug auf einem Drachenrücken bietet, nicht recht genießen konnte."[56] ("Melusine's style of speech reminded Beatrice of certain debates among the members of the Paris commune. Also, the armor-plated back was so sharp that Beatrice was soon suffering from seating discomfort, for which reason she couldn't properly enjoy the beauties of a nocturnal flight on a dragon's back.")[57] Beatriz condemns the rhetoric of many of the activists because instead of facing injustice and oppression they introduce yet another metastructure to discuss these issues. While the students were aware that language plays an important role in the political struggle, they were not able to escape its seductive qualities to cement power. The word ceremonies on all sides of the political spectrum merely disguise the attempts to hold on and to expand power. Only art is credited with enabling a more fluid and open use of language that expresses human hopes and dreams and outlines utopian expectations.

When Beatriz meets the East German Uwe Parnitzke, a regular participant at the evenings organized by the "Freundschaftsgesellschaft Frankreich–DDR" (Friendship Society France–GDR) in support of official recognition of the GDR, she is fascinated by his accounts of the GDR. In an ironic inversion she believes that it is not Paris but East Berlin that fulfills her desire to live in a utopian state. Therefore, she decides to leave Paris behind and to move to East Berlin where she meets Laura. From there, the second half of the novel unfolds.

Prague

Through Beatriz's move to the GDR, the student uprisings in Paris and Prague, usually thought of as distinct and different events, symbolically meet in East Berlin. The narrative positions East Berlin as the midpoint between these two cities, creating transnational sites of protest that transcend the physical border and the ideological barriers of the Cold War. With Beatriz as messenger, people in East Berlin were aware of the political tensions on both sides of the Wall in 1968, and the Eastern half of the city served as an, at least imagined, site of encounter for the activists and their ideas and ideals.

While Beatriz's move confirms the relevance of East Berlin during the 1960s, her move also signals the disappointment over the events in Paris. The end of the novel evokes the Prague Spring, another failed attempt to initiate change from below. The day after the celebration of the victory of the left in France in 1973, a moment that confirms the return to parliamentary democracy in France, Beatriz has a deadly accident while cleaning the windows of her apartment in a high-rise in East Berlin. Beatriz's death suggests the end of the hope that utopian ideals can indeed become reality. Paris and Prague now seem to stand only for the failed uprisings in the 1960s.

The novel concludes with nearly the same sentence it begins: "Denn natürlich war das Land ein Ort des Wunderbaren."[58] ("For, of course, this country was a land of miracles.")[59] Instead of being able to enjoy a utopian vision at the end, Emde suggests that the reader is led back to the beginning of the novel, to start reading again. "By refusing to give the reader a clear end to her story, Morgner rejects traditional notions of utopian visions as a type of counter-reality and instead constructs her utopia as a model of re-reading."[60] However, the first and the last sentence are not completely identical. The important difference between the last sentence and the first one, "Natürlich ist das Land ein Ort des Wunderbaren" ("For, of course this country is a land of miracles"), lies in the use of the tense and the addition of "denn."[61] Whereas the first sentence that opens the book suggests that the GDR is to be understood as a place that is marvelous, and as such a place where utopian ideals have already become reality, the last sentence shifts the focus to the past. The utopia ended and the word "denn" suggests that a critical reevaluation is necessary as to whether the country ever fulfilled utopian ideals. This last sentence places the story in a larger historical context. Beatriz's fall evokes the historical "Defenestrations of Prague" which in both cases were the starting points of wars.[62] Thus, even though the Prague Spring is not mentioned explicitly in the novel, its history is evoked. The aspiration of a peaceful rebellion is crushed by the violent responses of the states that felt the student protests on both sides of the Berlin Wall challenged their very existence. The sequel to *Leben und Abenteuer der Trobadora Beatriz nach Zeugnissen ihrer Spielfrau Laura*, called *Amanda. Ein Hexenroman* takes up the theme of the student movement as a global and transnational event by turning Berlin into the site of open political conflict.

Berlin

The second novel of the trilogy, *Amanda*, seems to build on the theme of failed revolutions, missed opportunities, and disappointed expectations. Compared with the first novel, the mood has changed completely. The utopian hopes that the 1960s student movement inspired across the globe have given way to a political and social reality that is characterized by the development of heterogeneous and often hostile political groups that either attempt to change society one step at a time, fight against society with violent means, or continue their opposition outside the political system without much promise of ever achieving their goals. This disappointment is reflected in the changes Beatriz undergoes. She reappears but has turned into a siren in the shape of an owl with a woman's face. She has lost her tongue and can no longer sing. Having fallen silent, she switches to written communication and finally commits to writing about her experiences instead of supporting the ongoing political struggle with her performances as a singer and songwriter. She now lives in a cage at the Berlin Zoo, laboriously scratching the words of her novel onto paper with her claws. The harmonious fusion of opposites envisioned in *Leben und Abenteuer der Trobadora Beatriz nach Zeugnissen ihrer Spielfrau Laura* was not successful and the motif of fragmentation, instead of symbolizing multiplicity and (reproductive) multitude, takes on a disabling meaning for the individual.

In order to make up for her missing half Beatriz, Laura has been reborn with a "hexische Hälfte," a female "doppelganger" who, under the name of Amanda, assumes an identity on her own. Due to this double fragmentation, Laura is unable to cope with the demands posed by the politically more radical figures who criticize her for attempting to find a niche in GDR society in order to solely focus on raising her son. In the end, she jumps out of the window, thus repeating Beatriz's deadly fall in the first part of the trilogy. Yet Laura's defenestration does not lead to a political or military conflict, but to a further retreat and the attempt for religious redemption in the vein of Goethe's *Faust*. At the end of *Amanda*, Laura collapses into a pathetic Gretchen figure who calls pitifully after Heinrich, the father of her child, who has been imprisoned. Sure enough, a disembodied voice informs her "Er ist gerichtet" ("He is judged").[63] This strand of the narrative suggests that there is no escape from the totalitarian state and as such, all utopian aspirations have to be buried.

And yet, the novel refocuses the attention on the student movements as suspended between Paris and Prague via East and West Berlin. The 1960s protests are now embedded in the Cold War and its ideological stalemate between East and West. East and West Germany and even more specifically East and West Berlin serve as the site of conflict that embodies the Cold War. Morgner continues to focus on the media as one of the most important tools in this conflict. Amanda, Laura's other half, is a witch who one day leaves Laura's apartment through the window on her broomstick. The West German TV station ZDF interprets this event as yet another defenestration. Spreading rumors concerning the motives for this political murder and the remains of the body, the commentator named Kleitgen uses the opportunity to connect the historical events in Prague with those that he reportedly witnessed in East Berlin, embedding Laura and Amanda firmly in the midst of world history.[64] In a highly ironic scene he reports from East Berlin:

> Prag ist nicht Berlin. Der Berliner Frühling muß dem Prager Frühling nicht gleichen, verehrte Zuschauer. Dennoch bin ich sicher, an einem historischen Ort zu stehen, der Weltgeschichte machen wird. Welche, steht noch in den Sternen, die ein trüber Himmel dieser traditionsreichen Stadt verbirgt. … Das Vorgehen der Ostberliner Behörden hat eine weltweite Kampagne ausgelöst. In allen europäischen Hauptstädten wurden bereits 'Komitees zur Befreiung von Laura Salman' gegründet.[65]

In his conclusion the commentator oversteps the boundaries of journalism and enters into activism by urging the citizens of the GDR to form "Bürgerinitiativen": "Wer will, kann seine Stellungnahme gegen die Verhaftung von Laura Salman, für einen menschlichen Sozialismus, auch direkt an die ZDF-Redaktion richten" (You are welcome to send your comment against the arrest of Laura Salman and for a socialism with a human face to the ZDF).[66]

Morgner's novel satirically exposes the media and their role during the late 1960s and 1970s. While parts of the 1960s student movement hoped to utilize the media for their goals, the media at the same time took advantage of the students with their ability to shape the public's perception of events and ultimately to influence world history. Hence, it is not art or the individual's creativity, but the media's ability to spin and frame stories and to mobilize the population in order to advance history. In a complete reversal of historical reality, the West German journalist aligns Prague and East Berlin in order to distract from the West German student movement. Emphasizing the dissatisfaction of the population in East Berlin with their own regime, the journalist conveniently appropriates the solution the population behind the Berlin Wall seeks. In a complete reversal of ideology, the journalist calls for a third solution of the conflict, for a "socialism with a human face." In an ironic inversion, the West German media, often highly critical of the West German student movement, took advantage of signs of rebellion on the other side of the Berlin Wall in order to advance Cold War ideology and turn into activists that support the East Germans' quest for freedom. This satirical representation debunks the myth of objective and independent journalism and at the same time connects the often neglected web of relations between Prague, Paris, and Berlin. Morger's second novel contributes to and shapes the truly global and transnational dimension of the 1960s student movement that overcomes and transcends the seemingly insurmountable Berlin Wall by emphasizing the real and imagined relations among the 1960s student protestors.

The Women's Movement and Its Representation in the Wake of 1968

The third part of Morgner's trilogy remains a fragment. Hence, it is hard to know which direction Morgner would have taken the final version of the text. Some of the fragments continue the story of Beatriz and Laura. Beatriz receives a less prominent role. She seeks fulfillment by falling in love with a man that was created from a female rib. He is called Desiree and is the one who is desired in order to fulfill utopian dreams. He also takes on the role of the harlequin in order to serve as the source of laughter in a world that lacks humor. Laura is sick since she is missing her other half, Beatriz, and hence is in the care of a home health aide who also serves as a male muse. He tries to stimulate her interest in the story of the man who was formed from a female rib and encourages Laura to write about this event. However, he cautions her that times have changed and that female readers do not want to read novels about women, but nonfiction books about men in order to improve their situation in a world that is marked by continued gender bias.

The fragments of the third part introduce another version of the creation of a man by a woman, namely the story of Hero and Leander, which takes a central place in the fragments. Hero had hoped to create a better world for herself by inventing Leander, a mirror image of Desiree, yet instead she is confronted with hatred because of her creation. With the reversed biblical image of a man created from a woman's rib, Morgner outlines the utopian hope for a renewed interest in more egalitarian relations between men and women. Hence, the fragments collected and edited by Rudolf Bussmann in *Das heroische Testament* reveal Morgner's intention to continue to work with the themes of protest and social change with a focus on gender relations. Immediately after its height, the student movement was widely considered a failure. The movement that was unified, albeit briefly, fell apart and utopian expectations had been disappointed and were abandoned. Political, social, and cultural engagement with the world developed in a variety of different directions. The fragments offer a creative reflection of subsequent events in the 1970s and 1980s, in particular the backlash against feminism and the women's movement. Morgner portrays this backlash as a disagreement among women about how to proceed after the emergence of a women's movement in the late 1960s and early 1970s which did not bring the radical immediate change that participants had hoped for. "Immer diese Politik und diese Emanzipation und diese Atomkriegssachen und ökologischen Katastrophen pipapo – nee. Wer davon nicht abschaltet, kommt nie zu Gemütlichkeit. Ich sag immer, in einer netten Wohnung mit Mann und Farbfernseher ist alles halb so schlimm" (At all times, this politics and this women's liberation and the nuclear war and the ecological disasters—no. If you don't disengage you will never find peace. I always say, in a nice apartment, with a husband and color TV, everything is much less worse).[67] In one of the few finished chapters, "Der Mann aus der Rippe" (The man from the Rib), Morgner returns to her main interest, namely to inscribe women into history. The chapter revolves around the news of a man that was created from a female rib. Hero is credited with this discovery and she worries about ways to import her self-made lover into the GDR. Women on both sides of the Berlin Wall are excited about the possibilities of creating men according to their own image, desires, and wishes. Other voices denounce these attempts of feminist self-determination and self-sufficiency. In a series of so-called *Dunkelweiberbriefe* (Letters of Obscure Shrews) Morgner reflects on the backlash, in particular among women, against advances made by women. In the aftermath of the 1960s student protest she considers efforts by the women movement to advance gender equity as threatened. With this title she alludes to the sixteenth century which witnessed the publication of the *Dunkelmännerbriefe* (Letters of Obscure Men) and hence inscribes her own text into a tradition of satire and religious, ethnic, and ideological conflict.

True to her attempt to open up reflective spaces with her writing Morgner references one of the most famous satires of the sixteenth century, the *Letters of Obscure Men*, which was published anonymously in 1515 and continues to provoke debates today. The work grew out of a controversy originated by Johann Pfefferkorn, a converted Jew, who denounced Hebrew books as tools of heresy and advocated their destruction. The emperor, whose authority had been invoked, sought the counsel of scholars in order to solve the conflict. Johann Reuchlin, a prestigious Hebraist, defended Hebrew literature and received the universal support of humanists; the theological faculties of several universities, on the other hand, sided with Pfefferkorn. Cologne, under the leadership of the Dominican Jacob Hoogstraten, a member of the faculty and inquisitor of the region, became Pfefferkorn's most zealous champion. At the height of the controversy, in 1513, Reuchlin published a volume of letters written by fellow scholars in defense of his position. He entitled the collection *Letters of Famous Men*. In 1515 another volume appeared under the title *Letters of Obscure Men*. At first glance it was a collection of epistles supporting Pfefferkorn. On closer inspection, however, it turned out to be a hoax calculated to ridicule the anti-Reuchlinists. The fictitious letters, written in atrocious Latin and portraying the writers as fools and scoundrels, were put together in the humanistic camp. Among the authors were Crotus Rubianus and Ulrich von Hutten, who politicized the religious struggle, pouring out a flood of pamphlets in the name of German liberty and finally advocating armed resistance against the clergy. Hutten's propaganda pieces were eagerly read in his own time, but fell into oblivion after his death, whereas the *Letters of Obscure Men*, with their timeless wit and humor, became a literary classic.[68]

By referencing these Letters, considered a "literary masterpiece produced during one of the most famous controversies in pre-Reformation Germany" and "still considered one of the classics of Western literature,"[69] Morgner writes her own trilogy into a historical and literary tradition that is full of satire and controversy and hence contradicts the assertion that women have no humor and are not equipped to participate in (academic) debates. Controversies surrounding the *Letters of Obscure Men* were grounded not only in religious and ethnic struggles, but also ideological ones, as Karl-Heinz Gerschmann points out in his comments about other "obscure letters" published in Germany during times of political upheaval.[70] Erika Rummel investigates the Reuchlin affair in terms of cultural diversity. She argues that meaning arises from the interpretation of the facts and the polemics surrounding the affair and explores its three different contexts, portraying the controversy alternatively "as a battle between orthodox Christians and Judaizers, between Catholics and reformers, or between representatives of scholasticism and champions of humanism."[71] In a similar vein, the controversy surrounding the women's movement in Germany in the late 1960s and 1970s and the debates ensuing during the process of memory construction in the 1990s after the fall of the Berlin Wall mirrors the diverse interpretations and the importance of the discursive structures that govern these interpretations.

Morgner describes her *Epistolae obscurarum feminarum* as "eine satirische Reaktion auf diesen beängstigenden Leistungszwang und auf gewisse gefährliche repressive Erscheinungen die Emanzipation der Frau betreffend" (a satirical reaction against the frightening performance pressure and against the repressive backlash against women's liberation).[72] In these letters, a variety of voices expresses concern about the news of the man created from a woman's rib. The letters are addressed to Dr. Gracia Ortwin, "Wissenschaftlerin für das Gute und Schöne,"[73] who developed a theory of silence as the adequate response to interactions with men. Her supporters question, illustrate, encourage, and advance Ortwin's position. In their letters, the women distance themselves explicitly from positions that were developed in the late 1960s and 1970s in conjunction with or as a response to the 1960s student movement. These women acknowledge women's limitations as being stupid by nature,[74] belittle working women as being too lazy to cook[75] and argue against theories that perceive "aussprechen" (vocalization) and not only "diskutieren" (to discuss), but also "ausdiskutieren" (to discuss fully) as progress.[76] Instead they embed Ortwin's theory of silence within their notion of a cultural heritage and tradition that governed the relation between men and women before the emergence of "Emanzen" (man-hating feminists). These female letter writers equate relationships between men and women with diplomatic relationships between states which are often determined by engaging in conversations without saying anything. In addition to advancing the theory and practice of silence, Ortwin's supporters also reshape other areas that the women's movement attempted to unmask in order to advance women's equality, namely the areas of women's beauty and sexual equality.

One "modebewusste Leserin" (fashion-conscious reader) argues that talking is silver and silence is golden. The key word gold then prompts her to argue that women who focus on their outward beauty, e.g., by wearing golden jewelry, are also good and truthful women. She reduces Plato's triad of beauty, truth, and the good to outer beauty of women created by fashion and skin and hair care. This argument reinstates the classical position of women as beautiful souls, undermining the women's movement's attempt to liberate women from the dictatorship of the fashion and beauty industry. Having learned from the feminist movement, Ortwin's supporter suggests a feminine approach to the philosophical imperative "Know thyself." The imperative is then understood as "Was steht mir, was kann ich tragen und was nicht, was kleidet mich vorteilhaft, welche Accessoires geben mir das gewisse Etwas" (What suits me, what can I wear, what makes me look attractive and which accessories add that special touch).[77] This letter also asserts that women in the GDR look toward the West. It plays with the notion that fashion and design advance with more innovation and speed in a market-driven economy. The GDR is described as provincial and stripped of its political significance as the site of revolutions; Paris is understood solely as the fashion capital of the world. Hence, social conflicts and inequalities are depoliticized, described in economic terms, and embedded in a cultural tradition that resists change.

Another letter engages with the idea of sexual liberation. The physician writing the letter cautions against the import of ideas from the West and considers sex not as a social, but a private act that should not be governed by the state. Nevertheless, he acknowledges the advantages of the sexual revolution for a general productivity. Hence, he functionalizes the quest for women to explore their sexuality and to find sexual satisfaction. "Die sogenannte sexuelle Revolution ist also nur ein verschwommener Begriff für das, was wissenschaftlich exakt 'Emanzipation der Frau' genannt wird und durch das Wohl des Mannes seine vornehmste Bestätigung erfährt" (The so-called sexual revolution is therefore only a vague term for what is scientifically accurately described as 'the liberation of women' which justifies its existence by guaranteeing the well-being of men).[78] Women's sexual liberation not only enhances men's sexual satisfaction, but also serves as a political weapon because people who let off steam sexually are less likely to notice the lack of other freedoms, such as the freedom to travel. Women's sexual liberation is understood as yet another weapon in the ideological conflicts of the Cold War in order to exercise disciplinary power over humans.

This backlash against the women's movement reaches another height with the letter from Gerhild Eiferbach from Cologne. She points not only to the ideological but also the religious and ethnic tensions that informed the satire of the *Letters of Obscure Men*. By exclaiming "Von der Inquisition lernen heißt gegen die Emanzen siegen lernen!" (To learn from the inquisition means to learn to win against feminists!).[79] Eiferbach suggests that violence is the ultimate tool in this struggle. Furthermore, she suggests that converts might be the most efficient investigators against their former allies. Citing the example of Johannes Pfefferkorn, the converted Jew who wanted to eradicate all Jewish scripture, she is proud to have been converted from being an ardent feminist to being an active opponent of all feminist aspirations. Eiferbach's letter foreshadows the violent confrontations that lead to the development of terrorism and push the limit of the public's acceptance of the use of force by the state.

Even though the third part of the *Salman* trilogy remains a fragment, the two parts that are most developed, the story of Hero and Leander and the *Dunkelweiberbriefe*, illustrate the utopian hope of gender equality which continues the discussion of art and its aesthetic strategies to contribute to political and social movements that marked the first two novels. The ambivalence between utopian hope and disappointed expectations is mirrored in Morgner's approach to art itself and its production as a happening, an art form that enjoyed increasing popularity in the 1970s. One of the letters sharply criticizes the happening as an aberration of artistic production and as a decadent phenomenon of the

West. Embedded in her story of Hero and Leander, Morgner describes how numerous artists follow Hero's footsteps and attempt to create men. In one of these happenings, the artist extends an invitation to the audience to participate in the creation of men out of bread rolls (a play with words on the German word for ribs [Rippe] and bread roll [Schrippe]) followed by a shared devouring of the communally created sculptures. The happening as a collective enterprise and as an event instead of a process which leads to the creation of an object that can be exhibited and sold on the market place challenges traditional notions of art. Its critique expressed in the satirical letter seemingly aims to reinstate classical notions of art, only to be dismantled through the use of irony. In addition, Morgner responded to criticism by other feminists who questioned her motives in creating men out of a female rib instead of women as companions for Hero and Beatriz. Morgner's response is very much in line with her hopes for a human, instead of a gendered, utopia. She insists on the duality of each human life whereby the female part in each woman is slightly larger and in each man, it is the male part that is larger. In the tradition of Jakob Böhme, Giordano Bruno, and Galileo Galilei who are alluded to at various points in the fragment, Morgner does not expect to be understood by her contemporaries but she nevertheless pursues her radical thinking and her utopian dreams regardless of negative repercussions. Despite the proclaimed end of all social utopias Morgner recognizes the continued existence and necessity of individual utopia that manifests itself in love. Since the desired other half is missing, both Hero and Beatriz create their other halves by taking the missing parts out of their own bodies. In this sense, both unhinge something literally and figuratively within their own bodies and both create someone out of their own bodies ("sich etwas herausnehmen"). On a symbolic level, this creative process serves as a performance of resistance that attributes to art transformative powers and political substance.

Montage, Fragmentation, Collaboration: The Narrative of Memory

Morgner's *Salman* trilogy has been read as a critique of classical, realist, or male aesthetic models of fiction writing since her text dismantles conventional notions of unified characters, narrators, time, place, and fixed genres in favor of montage, fragmentation, and collaboration. Silke von der Emde's analysis, for example, shows that the narrative structure reflects theoretical developments in the 1960s and 1970s and points to Morgner's interest in modern and postmodern thought and aesthetics. The intertextual references to novels of the European literary canon, most notably those representing the three prototypical male figures, Odysseus, Faust, and Don Quixote, have been interpreted as Morgner's attempts to create a space for the development of a female and, ultimately, a human aesthetics. This aesthetic privileges creative montage over forced unity, multiple fragmentations over deceptive wholeness, and artistic collaboration over workings of a man of genius. Fragmentation, montage, and collaboration are able to approximate a language that expresses the utopian longings of the 1960s protestors. Fragmentation, montage, and collaboration also account for the silences and the voids of those words that are not explicitly and directly expressed in political, social, and cultural moments of protest and rebellion. Morgner's narrative technique makes a unique contribution to the cultural memory of 1968. Placing Morgner's trilogy in the context of 1968 emphasizes the discursive elements that connect dissent and resistance in the GDR with other protest movements in Europe and the world.

Morgner's text suspends the separation of the real and the imaginary, of fact and fiction.[80] Travel through time and space, gender changes, and elements taken from fairy tales, legends, and myth are treated on the same level as very realistic descriptions of everyday life in the GDR and elsewhere. Thus, Morgner's novel was both praised and condemned for its overabundance of fantasy. The use of the fantastic enables Morgner to develop an aesthetic that responds to and comments on the cultural policies in the GDR in the 1960s and 1970s. The humanist legacy of Weimar classicism, whose innocence had been preserved throughout the Third Reich, at least according to official GDR doctrine, served as the basis for the state's position on culture and for its national legitimacy. After the failure of the so-called *Bitterfelder Weg*, which proclaimed the dual goal of familiarizing authors with the world of the workers and of encouraging workers to write about their experiences at the work place, the SED aimed to restrict the arts at the eleventh plenary session of the Central Committee in December 1965. Fiction, film, and popular music were sharply criticized for their tendency to follow trends in the West and, in doing so, to undermine socialism. Subsequently, censorship was more widely exercised again after a relative détente in the first half of the decade. It was also clear that the state aimed to curtail any expressions of sympathy or support for the reform movements in neighboring countries, mainly the Czechoslovak Socialist Republic. After the change of guard in 1971, a brief, yet more liberal approach to cultural policies came to a rapid end with the forced expatriation of Wolf Biermann in 1976. His expulsion caused tremendous tension between the state and its artists, a conflict that never really ended again until the fall of the Berlin Wall.

The trilogy's suspension between fact and fiction is mirrored in its narrative aesthetic which highlights Morgner's own understanding of storytelling and its relation to history, politics, and the public discourse. During the contract negotiations for the book that Beatriz and Laura write, Laura describes their literary technique to the editor of the publishing house *Aufbau* who challenges their book proposal. Laura argues: "Die orthodoxe Romanform verlangt Festhalten an einer Konzeption über mehrere Jahre. Das kann angesichts heftiger politischer Bewegungen in der Welt und einer ungeheuren Informationsflut heute nur trägen oder sturen Naturen gelingen. Was ich anbiete, ist die Romanform der Zukunft. Die zum operativen Genre gehört."[81] ("The orthodox novel form requires sustaining a concept over several years. In view of violent political movements throughout the world and an appalling information explosion, that is possible nowadays only for lethargic or stubborn characters. What I'm offering is the novel form of the future. Which is part of the operative genre.")[82] She continues that all changes, omissions as well as additions, could be accepted without problem since the genre of their text, which she defines as "operative[r] Montageroman"[83] ("operative montage novel")[84] is a resilient genre that is flexible without ever losing its meaning.

The techniques of montage, fragmentation, and collaboration adequately represent the ruptures of the 1960s student protests. Instead of creating a well-balanced, comprehensive, and complete story, stories of collisions, abrupt changes, and conflicting truths are told and negated from various angles. Speeches, interviews, poems, excerpts from army reports and scientific research, and intertextual references mingle with fairy tales, legends, myth, and dialogues between historical and fictional figures. The interruption of the flow of the narrative and the introduction of heterogeneous materials blur the lines between fact and fiction and achieve an alienating effect. Each new fragment comes as a surprise, looks out of place, and cannot be assimilated easily, pointing to the procedural character of both storytelling and history. Laura's definition also points to another advantage of making montage, fragmentation, and collaboration the central characteristics of the genre "operativer Montageroman." On the one hand, Laura indicates her willingness to make changes to the text and thus to work constructively not only with the editor but, if necessary, also with the censor. On the other hand, this openness and flexibility also indicates that censorship will not be able to destroy the novel completely. Since its narrative is so fragmented, meaning is not created at one concrete point such as at the word, sentence, or paragraph level but within the imaginary space that develops during the process of writing and reading. Read in conjunction with the discourse on 1968, there is a tremendous—maybe overly optimistic—belief in the transformative power of creative expression.

As the conversation with the editor of the Aufbau-Verlag continues Laura places special emphasis on the kind of reader their novel requires: "Lesen soll schöpferische Arbeit sein: Vergnügen."[85] ("Reading should be creative work: Pleasure.")[86] Morgner's use of montage, fragmentation, and collaboration relies upon an active reader who is aware of this playful and creative opportunity and who is willing to devote himself or herself to the work of reading for pleasure. Morgner herself commented on the need to read her novels slowly, contemplatively.[87] Thus, it is not the author who determines meaning but it is the reader who constructs the narrative while and as long as he or she is reading. The confusion of authorial positions and narrative voices, including that identified as Morgner's own, further contributes to the emphasis placed upon the process of reading as interpretation and analysis. Morgner's art demands that the reader engages productively with the fragmented text, adding meanings and creating coherent snapshots of meanings that are not apparent in "real life."

Emde calls this narrative process "überschreiben" ("overwriting," also in the sense of "transcribing" and "overstriking") and convincingly argues that one has to understand this process as a form of utopia. This process hinges on processes of remembering that constitute layers of memories and serves as a reflection on Morgner's aesthetics: "Morgner rejects traditional notions of utopian vision as a type of counter-reality and instead constructs her utopia as a model of re-reading. In fact, re-reading, re-writing, and "wondering" about the conditions in which we live constitute the utopian process that Morgner promotes in her *Salman* Trilogy."[88] Emde's notion of rereading mirrors my own proposition to re-read, and as such, to remember Morgner's trilogy in order to gain an understanding of the contributions to the discourse on 1968 by writers of the former GDR.

With the notion of "operativer Montageroman" Morgner's novels challenge traditional definitions of literary productivity as creative expression by emphasizing the work that is done on part of both the writer and the reader and by placing emphasis on the intertextual references and the context of the text. Writing and reading are not forms of individual expression, but always occur in dialogue with other voices and in a social context. The notion of the author as the creator of an original, authentic, and autonomous piece of art is challenged since the novel develops at least three authorial figures: Beatriz, the professional singer and song writer who contributes part of the material, Laura who negotiates the contract with the publisher and who outlines the aesthetic of reading and writing, and Irmtraud Morgner, the author who writes herself into the novel.

The novel invites its readers to challenge traditional notions of political or engaged literature. The novel reintroduces the importance of the narrative, that is, of the literary form that transcends the confinements of a sociopolitical analysis. With its use of montage and fragmentation, Morgner's text resists the dominant discourses of ideological appropriation by constructing a mosaic that is "mehr als die Summe seiner Steine"[89] ("more than the sum of its stones").[90] Morgner proposes that the aesthetic of the narrative determines what becomes accepted truth and which stories shape cultural memory and a shared history. In her writing, we are not witnessing the attempt to streamline processes of remembering and forgetting by privileging a dominant narrative over all others, but the attempt to create opportunities for storytelling by weaving a fabric with a rich texture consisting of many different colorful threads. The reader is invited to continue the author's work by adding his or her own threads while reading. Montage and fragmentation do not create an incomplete narrative, but rather a narrative with multiple meanings and multiplying stories collocated by many voices.

Writing Novels, Creating Memories

The perceived or real absence of massive student protests in the East does not mean that the West German, European, and global political and social unrest did not affect East Germany's youth, artists, and intellectuals. As my close reading of Morgner's trilogy suggests, East German discourses of protest and opposition of the time were firmly embedded within a German, European, and global context. One of Morgner's motivations for writing was, in her own words, to support the "Eintritt der Frau in die Historie" (the entry of woman into history).[91] Women, she argues, have played virtually no active part in the creation of history of mankind. If they appear at all in the narratives of our traditions, it is invariably only in an oblique way, in the position of an object perceived by a male subject. Morgner's *Salman* trilogy represents an experimental attempt to redress this imbalance. The text creates a historical, mythological, and legendary space for womanhood. This space makes an important contribution to the cultural memory of 1968 since the 1960s student movement did not recognize its own gendered approach to the sexes. Rather, despite all opposite claims, the students perpetuated some of the rather hierarchical gender biases that shaped mainstream society at that time. Morgner's voice from behind the Berlin Wall emphasizes this lack of gender equality by privileging the female voice to participate in the discourse on 1968.

In addition to successfully writing women into history and challenging traditional, male conceptualizations of writing, the trilogy accomplishes another goal that is at the center of this study. The novels create an imaginary space for all those movements that inspired and shaped the 1960s and 1970s in East and West. This space invites the reader's critical, yet playful, engagement with these movements that currently tend to be either depoliticized, demonized, or subsumed in the mainstream of society and thus lose their potential to initiate change. Excluding Morgner's novel from the various attempts to present rereadings of so-called GDR literature would have two effects: the exclusion of literature written in the GDR within the discourse on 1968 and the exclusion of women as active participants in this discourse.

Furthermore, the novel not only shapes the reader's understanding of a different perspective on German history during the Cold War, but also allows us to reflect on our contemporary situation marked by the devastations of war and genocide, large-scale environmental destruction, and grave economic inequalities—problems that cannot be solved by nation states alone, but that deserve and require global attention. As the novel begins with detonations that wake Beatriz and destroy her castle which contains the traces of the troubadour's earlier life in the Middle Ages, Morgner reminds us that it only seems to be faster, more convenient, and cheaper to destroy historical sites and the nature surrounding and embedding it. Yet, ultimately, as her novel demonstrates, it is impossible to silence the voice of the troubadour who sings in order to remind those who listen of the past, encouraging them to anticipate the future. The figure of the troubadour embodies the utopian moment that permeates the cultural memory of the 1960s as a way to remember the 1960s student protests.

Positioning Morgner's trilogy within the cultural memory of 1968 suggests that there are distinct differences that challenge the demarcation between traditional notions of political and engaged literature in the West, as a result and consequence of the 1960s, and the notion of GDR literature as solely a reaction to official cultural politics or as an attempt to finding niches in the socialist state. Rather, literary expressions in both East and West need to be reread as political statements within the frames of their narratives. This allows us, the readers, to focus on their discursive fields between Paris and Prague via East Berlin instead of on the ideological battles of their reception. The act of rereading triggers memories and creates postmemories that shape the cultural memory of 1968 as a transnational German–German affair that recognizes its European and global repercussions.

Notes

1. The Paris Commune is in Prague. The Paris Commune is in Prague, it is still alive/ The revolution liberates itself/Marx himself and Lenin and Rosa and Trotsky/provide support for the communists. Communism holds tight/freedom and impregnates her with a child that laughs/life without bureaucrats becomes/liberated from exploitation and the power of despots. The Pharisees, the fat ones, they tremble/and smell the truth. The day will come/At the bottom of the Vltava the stones go hiking/There are four kings buried in Prague. We breathe again, comrades. We laugh/the laziness out of our chest/Man, we are stronger than rats and dragons!/And had forgotten and always knew. Wolf Biermann, *Alle Lieder* (Köln: Kiepenheuer & Witsch, 1991): 209.
2. Other prominent East '68ers are Erika Berthold, Thomas Brasch, Frank Havemann, Rosita Hunzinger, and Sandra Weigl. The book by Ute Kätzel, *Die 68erinnen. Portrait einer rebellischen Frauengeneration* (Berlin: Rowohlt, 2002) contains an interview with Erika Berthold who, together with Frank Havemann and Franziska and Gert Groszer, founded the Commune I East. This emphasizes the numerous exchanges between East and West during the 1960s and 1970s. Others remain skeptical, e.g., Ulrich Ott and Roman Luckscheiter's edited volume *Belles lettres/Graffiti. Soziale Phantasien und Ausdrucksformen der Achtundsechziger* (Göttingen: Wallstein, 2001), a collection of essays originally presented at a conference in conjunction with the exhibit "1968" in Marbach, documents the result of the discussion on 1968 and the GDR as a consensus that it is problematic to talk about an East German 1968. Hans Peter Krüger is quoted with his response to the topic "1968 and the GDR:" "Die ostdeutschen Achtundsechziger seien eine schwer zu definierende Gruppe, die von in den Westen gegangenen 'Kindern der Nomenklatura' (etwas Monika Maron) bis zu den beiden 'inneren Formen geistiger Opposition' gereicht habe, sei es in der Nähe des kulturellen Milieus der protestantischen Kirche (z.B. Christoph Hein) oder frei davon (unter Theaterautoren z.B. Bernd Tragelehn oder

Lothar Trolle). Die Mehrzahl von ihnen, so Krüger weiter, sei 'aber in den Säuberungen 1968–71 einfach untergegangen' oder stark diszipliniert worden. Die ostdeutschen Achtundsechziger hätten dann auch 1989/90 nur im Zusammenspiel mit ihren Vorgänger- und Nachfolger-Generationen eine auslösende Rolle gespielt" (The East German Sixtyeighters are a group that is hard to define. It included children of the nomenklatura who moved to West Germany (for example Monika Maron) and groups of inner opposition, for example close to the cultural milieu of the protestant church (Christoph Hein) or free of any affiliation (Bernd Tragelehn or Lother Trolle). In the years 1968–71, most of its members simply disappeared or had been disciplined. Hence, the East German Sixtyeighters only played the role of incubator in the context of previous and later generations) (ibid.: 8). McDougall interprets the relative anonymity of the protestors in the following way: "The East German ''68ers' had done most of their growing up in the post-Berlin Wall era of GDR history. In a climate dominated by political conformity, most of them were acutely aware of how far they could push their luck when it came to voicing their opposition to the invasion of Czechoslovakia. What is most striking about dissent among the youth at this time is precisely the fact that it was open and provocative, rather than secret and conspiratorial, in character—almost as if young people recognized the futility of organized 'resistance' and confined themselves to venting their frustration via anonymous (and relatively risk-free) graffiti and leaflets." Alan McDougall, *Youth Politics in East Germany: The Free German Youth Movement 1946–1968* (Oxford: Clarendon Press, 2004): 231f. See also Paul Kaiser and Claudia Petzold, ed., *Boheme und Diktatur in der DDR. Gruppen, Konflikte, Quartiere. 1970-1989* (Berlin: Verlag Fannei & Walz, 1997); and Ilko-Sascha Kowalczuk, "Wer sich nicht in Gefahr begibt …" Protestaktionen gegen die Intervention in Prag und die Folgen von 1968 für die DDR-Opposition" in *Widerstand und Opposition in der DDR*, ed. Klaus-Dietmar Henke, Peter Steinbach, and Johannes Tuchel (Köln, Weimar, Wien: Böhlau, 1999): 257–274.
3. Florian Havemann, *Havemann. Eine Behauptung* (Frankfurt a.M.: Suhrkamp, 2007): 857.
4. Ibid.: 858.
5. Dorothee Wierling, "How do the 1929ers and the 1949ers differ?" in *Power and Society in the GDR. 1961–1979. The 'Normalisation of Rule'?* ed. Mary Fulbrook (New York: Berghahn Books, 2009): 204–219, 214.
6. Thomas Brasch, *Vor den Vätern sterben die Söhne* (Berlin: Rotbuch Verlag, 1977): 36.
7. Ibid.: 59f.
8. For a detailed account of Brasch's 1968 see the article by Stephan Suschke in the *Berliner* Zeitung on 26 January 2008, <http://www.berlinonline.de/berliner-zeitung/spezial/dossiers/1968/92887/index.php> (accessed 16 March 2011).
9. Barbara Köhler, "A la recherché de la révolution perdue. Ein innerdeutscher Monolog," in *Women and the Wende: Social Effects and Cultural Reflections of the German Unification Process: Proceedings of a Conference held by Women in German Studies, 9–11 Sept 1993 at the University of Nottingham*, ed. Elizabeth Boa and Janet Wharton (Amsterdam, Atlanta: Rodopi, 1994): 1–5.
10. Ibid.: 4.

11. Konrad Jarausch, "Divided, Yet Reunited–The Challenge of Integrating German Post-War Histories," posted on H-German@H-Net.msu.edu, 1 February 2011. Other contributors included Christoph Klessmann and Peter Lautzas.
12. A conference organized by the Stiftung Sozialgeschichte für das 20. Jahrhundert in Bremen on 22 and 23 February 2008 with the title "Das Jahr 1968 aus der Perspektive der Gesellschaften Mittel-, Ost- und Südosteuropas:" <http://www.ahf-muenchen.de/Tagungsberichte/Berichte/pdf/2008/059-08.pdf> (accessed 18 July 2008).
13. Florian Havemann is an excellent case study of the intricate layering of memories that this study seeks to illuminate. Memorialized in Thomas Brasch's novella *Vor den Vätern sterben die Söhne* Havemann wrote the autobiographical account *Havemann* in the disguise of a family novel in which he recounts his family's history in three generations. From his perspective as an East '68er he dismantles his famous dissident father Robert Havemann. This is yet another example for the continuing interest in the literary father-son struggle. See the review by Christoph Dieckmann, "Das uralt kluge Kind. Florian Havemann ermordet seinen toten Vater, auf dass er lebe," *Die Zeit* 51 (2007) <http://www.zeit.de/2007/51/L-Havemann> (accessed 18 July 2008).
14. Marc-Dietrich Ohse, *Jugend nach dem Mauerbau: Anpassung, Protest und Eigensinn (DDR 1961–1974)* (Berlin: Ch. Links Verlag, 2003); Bernd Gehrke, "1968. Die 68-er Proteste in der DDR," *Aus Politik und Zeitgeschichte* 14–15 (31 March 2008): 40–46; Bernd Gehrke, "1968—das unscheinbare Schlüsseljahr der DDR," in *1968 und die Arbeiter. Studien zum proletarischen Mai in Europa*, ed. Bernd Gehrke and Gerd-Rainer Horn (Hamburg: VSA-Verlag, 2007): 103–130; and Michael Hofmann, "'Solidarität mit Prag.' Arbeiterproteste 1968 in der DDR," in *1968 und die Arbeiter. Studien zum proletarischen Mai in Europa*: 92–102. While Gehrke considers 1968 as central to GDR history, Ohse and Hofmann recognize that it does have a function, yet it was not a central experience, in particular when compared with the West.
15. Ina Merkel, "The GDR—A Normal Country in the Centre of Europe," in *Power and Society in the GDR. 1961–1979. The 'Normalisation of Rule'?* ed. Mary Fulbrook (New York, Oxford: Berghahn Books, 2009): 194–203, 196.
16. Wierling, "How do the 1929ers and the 1949ers Differ?": 210.
17. Christa Wolf, "Nur die Lösung: Sozialismus," *Neues Deutschland*, 4 September 1968: 4.
18. Wolfgang Emmerich, *Kleine Literaturgeschichte der DDR*. Erweiterte Neuausgabe. (Leipzig: Gustav Kiepenheuer Verlag, 1996).
19. For a discussion of the relation between 1989 and 1968 with respect to the GDR, see Günter Minnerup, "Germany 1968 and 1989: The Marginalized Intelligentsia Against the Cold War," in *Student Protest. The Sixties and After*, ed. Gerard J. DeGroot (London, New York: Longman, 1998): 201–215. For research that shows that the Berlin Wall was less impenetrable during the 1960s than usually thought, see Paulina Bren, "1968 East and West. Visions of Political Change and Student Protest from across the Iron Curtain," in *Transnational Moments of Change. Europe 1945, 1968, 1989*, ed. Gerd-Rainer Horn and Padraic Kenney (Lanham: Rowman and Littlefield, 2003): 119–135.

20. Ulrich Plenzdorf's *Die neuen Leiden des jungen W.* (Rostock: Hinstorff, 1973) was a huge success in both states and caused significant debates about youth and youth culture in the GDR. The example of the jeans shows how popular culture contains traces of power relations, makes them visible, and participates in social change. Ina Merkel outlines a historical progression from wearing jeans in the 1960s as a sign of virtual border transgression, in the 1970s, jeans were regarded as a "normal" part of internationalization, and in the 1980s, Erich Honecker had them imported into the GDR. (Merkel, "The GDR—A Normal Country in the Centre of Europe:" 199f.) However, the variety and the depth of cultural production in the East that contributes to the discourse on 1968 has not yet been fully recognized, e.g. the insightful study by Janine Ludwig, *Heiner Müller, Ikone West* (Frankfurt a.M.: Lang, 2009), who reads Müller's work in the context of the intellectual climate of the 1970s, e.g., the New Left, terrorism, feminism, and the global uprisings.
21. Compare the essays by Angelika Bammer, "The American Feminist Reception of GDR Literature (with a Glance at West Germany)," *GDR Bulletin* 16.2 (1990): 18–24; Wolfgang Emmerich, "Affirmation-Utopie-Melancholie. Versuch einer Bilanz von vierzig Jahren DDR-Literatur," *German Studies Review* 14.2 (1991): 325–344; Patricia Herminghouse, "New Contexts for GDR Literature: An American Perspective," in *Cultural Transformations in the New Germany: American and German Perspectives*, ed. Friederike Eigler and Peter C. Pfeiffer (Rochester, NY: Camden House, 1993): 93–101; and Frank Hörnigk, "Die Literatur bleibt zuständig: Ein Versuch über das Verhältnis von Literatur, Utopie und Politik in der DDR—am Ende der DDR," *The Germanic Review* 67.3 (1992): 99–105.
22. Others have joined in Emmerich's call, see Siegrun Wildner, *Experimentum Mundi: Utopie als ästhetisches Prinzip: zur Funktion utopischer Entwürfe in Irmtraud Morgners Romanwerk* (St. Ingbert: Röhrig, 2000): 35. Thomas C. Fox, "Germanistik and GDR Studies: (Re)Reading a Censored Literature," *Monatshefte* 85.3 (1993): 284–294, suggests several theoretical approaches in order to broaden the horizon of understanding GDR literature and to create a more interdisciplinary research frame. Recent publications incorporate these and other approaches in order to re-contextualize GDR literature, e.g., Janine Ludwig and Mirjam Meuser, ed., *Literatur ohne Land? Schreibstrategien einer DDR-Literatur im vereinten Deutschland* (Freiburg: FWPF, 2009). In their introduction, the editors suggest to utilize a generational model in order to analyze the *littérature engagée* that emerged in the GDR before and after 1989.
23. Emmerich, *Kleine Literaturgeschichte der DDR. Erweiterte Neuausgabe*: 245.
24. Irmtraud Morgner, *Leben und Abenteuer der Trobadora Beatriz nach Zeugnissen ihrer Spielfrau Laura: Roman in dreizehn Büchern und sieben Intermezzos* (Darmstadt: Luchterhand, 1974); *Amanda: ein Hexenroman* (Darmstadt: Luchterhand, 1983); *Das heroische Testament: Roman in Fragmenten,* ed. Rudolf Bussmann (München: Luchterhand, 1998); *The Life and Adventures of Trobadora Beatrice as Chronicled by her Minstrel Laura: A Novel in Thirteen Books and Seven Intermezzos*, ed. Jeanette Clausen and Silke von der Emde, trans. Jeanette Clausen (Lincoln: University of Nebraska Press, 2000).
25. Helen Bridge, *Women's Writing and Historiography in the GDR* (Oxford: Clarendon Press, 2002).

26. A conference organized by the Stiftung Sozialgeschichte für das 20. Jahrhundert in Bremen on 22 and 23 February 2008 with the title "Das Jahr 1968 aus der Perspektive der Gesellschaften Mittel-, Ost- und Südosteuropas:" <http://www.ahf-muenchen.de/Tagungsberichte/Berichte/pdf/2008/059-08.pdf> (accessed 18 July 2008).
27. Ute Frevert, "Umbruch der Geschlechterverhältnisse? Die 60er Jahre als geschlechterpolitischer Experimentierraum," in *Dynamische Zeiten. Die 60er Jahre in den beiden deutschen Gesellschaften*, ed. Karl Christian Lammers, Axel Schildt, and Detlef Siegfried (Hamburg: Christians, 2000): 642–660.
28. Alice Schwarzer, "Vor 40 Jahren: Wir haben abgetrieben!" *EMMA* February 2011, <http://www.emma.de/index.php?id=6173> (accessed 26 June 2012).
29. Nikolaus Markgraf, "Die Feministin der DDR," in *Irmtraud Morgner. Texte, Daten, Bilder*, ed. Marlis Gerhardt (Frankfurt a.M.: Luchterhand, 1990): 150–155, 153.
30. Patricia A. Herminghouse, "Die Frau und das Phantastische in der neueren DDR-Literatur. Der Fall Irmtraud Morgner," in *Die Frau als Heldin und Autorin: neue kritische Ansätze zur deutschen Literatur*, ed. Wolfgang Paulsen (Bern: Francke, 1979): 248–266.
31. For a detailed literature review, see Doris Janssen, *"Blue-Note-Akrobatik." Irmtraud Morgner im kulturellen Kontext der sechziger Jahre* (Marburg: Tectum Verlag, 1998); Wildner, *Experimentum Mundi*; and Ute Wölfel, *Rede-Welten. Zur Erzählung von Geschlecht und Sozialismus in der Prosa Irmtraud Morgners* (Trier: Wissenschaftlicher Verlag, 2007).
32. Agnès Cardinal, "'Be Realistic: Demand the Impossible'. On Irmtraud Morgner's Salman Trilogy," in *Socialism and the Literary Imagination. Essays on East German Writers*, ed. Martin Kane (New York, Oxford: Berg, 1991): 147–161.
33. Wildner, *Experimentum Mundi*.
34. Beth V. Linklater, *"Und immer zügelloser wird die Lust": Constructions of Sexuality in East German Literatures; with special reference to Irmtraud Morgner and Gabriele Stötzer-Kachold.* (Bern: Lang, 1997): 212f.
35. These themes also include the influence of the Civil Rights movement and the colonial and postcolonial struggles in South America. Parts in *Beatriz* that thematize the Vietnam War are all authentic texts taken from newspaper articles and official army reports (e.g., Book 11, chapter 17). Book 1, chapter 21 contains an interview with a chemical weapons expert. Book 9 quotes Heinrich von Kleist's *Penthesilea* with reference to the Vietnam War and describes Penthesilea as a woman with an "Afro" hairstyle, and Book 11, chapter 25 summarizes the cost of the Vietnam War.
36. The Schengen Agreement was a treaty signed on 14 June 1985 near the town of Schengen in Luxembourg between five of the ten member states of the European Economic Community. It was supplemented by the Convention implementing the Schengen Agreement five years later. Together these treaties created Europe's borderless Schengen Area which operates very much like a single state for international travel with border controls for travelers travelling in and out of the area, but with no internal border controls
37. Merkel, "The GDR—A Normal Country in the Centre of Europe:" 198.
38. Morgner, *Beatriz*, Book 1, Chapter 6.
39. Ibid.: Book 1, Chapter 12.

40. Ibid.: Book 1, Chapter 16.
41. Ibid.: Book 1, Chapter 23: 70.
42. Morgner, *Beatrice*, Book 1, Chapter 23: 44.
43. Morgner, *Beatriz*, Book 1, Chapter 23: 70.
44. Morgner, *Beatrice*, Book 1, Chapter 23: 44.
45. Morgner, *Beatriz*, Book 1, Chapter 8: 32.
46. Ibid.: Book 1, Chapter 8: 18.
47. Ibid.: Book 1, Chapter 8: 32.
48. Morgner, *Beatrice*, Book 1, Chapter 8: 18.
49. Morgner, *Beatriz*, Book 1, Chapter 8.
50. Ibid.: Book1, Chapter 8.
51. Ibid.: Book 1, Chapter 25: 73.
52. Morgner, *Beatrice*, Book 1, Chapter 25: 46.
53. Morgner, *Beatriz*, Book 2, Chapter 4: 93.
54. Morgner, *Beatrice*, Book 2, Chapter 4: 60.
55. Morgner, *Beatriz*, Book 2, Chapter 7: 97.
56. Ibid.: Book 4, Chapter 13: 160.
57. Morgner, *Beatrice*, Book 4, Chapter 13: 107.
58. Morgner, *Beatriz*, Book 13, Last chapter: 688.
59. Morgner, *Beatrice*, Book 13, Last chapter: 468.
60. Silke von der Emde, "Places of Wonder: Fantasy and Utopia in Irmtraud Morgner's Salman Trilogy," *New German Critique* 82 (Winter 2001): 167–192, 167.
61. Morgner, *Beatriz*, Resolutions: 9. Morgner, *Beatrice*, Resolutions: 3.
62. The First Defenestration of Prague involved the killing of seven members of the city council by a crowd of radical Czech Hussites on July 30, 1419. It led to the Hussite Wars which lasted until 1436. The Second Defenestration of Prague was central to the start of the Thirty Years' War in 1618.
63. Irmtraud Morgner, *Amanda: ein Hexenroman*, Chapter 139: 676.
64. Named after Fritz Pleitgen, a journalist for the ARD who worked in Moscow and in East Berlin during the time of the Cold War.
65. Irmtraud Morgner, *Amanda: ein Hexenroman*, Chapter 118: 578. (Prague is not Berlin. The Berlin Spring does not have to be similar to the Prague Spring, dear audience. However, I am sure to stand on historic ground, on a site that will enter world history. Which, only the stars know, however, they are clouded by a gray sky over this city with such a rich history. … The action by officials in East Berlin triggered a worldwide campaign. All European capitals witnessed the founding of solidarity committees to free Laura Salman.)
66. Irmtraud Morgner, *Amanda: ein Hexenroman*, Chapter 118: 579.
67. Morgner, *Das heroische Testament*: 17.
68. Erika Rummel, *Scheming Papists and Lutheran Fools. Five Reformation Satires* (New York: Fordham University Press, 1993).
69. James V. Mehl, "Language, Class and Mimic Satire in the Characterization of Correspondents in the *Epistolae obscurorum virorum*," *Sixteenth Century Journal* XXV.2 (1994): 289–305.
70. Karl-Heinz Gerschmann, "Wenn Dunkelmänner Briefe schreiben…" *Neophilologus* 81 (1997): 89–103. He mentions two other instances of letters written by obscure men, 1848/49 addressed to the radical democrat Arnold Ruge, member of the par-

liament in the Frankfurt Paulskirche and 1935 written by Alfred Rosenberg as propaganda against the churches.
71. Rummel, *Scheming Papists*: vii.
72. Morgner, *Das heroische Testament*: 334.
73. Ibid.: 15.
74. Ibid.: 14.
75. Ibid.: 72.
76. Ibid.: 24.
77. Ibid.: 16.
78. Ibid.: 64.
79. Ibid.: 64.
80. "Mein Antrieb wäre nicht, Kunst zu machen, mein Antrieb wäre, Welt zu machen," quoted in Herminghouse, "Die Frau und das Phantastische:" 252.
81. Morgner, *Beatriz*, Book 8, Chapter 6: 257f.
82. Morgner, *Beatrice*, Book 8, Chapter 6: 175.
83. Morgner, *Beatriz*, Book 8, Chapter 6: 258.
84. Morgner, *Beatrice*, Book 8, Chapter 6: 175.
85. Morgner, *Beatriz*, Book 8, Chapter 6: 259.
86. Morgner, *Beatrice*, Book 8, Chapter 6: 176.
87. In an interview with Eva Kaufmann, "Interview mit Irmtraud Morgner," *Weimarer Beiträge* 30 (1984): 1494–1514.
88. Emde, "Places of Wonder:"167f.
89. Morgner, *Beatriz*, Book 8, Chapter 6: 259.
90. Morgner, *Beatrice*, Book 8, Chapter 6: 176.
91. Morgner, quoted in Joachim Walter, "Interview mit Irmtraud Morgner," *Weltbühne* 32 (1972): 10–11.

Chapter 3

Transatlantic Encounters between Germany and the United States as Intercultural Exchange and Generational Conflict

> Amerika, du hast es besser
> Als unser Kontinent, das alte,
> Hast keine verfallene Schlösser
> Und keine Basalte.
> Dich stört nicht im Innern,
> Zu lebendiger Zeit,
> Unnützes Erinnern
> Und vergeblicher Streit.
> *Johann Wolfgang von Goethe*[1]

This chapter explores the representations of the United States and of the transatlantic relations between Germany and the United States within the literary discourse of 1968. 1968 memory novels contribute to the construction of an imagined transnational community of protest that has historical roots in the 1960s and shapes the cultural memory of 1968 in significant ways. The interpretation of 1968 memory novels reveals different temporal layers that articulate the different stages that American–German relations in the twentieth century underwent. This transatlantic relationship is rooted in space, and through the transfer and exchange of ideas and people, the literary representation of the United States serves as a topos, a projection screen of the German imagination, a site where Germans negotiate their relationship with the other and with one another. Hence, this chapter asks how and why, in the 1990s, West German encounters with the United States were crucial to reconstructions of a unified German identity.[2]

The academic interest in the notion of encounter is grounded in travel literature, anthropology, and colonial and postcolonial studies. Of particular impact was Edward Said's *Orientalism*, analyzing (colonial) cultural encounters as an unparalleled influence on the construction of the other.[3] Since its publication in 1978, scholars with diverse academic backgrounds have turned to the question of "the encounter."[4] My reading places the encounter within the discourse on the cultural memory of 1968. The notion of encounter emphasizes the dynamic nature of this cultural memory and its foundation in time and space. The cultural memory of 1968 relies on the individual memories of former activists and the trigger and negotiations of these memories as they enter a transnational dialogue in contemporary fiction.

Historical scholarship analyzes the relationship between the 1960s student movement and the Cold War, and the converging processes of Westernization, often narrowly understood as Americanization, in countries like Great Britain, France, Italy, Germany, and the United States during the 1960s.[5] They emphasize the concurrent, yet contradictory, attitudes of Americanization and anti-Americanism that prevailed in Germany during the 1960s. The inspiration that the German student movement drew from across the Atlantic has found a lot of attention in historical research.[6] Some historians point to the very distinct conceptions of America that came into play in the 1960s in Germany.[7] Claus Leggewie claims that the "explosive rage of the times [the 1960s and 1970s] came less from some fundamental anti-Americanism than from the disappointment over a fallen idol [the United States and its engagement in the Vietnam War] by a generation that had grown up under the influence of cultural Westernization and had admired men such as John F. Kennedy and Martin Luther King, Jr."[8] Philipp Gassert agrees that:

> the accusation of fascism directed against the United States was thus certainly not an expression of a genuinely nationalist or possibly apologetic tendency in the German Left, but a sign of the times, however objectionable. Leftists across the Western world used the catchword of "fascism" to polemize against dubious practices and undemocratic conditions in the name of an undifferentiated and rash critique of "the system."[9]

Hodenberg and Siegfried also point to the contradictory treatment and approaches of the German activists toward the United States which they understand as yet another example of the Janus-faced student movement in Germany.[10] These contradictory attitudes during the 1960s are reflected in the novels *Eduards Heimkehr* (Peter Schneider), *Frühstück mit Max* (Ulrike Kolb), and *Der Vorleser* (Bernhard Schlink). These novels construct memories of 1968 that enable the narrators to reconsider their former attitudes and to shift the focus of the literary image of America to acknowledge the importance of the United States as the land of exile for Jewish-German survivors of the Third Reich. The third generation challenges the parents' revolutionary attitudes by adhering to notions of life, liberty, and the pursuit of happiness within a democratic and capitalist Western state.

These novels construct the United States as a geographical location, as well as an imaginary space, allowing critical reflection on the 1960s student movement and the transatlantic relationship. I propose to read these literary texts as a contribution to the discourse on processes of cultural transfer and as an invitation to reflect on the construction of identities within a historical and geographical perspective. The palimpsest, structured around the years 1933, 1945, 1968, and 1989, questions, critiques, and reshapes recollections of German history and of the image of the United States in contemporary German literature.

Eduards Heimkehr and *Der Vorleser* revive memories as well as silences, absences, and voids that are often understood as forgetting. Most importantly, the novels include a voice that was previously forgotten, absent, or silenced because the narrators complement their postmemories with the memories of Jewish survivors. Yet these encounters do not take place in Germany but in the United States, and thus shed light on the importance of the United States for the German literary imagination. This representation stresses the ongoing responsibility of the second and third generation for a past that will not go away. Revisiting 1968 emphasizes that without the dialogue between the second and third generation, the survivors and their descendants, and without the engagement with their experiences, memories, and postmemories, the debate about the Nazi past will remain incomplete. In Ulrike Kolb's novel *Frühstück mit Max*, Manhattan serves as the site of the encounter between Nelly, a former '68er, and her stepson Max. The chance meeting between two people who lived in the same communal living project in West Berlin during the 1970s triggers a wave of memories and emotions, some of which they share with each other, while others are only revealed to the reader. This American–German encounter shapes the plot and the narrative structure of *Frühstück mit Max* and uses the United States as a site in order to critique the past.

Representations of the United States in German Literature

In the German imagination, the United States has always claimed a privileged space, simultaneously a promising yet uncanny new home[11] and a literary topos. Ever since Columbus arrived in America in 1492 and in particular beginning in the eighteenth century with Goethe, there is hardly a major writer in the German language who did not address the topic of "America" regardless of whether authors relied on travel reports and other accounts from the New World or on personal experiences. While Goethe, in *Wilhelm Meisters Lehrjahre* (Wilhelm Meister's Apprenticeship),[12] is full of enthusiasm regarding the opportunities in and the future of the United States, novels published in the nineteenth century document the beginnings of disillusionment with America and the ideals it stood for.[13] However, this disillusionment did not lead to a decline in literary engagement with the United States in the twentieth century. Since it was very often not the interest in the historical reality of the United States but rather the attempt to construct a (utopian) counter-image to a specific state of things at home that spurred representations of the United States in German literature, literary representations of the United States continue to remain popular in contemporary literature written in German.

In most of these texts we learn more about the authors and their particular psychological, social, and historical dispositions than about the United States itself. Often the United States functions as a catalyst that sets in motion the exploration, not of the foreign country, but of the visitors themselves and their home country. The United States serves as a playground for the imagination and as a site where the subject comes to understand him/herself. However, at the same time, there is also recognition of America as a land that promises life, liberty, and the pursuit of happiness to everybody who arrives there. These processes are further complicated by the fact that the American–German relationship is conducted on a governmental level as well as on an unofficial level that can be described as transnational. Beginning in the 1950s, government-sponsored student exchange programs enabled contact between students and civil rights activists on both sides of the Atlantic. These encounters contributed to the development of a transnational sphere that challenged official politics and acquired a global reach. Parallel to the continuously changing fate of the transatlantic relations, oscillating between friendship and war, between processes of Westernization often understood as Americanization and feelings of anti-Americanism, literary representations of the United States participated in these public debates by constructing and deconstructing the extremes associated with "the United States:" used as a synonym for mass culture that is characterized by commodification, reification, materialism, consumerism, imperialism, and pollution, the United States also offers the hope of continuous beginnings, endless transformations, and permanent renewals.[14]

The generational differences between attitudes in the 1960s and in the 1990s, already discussed in chapter 1, are also expressed in the literary representations of the United States. For the 1970s, Heinz D. Osterle identifies three attitudes towards the United States that he considers characteristic for West German writers after 1945: "[O]utright rejection, ironic detachment, and cool reassessment."[15] Osterle observes the attitude of cool reassessment in Uwe Johnson's novel *Jahrestage*, which combines utopian, dystopian, and pseudo-utopian themes.[16] Pseudo-utopian representations of the United States emerge, telling stories of private and introverted pursuits of happiness in an American setting, yet with an ironic inversion, by ignoring the public aspects of the American dream of the good society.[17] At the same time, anti-utopian or dystopian views of the United States emphasize the negative images of the country, replacing the old utopian dream of the good society with new nightmares of alienation and exploitation. Osterle observes that these latter texts are not isolated examples but part of a trend of the New Left dominating the literary scene in West Germany during the late 1960s and 1970s.[18]

One of the most prevalent political simplifications the students proclaimed was the equation of capitalism and fascism. The fact that members of the German student movement described the United States as a state with "fascist tendencies" can be understood as attempts to divert attention from the German past. Gerd Gemünden interprets these discursive strategies as an attempt to ease the burden of guilt and of the ongoing responsibility of those born after 1945. This attitude toward the United States also awards the activists in the 1960s the opportunity to point their fingers at the parents' generation, thus indicating that had the '68ers had the opportunity, they would have resisted Hitler.[19] 1968 memory novels support this reading. In their representations of the United States thirty to forty years later, the narrators paint differentiated images of the United States and emphasize the dynamic of the transcultural exchange as a necessary ingredient for a cultural memory of 1968 that is diverse and fluid rather than homogenous and static. The narrators reassess their own motivations in the ambivalent struggle with the United States during the 1960s and reconsider the role of the United States and the transatlantic relationship between Germany and the United States

Representations of the United States in 1968 Memory Novels

Remembering 1968 in the three novels by Kolb, Schlink, and Schneider serves as the focus through which American–German relations in the twentieth century are remembered and reevaluated. In fact, the texts seem to suggest that it is impossible to remember 1968 without also remembering the United States and its importance for Germany in the twentieth century. Representations of the United States form three distinct yet intersected layers that correspond temporally with the Third Reich, the 1960s, and the 1990s, and the respective generations that symbolize these decades. The novels construct the United States as the land of exile for those members of the first generation who were forced to leave Nazi Germany. The second generation remembers their ambivalent attitude toward the United States during the 1960s; whereas the third generation does not seem to be burdened by history and views the United States as the utopia of the globalized twenty-first century.

Fictional texts construct the United States as a literary projection screen for the German imagination. These representations entail a dynamic dimension because the United States is depicted as a country that enables the encounter of estranged humans. In *Der Vorleser* and in *Eduards Heimkehr* the United States serves as the meeting ground for the second generation of Germans and the survivors of Nazi Germany. The novel *Frühstück mit Max* tells the story of the encounter of Nelly and Max, members of the second and third generation respectively. The United States as the host of these encounters enables the dialogue between people whose memories of a shared past separate and tie them together simultaneously.

Whereas the different generations provide a temporal structure, the transatlantic encounter adds the spatial dimension. The dynamic nature of these representations plays an important role in the dialogue about the German past in the twentieth century. This dialogue and its creative appropriation in 1968 memory novels visualizes silences, spurring a renewed interest in the past and outlining different ways to remember it. In the 1990s, representations of the United States within the cultural memory of the 1960s student movement function as representations of a transatlantic exchange that is an integral part of personal and public identity construction in German literary discourse. These two dimensions, the representation of the United States and the representation of various transatlantic encounters initiating dialogue and exchange, emphasize that the cultural memory of the 1960s is inherently dynamic in its negotiation of time and space and their interrelatedness. Aligning the experiences of the United States with the generational experiences of Germans during the 1940s, the 1960s, and the 1990s demonstrates that these two dimensions cannot be looked at in isolation. Literary texts offer unique opportunities to create realities that put both dimensions—the temporal and the spatial—into play with each other.

Temporalities and Topographies in the Discourse on Memory

Literary texts that are embedded in the discourse on memory create a meeting place for individual and culturally mediated memories. They connect personal experiences and historical events and shed light on the political ramifications of personal memories and the significance of historical and political events for the individual. Yet literary texts differentiate themselves from autobiographies as well as from historiographies because they create possible worlds and thus are typically not confronted with claims or questions regarding their truth value or validity in terms of their representation and interpretation of the past. In fact, the interpretation of literary texts depends on the analysis of the specific qualities of the genre, its language use, the position of the narrator and the literary figures, and its intertextuality and historical context.

Two theoretical considerations form the basis for my claim that literary remembering is structured both temporally and spatially. The process of remembering constructs a three-dimensional palimpsest of layered memories that can be unearthed in the manner and with the implications that Walter Benjamin proposes in his short essay "Ausgraben und Erinnern" (Excavate and Remember).[20] On the one hand, fiction, as one medium among others, such as holidays, memorials, museums, art, films, music, and architecture, contributes to the continuous construction and deconstruction of cultural memory. The model of the palimpsest thus visualizes the relations among literary texts that obtain additional meaning and significance through their reception and in literary histories. This model is also applicable to the representation of 1968 in German literature.

On the other hand, in certain literary genres, processes of remembering and forgetting often structure the narrative and form the basis of the plot. This is particularly true for autobiographies, autobiographical fiction, and fiction that is told from the perspective of the first-person narrator looking back at his or her life.

The Temporal Dimension of Memory

The first-person narrators not only remember events that shaped their lives—mainly the student movement in the 1960s—but they also seem to "remember" the Nazi past which, if at all, they only experienced as very young children. Thus, the narrators tell stories based on their own memories of the student movement and on postmemories of the Nazi past. Their intersections construct the temporal dimension of the intricate layering that determines the narratives. These layers question and critique each other and create problematic fusions and confusions because they encounter each other during processes of remembering and memory construction.

As former members of the student movement, the narrators revisit the memories of their involvement in the student movement. This process leads to a reassessment of their roles within the movement and the movement's function for Germany before and after the fall of the Berlin Wall. In particular, the narrators reevaluate their attitudes towards the Nazi past. In the 1960s, the students protested against what they perceived as either the inability or the unwillingness of their parents' generation to confront their involvement in and with the Third Reich. They also protested against the continuation of fascism in West Germany even after 1945. In contrast, thirty years later the narrators focus on their own shortcomings first, before condemning their parents and society as a whole.

These second-generation narrators emphasize the problematic aspects of their engagement with the past that was also marked by silences, in particular because of their inability and unwillingness to engage in a dialogue with their parents. In *Frühstück mit Max*, Nelly's parents are only mentioned in passing, described as the clichéd family of the fifties, focusing on the future, the "Wiederaufbau" and the "Wirtschaftswunder" (the reconstruction and the economic miracle after the Second World War).[21] In *Der Vorleser*, Michael Berg seeks a conversation with his father, a professor of ethics, in order to find an answer to the question of whether Berg has the responsibility to reveal Hanna's illiteracy to the court. However, since the relationship between Berg and his parents is marked by emotional distance, he describes his dilemma on a very abstract level and avoids mentioning Hanna and his relationship with her, and thus only receives a very abstract answer from his father.[22] In *Eduards Heimkehr*, Eduard Hoffmann only learns more about the grandfather who bequeathed him an apartment complex by talking with a Jewish survivor.[23] His grandfather, who was excluded from the family memory, was not included in Eduard's interest in the past either, since as a member of the student movement Eduard was dealing with a general "Vergangenheitsbewältigung" (coming to terms with the Nazi past) and not with his own family history. Even his marriage to the daughter of Holocaust survivors does not spur a more personal discussion of Germany's past.

In addition, by posing as victims of the perceived fascist structures in West Germany, the students displaced the historical victims of National Socialism, who did not find a space within the German discourse about National Socialism and the Holocaust in the 1960s. Literary texts bring alive memories as well as silences, absences, and voids that are often understood as forgetting. Revisiting their postmemories, the narrators question the sources that mediated them originally. Furthermore, they attempt to include voices that were previously consigned to oblivion, in particular those of the victims of the Third Reich and their families. The narrators reassess their postmemories—which were often mediated through their own families—and complement them with the memories of the victims of the Nazis. I read this as an attempt to gain a more comprehensive understanding of the past and to give the victims a voice within the German discourse on National Socialism and the Holocaust as represented in German literature. These representations stress the ongoing responsibility of the second and third generation for a past that will not go away.

The Spatial Dimension of Memory

In addition to the temporal dimension, the literary palimpsest of memories contains a spatial dimension. Pierre Nora agrees with Maurice Halbwachs that individual memories are established within a social framework and thus gain their meaning from this social context.[24] At the same time, the construction of memory within a society is based on a variety of individual representations of the past. These form narratives that are negotiated, accepted, and refuted by the public discourse. Nora argues that in premodern times societies experienced memory as a continuous reliving of the past through rituals, the passing on of traditions from one generation to the next, and the reliance on traditions that resist modernization.[25]

Conversely, modern society, according to Nora, separates the past from memory. Due to this loss of the "milieux de mémoire" in which the past is never really past, modern societies are forced to create "lieux de mémoire," specific locations and occasions of remembering in order to enable individuals and groups to gain access to the past.[26] Nora concludes that this loss of the everyday experience of remembering as a lived and living tradition initiated the contemporary discourse on memory and remembering.

Nora's definition of memory as a primitive or sacred form of accessing the past that is in opposition to modern historical consciousness expresses a nostalgic longing for a past that has probably never existed in the proposed form. And while I disagree with his fundamental critique of history and historiography as having destroyed the "milieux de mémoire," his concept of "lieux de mémoire" is a useful analytical tool for analyzing the representation of space in literary texts and its importance for the construction of a cultural memory of 1968.

In my reading, particular locations in the United States and Germany serve as topographies of memories that evoke the personal experiences of the narrators and their literary figures and point to questions of personal and national identity. Analyzing the literary representations of the United States and Germany as "lieux de mémoire" emphasizes their constructedness through processes of remembering and forgetting. These memories and postmemories evoke the geographical locations and their national boundaries and the controversial images associated. Representations of the United States after 1989 also evoke a displaced discussion about the nation, national history, and national identity in Germany. In particular, the novels conceptualize the United States as a meeting place for the three generations and as a site of generational conflicts. While the second generation revisits their ambivalence toward the United States in the 1960s, the narrators recognize the importance of the country for the members of the first generation who emigrated to the United States in the 1930s and 1940s. The third generation places their dreams and hopes onto a country that promises life, liberty, and the pursuit of happiness. The representations of the United States do not offer access to historical, political, or social authenticity, yet the country serves as "lieux de mémoire" and thus adds layers to the palimpsest of memories and postmemories that structures 1968 memory novels.

Markers of space such as countries, regions, cities, neighborhoods, and homes take on particular significance within the discourse on memory. Furthermore, face-to-face encounters between individuals, both chance meetings and arranged visits, serve as representations of these overlapping time/space constructions. These sites of memory have the potential to challenge generally accepted, yet always insufficient, interpretations of the past; to initiate dialogues between individuals and communities in the present; to overcome fixed and preconceived notions of identity; and to allow for identity formation to be an ongoing, fluid, transformative, and transforming process.

Remembering the United States: A Site of Generational Conflicts

The three generations that mark the temporal structure of these 1968 memory novels evoke very different images of "America." The United States serves as a site of generational conflicts both within a generation and among the generations. These projections onto and appropriations of the United States point to the self-definitions of the three generations. I propose to read the three novels in light of their differentiated construction of the United States as a utopian imagination, as a land of exile and immigration, and as a country that very often seems to entail political, social, and cultural extremes.

In the representations of the United States through the recollections of the second generation, the '68ers revisit their own past and their image of the United States in the 1960s. During the time of the student movement, the focus on the country's perceived fascist tendencies often overshadowed the awareness that the United States was also the country that initiated and inspired the worldwide protest movements. Revisiting this split allows the narrators to recognize the complexities of the transatlantic relation and to add a historical dimension that was often missing in the debates: the important role the United States played as the host to many emigrants and victims of the Nazi regime. In *Der Vorleser* and in *Eduards Heimkehr*, both narrators visit the United States in order to meet survivors of the Holocaust who emigrated there during the 1930s and 1940s. In addition, the third generation questions the ambivalence of the second generation toward the United States. Members of the third generation emphasize the utopian opportunities of a country that does not burden its inhabitants with the demands of a long history and promises individual freedom and the limitless pursuit of happiness.

The United States during the 1960s: Land of Extremes

All three narrators remember the contradictions and ambivalences toward the United States in the 1960s. Even though the United States liberated Germany from National Socialism—something the Germans had failed to accomplish themselves—and supported the democratization of West Germany, the members of the student movement did not perceive the United States as a liberator, but rather as an imperialist and colonialist force. At the same time, members of the 1960s student movement in Germany failed to acknowledge that the movements on both sides of the Atlantic shared the same goals, e.g., the struggle against imperialism and colonialism and the fight for equality and peace. In fact, the American Civil Rights Movement and the American student movement inspired the German movement, and German activists acquired American methods of civil disobedience and of changing hierarchical structures at universities by using teach-ins, sit-ins, and other forms of protest in order to demand radical reforms of the universities, the education system, and society in general.[27] Thirty years later, in their memories, the narrators acknowledge that what looked like an outright rejection of the United States in the 1960s was a much more complex process of rejection and appropriation that did not juxtapose Germany and the United States but rather unified the younger generation in both countries against their respective governments in power. The extremes that characterized the activists' perception of the United States ultimately fueled their political engagement.

In the wake of the 1960s student protests, the United States served yet again as a safe haven for German emigrants as numerous young Germans left Germany in the mid to late 1970s. In 1972, the German government enacted the so-called Decree Against Radicals that led to a wave of professional bans by preventing some participants of the protest movement from becoming government employees, including civil servants, teachers, and professors. Hence many of the former protestors could not find work in their home country but found opportunities in the United States, which seemed more capable of reintegrating the protestors into mainstream society.[28] In *Eduards Heimkehr,* Eduard works as a professor of genetics in California, emphasizing that he did not leave Berlin on his own account, but rather he was denied an academic career in Germany because of his political past.[29] Thus, the United States is able to confirm its image as the country of personal freedom and opportunity for everybody, even for those who previously challenged American society.

The United States as the Land of Exile and Immigration

Despite the many shared aspects among the student movements in the various countries, and the close relationship between the American and the German activists in particular, each student movement was still distinct in its historical, cultural, and local situatedness. In Germany, the protests were marked by the attempt to come to terms with the Nazi past. In the 1990s, literary texts engaged critically with the former activists who reconsidered their assessment of the Third Reich during the 1960s. Michael Berg, the narrator in *Der Vorleser,* is probably the best-known figure to represent this aspect of the cultural memory of 1968. Feelings of guilt, shame, embarrassment, and complicity accompany him his whole life. Hanna Schmitz, his former lover and a convicted concentration camp guard, kills herself on the day she is to be released from prison. She has named him as executor of her will and Berg travels to New York City to deliver Hanna's possessions—an old tin can and some money—to the survivor of the concentration camp where Hanna was a guard.[30]

Even though Berg recounts the visit to New York City relatively briefly, the visit receives a prominent place at the end of the novel and gains significance because it is the only foreign travel described by the narrator. During the meeting, the atmosphere is cold, and Berg and the survivor remain rather distant, a feeling emphasized by the fact that the woman's name is not mentioned once. This distance is mirrored through the description of her neighborhood, which consists of modest and orderly apartment buildings leaving a rather clinical impression. Her neighborhood does not evoke the New York City that is often described in German novels depicting its energy, its fast pace, and its diversity.[31] This contrast shows that *Der Vorleser* departs purposefully from the typical depiction of New York City in German fiction by focusing on the daily reality of those who came to New York City because they lost their home for political reasons. After all, Jewish emigrants in the 1930s and 1940s did not chase the American dream, but were forced to leave Germany by the Nazis.

The conversation focuses on Berg's relationship with Hanna. Prompted by the survivor, Berg reveals his relationship with her for the first time in his life.[32] As an allusion to Peter's denial, Berg has had three opportunities to speak about his relationship but each time he either avoids the conversation or disavows the relationship. Neither during the time of the relationship with Hanna, nor during the trial, nor long after the trial when he meets a former fellow-student at the funeral of the professor who taught the seminar accompanying the trial, was Berg able to tell his parents, his professor, or any of the other students about Hanna.[33] Thus it is at first surprising that Berg readily tells a complete stranger about Hanna.

The survivor attempts to interpret Berg's experiences in light of her own experiences as a victim of National Socialism. She insinuates that Berg suffered throughout his life because of Hanna.[34] Even though Berg rejects this interpretation, the fact that he decides to tell his story to someone who is connected to Hanna through historical events remains puzzling and invites this interpretation. His confession could be seen as yet another attempt by a '68er to align himself with a historical victim of the Holocaust. It also points to the importance of the United States as a place where the individual is not burdened by history, or by the many attempts to come to terms with it. Since Berg is dislocated, albeit only temporarily, he is free to tell his life story. Furthermore, Berg seems to trust the survivor to understand the complexity of the emotions with which he is struggling.

Even though this is an important step in working through his own life and a sign of dissolving identity constructions fixed by essentialist notions of national identity, it is still problematic that his life story is the main topic of conversation between a German and one of the victims of National Socialism, in particular since this is their first encounter. It seems symptomatic of the contemporary German approach to the past that the German perspective is emphasized. Often expressed as German suffering, this particular German perspective seems to trivialize the suffering of those who did not have any or as many options for resistance as the Germans and who instead were persecuted by the Nazis. At the end of the visit, the survivor refuses to accept the money because she does not want to exchange money for redemption. However, she does accept the tin can which replaces the one she lost in the camp.[35] While money is not able to carry memories or to buy forgetting, a concrete object such as a tin can, even if it is not identical with the one that was lost, can serve as an object of memory, as a reminder of the past, and as a commemorative token that reinforces the relevance of the past for the future.

This visit in New York City is Berg's first encounter with a Jewish survivor. This is noteworthy since the generation of the student movement emphasized the need to come to terms with the past. However, their approach did not include the establishment of a dialogue with those who suffered most during the

Third Reich.[36] Instead of talking with survivors of the Holocaust, Berg visited a concentration camp twice during the time of Hanna's trial. On one of his trips to a camp, he angrily engages in an argument with a male member of his parents' generation that leads to a rapid end of the conversation, signaling the breakdown in communication between the first and the second generation.[37] Berg is disappointed that visiting the concentration camp does not grant him access to the past nor does it allow him to engage in a dialogue with the past. Historical locations do not contain significance just because they were the locations of historical events; however, they gain significance because their visitors attribute meaning to them by remembering. Since the Holocaust was not publicly and explicitly acknowledged and discussed in Germany for a long time, there are no personal or familial postmemories associated with the historical locations that Berg could refer to in order to access the past.[38] The sites of the Holocaust are neither "lieux" nor "milieux de mémoire" for Berg.

Following Benjamin's dictum that "das Gedächtnis nicht ein Instrument zur Erkundung der Vergangenheit ist sondern deren Schauplatz" (memory is not an instrument for the exploration of the past, but its stage),[39] I am using the notion of "Schauplatz" as meaning stage or site of memory in order to point to and analyze the interconnectedness of spatial and temporal aspects of cultural memory. Since history, or rather snapshots of historical developments, according to Benjamin, are captured on stage and hence in a spatial representation, they can also be analyzed within this setting. Thus, cultural memory is not just an addition of time and space, but rather an intricate entanglement, spatial in its representation of temporal aspects of remembering and dependent on the performative act of remembering.

Read in conjunction with Benjamin's "Berliner Chronik," the site of memory obtains the status of an analytical category that enables the reader to dissect and understand the significance of memories and to observe processes of forgetting.[40] Two aspects are of particular importance for my interpretation. First, the fact that the sites of memory of Benjamin's youth take on meanings beyond his own life. In his account, personal spaces such as apartments and family homes gain as much significance as embodiments of history as public spaces do. They point to, signify, and permeate the historical developments in the first half of the twentieth century. In a similar vein, in *Eduards Heimkehr*, the apartment building in Berlin and Edita's apartment in Florida represent memories and history and thus serve as sites of memory. Whereas both spaces, the apartment building and Edita's new home, force their inhabitants, visitors, owners, and prospective owners to revisit history, Edita's apartment also serves as the backdrop of her encounter with Eduard. This leads to the second important aspect of Benjamin's site of memory. In his "Berliner Chronik," Benjamin states that it is the "Schauplätze … an denen wir andern oder uns begegnen" (the stages of history … where we encounter ourselves or others).[41] Thus, the site of memory also entails the encounter, not just as a personal matter but as an image and performative act that represents historical and social constellations and thus obtains significance beyond the personal. The encounter prevents memory from being static and instead propels memory through time and space through the convergence of people and their shared memories, which either unite or divide them.

In *Eduards Heimkehr*, the encounter between Eduard and Edita enables the exploration of memory and identity. Eduard is faced with various obstacles during the attempt to claim his inheritance, an apartment building located in former East Berlin. Even though it is not clear whether Eduard's grandfather ever lived in the building himself, the house gains a Benjaminian significance as an object that captures a moment of the merging of personal and public history and hence serves as a site of memory. While ownership in a capitalist society is always personal, it is still made public in order to guarantee the successful functioning of exactly this society. During the Third Reich, the public marketplace was increasingly dominated by anti-Semitic and other racist rules and, therefore, Jewish property was endangered and ultimately seized. It is this legacy of anti-Semitism that haunts Eduard and that stands between his claim and his lawful and legitimate ownership of the building.

As a first step to claim his inheritance, Eduard hires a lawyer in order to evict the squatters.[42] He visits the registry of deeds and the Document Center in order to confirm his grandfather's legal and legitimate ownership of the apartment building. As a result of his archival research, Eduard finds the deed for the house and numerous letters documenting the transaction involving the Jewish family Marwitz and Eduard's grandfather.[43] Yet, even with these documents, Eduard is not able to reconstruct a coherent narrative that would confirm his grandfather's innocence and good intentions in purchasing the house at a time when Jewish property had already been seized by the Nazis. This inability points to the insufficiency of historical documents and their need to be interpreted since their mere existence does not guarantee the coherent and comprehensible access to the past. In conjunction with the notion of postmemory, the novel thus challenges the assumption that documents can provide a meaningful access to the past. Rather, in line with Hirsch's argument, postmemories always depend on stories, eyewitnesses, and a variety of documents and artifacts. They make significant contributions to the reconstruction of memory and to the historiographical reconstruction of the events.

In order to shed light on the situation, Edgar travels to Florida to meet with Edita Marwitz, the last surviving eye witness.[44] This visit represents the slow destruction of clearly delineated markers of time and space. This destruction does not leave a void, yet allows both Eduard and Edita to remember the past and Germany in new ways. The encounter constructs a site of memory in Benjamin's sense. For Edita, it brings the past, or at least a potential trait of the past, in the form of her former lover's grandson, to her exile. For Eduard, it emphasizes the need to leave Germany one more time in order to be able to approach his family's history, his country's past, and his own life from a new perspective.

Already on his trip to the United States, Eduard is confronted with the collapse and confusion of exact categories and clearly identifiable identities. At his departure in Berlin he is able to, or at least he claims to be able to, distinguish between American and German travelers, yet, as the passengers leave the plane in Florida, Eduard cannot "recognize the passengers disembarking ahead of and behind him, … he now saw that nearly all of them had boarded the plane in the standard dress affected in Florida all year around, irrespective of the wearer's sex or age group: sneakers, shorts, T-shirts."[45] While this is a not so subtle cliché describing American fashion, in this moment it is first and foremost used to point to the dissolution of markers of identity: Americans and Germans look alike. This fusion and confusion continues on the way to Edita's apartment: "Eduard hatte noch nie so viele reiche Häuser in so vielerlei Baustilen nebeneinander gesehen. … Ein Privathaus im Stil einer türkischen Moschee zog den Blick vom benachbarten Alterssitz, der nach Art einer gotischen Kirche gestaltet war, eine toskanische Villa mit Kupferdach versuchte, neben einem griechischen Tempelbau zu bestehen."[46] ("Eduard had never seen such a juxtaposition of opulent homes in so many different architectural styles. … A private residence in the style of a Turkish mosque drew the eye away from its neighbor, a retirement home resembling a Gothic church; a Tuscan villa with a copper-sheathed roof strove to hold its own beside a Greek temple.")[47] This motley array of houses can be understood as a reference to rather stereotypical notions of American identity as an unruly mixture of European and other identities with random historical references to all previous centuries. Eduard's journey is a trip through time and space that in its seemingly chaotic mix forces him to focus on his own identity, in particular his relation to the Nazi past, and to challenge same basic premises that until then governed his life. Travel seems to be one prerequisite in order to be able to acknowledge one's own limited perspective and to understand oneself from a different viewpoint.

Upon entering Edita's apartment Eduard is confronted with another displaced reconstruction of the past: her apartment is a mixture of greenhouse and museum, as Eduard observes, complete with tropical flowers, embroidered slipcovers, and crocheted table clothes.[48] Yet it is only a recreation of her past, in particular her past home, a fact that is emphasized by the numerous photographs that serve as daily reminders for all those who did not escape the Nazi terror. Her home thus serves as a "lieux de mémoire," a deliberate creation and recreation of the past that allows her to remember the past and to reconnect it with her present life at a different location.

The historical distance, which is at the same time a temporal layering and overwriting, is also indicated by Edita's searching in Eduard for traces of his grandfather, whom he had never met in person. She is disappointed: there are none. Edita shows Eduard a photo of his grandfather of whom he had never seen an image before. Thus, she provides Eduard with some access to his family's past that his own family had obliterated.[49]

He is the welcome audience for her story, to which no one has yet bothered to listen. After he enters the apartment, their conversation switches from English to German when Edita remarks: "Es ist doch komisch, wenn zwei Leute, deren Muttersprache Deutsch ist, sich gegenseitig vormachen, wie gut sie Englisch können."[50] ("It is silly for two people whose mother tongue is German to show off their English.")[51] The process of historical distancing and layering is further emphasized by the fact that even though they both speak German it is not the same language: "Ihn wiederum verwirrte der Klang ihres Deutschs. Die Vokale und die harten Rachenlaute erinnerten ein wenig an jene Version des Deutschen, die man aus Hollywoodfilmen über den Zweiten Weltkrieg kannte."[52] ("Eduard was puzzled by the sound of her German. The vowels and harsh gutturals reminded him a little of the German favored by Hollywood movies set in World War II.")[53] Here, it is not only the historical distance that is noteworthy but also the fusion of temporal and spatial structures which create a site of memory: Eduard is not only confused because it seems to be the language of a time long gone but also because Edita seems to use the performative language he associates with movies made in California. Since language is an integral part of one's identity and at the same time conveys one's identity, Eduard's feelings suggest that it is not so much the language per se, but the performance of a German identity that confuses him. This confusion further emphasizes that during the 1960s the students did not comprehend that the Jews that either perished in the Holocaust or were exiled were not really the other, but were Germans just like those that claimed to be Aryans. The encounter with Edita forces him to acknowledge the diversity within German identity that counters any claims of a homogenous German identity.

During his visit with Edita, Eduard is continuously challenged in his notions of identity. He slowly realizes that he has not yet approached his own family's past in relation to the German past. He understands that, maybe unwittingly, he followed his grandmother's lead in excluding his grandfather from his family's memory, albeit for different reasons. His grandmother refused to remember her husband because he was a gambler and womanizer and hence considered him to be of loose moral character. Eduard reveals that his own motivations were guided by the trend in the 1960s to accuse the parent's generation collectively rather than to engage with one's individual family history.[54] The visit with Edita challenges Eduard to engage with his own family history.

The atmosphere during the visit is characterized by an ironic distancing on Edita's part. She comments on the Germans' need to receive a pardon by Jewish survivors at a time when it is convenient and necessary for the Germans.[55] She assures Eduard that his grandfather did not profit unduly from the political situation. In fact, he helped her father by buying the house at a fair price, at a time when Jewish property was already being confiscated by the Nazis without compensation.[56] She also adds her personal story to the mere legal facts and emphasizes that Eduard's grandfather did not help solely out of humanitarian reasons, but because, secretly, he was in love with her.[57] This revelation underscores the effect of shared memories on those who experience a situation from vastly different points of view. Whereas Eduard's grandmother bans her husband from entry into the family history because of his adultery, Edita remembers Eduard's grandfather because of their romance and his support for her family during the Third Reich when most Germans turned a blind eye or actively supported the persecution of Jews.

Eduard learns about his family history from someone who was not officially part of his family yet who knows details about his grandfather that are not preserved in Eduard's family memory. His visit provides Edita with the chance to tell her side of the story and underscores the importance of storytelling, in this case female storytelling, in order to construct a more complete memory of the past. The encounters described in the two novels, *Eduards Heimkehr* and *Der Vorleser*, not only share the similarity that they both take place in the United States, but they also both involve a male narrator and an older Jewish woman. The women are the eye witnesses who are asked to grant redemption and to share their recollections in order to gain access to the historical truth. Both women initiate a switch in the language that is spoken during the encounters. They greet their visitors in English and tell their stories in German, the shared mother tongue of those exiled and those who stayed, as Edita emphasizes.[58] As such, the figure of the largely absent and silent survivor turns into a storytelling witness whose recollections are valued by those members of the second generation who reconsider their activist attitudes originating in the 1960s.

These literary representations of the meetings between the survivors and members of the second generation constitute an ironic inversion and a gendered critique of constructions of history and historiography traditionally dominated by male voices. As the narrators' attempts to rely on "objective" representations of history fail, such as historical locations and documents, they need to seek out the female voices that were until then forgotten. These encounters add female memories to the historiography of the Holocaust and emphasize the necessity of storytelling in order to create a more complete and complex image of the past.[59]

As in *Der Vorleser*, storytelling in *Eduards Heimkehr* adds another piece to a history that will not go away as long as it is preserved in various layers of memories and postmemories. Yet Edita focuses her story not on herself, but on those Germans who are forgotten in their own country. She claims that the Germans know the perpetrators better than those who attempted to resist and to support those faced with persecution, deportation, and death. With this stance, Edita serves as the author's spokeswoman since Peter Schneider makes this point in his writing at other occasions. In "The Good Germans: Saving Konrad Latte" and *'Und wenn wir nur eine Stunde gewinnen...' Wie ein jüdischer Musiker die Nazi-Jahre überlebte*, Schneider shows how the Germans focus on the perpetrators in an attempt to understand how the Holocaust could have happened and how similar atrocities can be prevented in the future.[60] This focus obliterates those few who did not support the Nazi state even though their actions are worthy of our investigation and memory, too. Eduard discovers how difficult it is to understand behavior retrospectively. It seems impossible to decide with certainty whether his grandfather helped the Jewish family to save their lives and their belongings because of his love interest in the daughter or because of his political convictions. Even the eyewitness Edita, who serves as Eduard's most important source of information about his own family history, cannot tell with certainty.

These first attempts of a Jewish–German dialogue are problematic because they are seemingly self-serving. Without the need for information in Hoffmann's case or the obligation to pass on an inheritance in Berg's case, the Germans of the second generation would still not have sought the direct contact with the victims of the Third Reich. Both narrators comment on this failure and interpret it as a continuation of the problematic silence, neglect, and avoidance strategies inherited from the parents' generation. This continuation decries all opposite assurances by the second generation. In that context, Ulrich Baer offers a highly instructive comparative discussion of Günter Grass and Peter Schneider as both writers of fiction and participants in the public discourse. Baer asks whether it is possible "to write about victims and perpetrators with the same degree of imaginative empathy necessary to create morally true fiction."[61] Pointing to David Grossman's novel *See Under: Love?* Baer treats this text as an example of morally true fiction. Yet with respect to Schneider's novel and also Grass's writing, to a certain degree, Baer concludes that, for different reasons, these writers each fail to accomplish this goal. Without giving *Eduards Heimkehr* overall much attention, Baer interprets Eduard's visit with Edita as yet another piece of evidence that "the perpetrator's problems with guilt, shame, and forgiveness cannot be expected to be solved by the victims."[62] Baer is interested in the fundamental and principal concern that all discussions of atonement, guilt, and forgiveness are "necessarily haunted and threatened by the unstated presumption that the other side [the side of the victims] is capable of participating and listening."[63] According to Baer, Schneider's position exemplifies that of the generation of Germans born after 1945 who worked through its own sense of powerlessness in a nation that committed genocide by confronting its parents collectively. According to Baer, the encounter between Edita and Eduard has to be interpreted as an unwelcome appropriation of the survivor and as a morally and ethically outrageous impertinence.

Yet by focusing solely on this one scene of the novel Baer fails to acknowledge that Schneider's text engages critically with exactly that position of the former '68er who, maybe for the first time, understands the implications of his former attitude towards the Nazi past during the 1960s. While one can certainly read Schneider's rendition of German–Jewish reconciliation either as "refreshingly unburdened" or "flippant,"[64] the notion of "morally true fiction" deserves more attention.[65] While Baer distances himself from Ernestine Schlant's notion of the real or perceived silence about the Holocaust in German literature after 1945 one wonders whether both critics are ultimately guided by the conviction that there is only one way to write about the Holocaust. If this is so then fiction about the Holocaust would subscribe to an a priori or prescriptive aesthetics that is guided by moral and ethical considerations and not by questions of form and representation.

While Baer provides a thought-provoking discussion I maintain that Schneider's novel exemplifies the kind of self-questioning that his generation currently undergoes, thus shaping a process of remembering and forgetting that will affect historiography. In contrast to Baer, I read *Eduards Heimkehr* as a literary text that reveals contradictions, constructs complexities, and creates precarious suspensions via processes of remembering and forgetting and of writing and omitting language. I share Siegfried Mew's cautiously optimistic reading of *Eduards Heimkehr* in which he argues that Schneider intends to shift the focus to a more productive, less inhibiting and paralyzing approach to the German past. Even though these encounters are problematic and characterize the Germans as naive at best or vicious at worst, they nevertheless give Jewish survivors a voice in contemporary German literature. The members of the generation who thought to differentiate and distance themselves from their parents' involvement in the past reevaluate their behavior in the 1960s and change their approach via reflections and actions. The actual encounters take place in the United States, thus acknowledging the difficulty of the German–Jewish dialogue in Germany and the important role the United States played in offering exile to refugees in the 1930s and 1940s. Furthermore, the United States serves as the "lieux de mémoire" because only the distance from Germany and the visit to the homes of the survivors and refugees in the United States allow the second generation of Germans to remember their own life and to reassess their own approaches to the past.

The United States as Utopian Imagination

Ulrike Kolb's novel *Frühstück mit Max* takes place in Manhattan and places the encounter between the second and the third generation of Germans in the center of the story. The chance meeting triggers the narration of their memories. Nelly, who is visiting New York City as a tourist, was the girlfriend of Max's father and participated in raising Max. Max lives with his family in Brooklyn and works in Manhattan as an architect. Taking turns in narrating the novel, they remember the years they lived together in a communal living project in Berlin named "Mommsen" after their street address, and they tell each other their life stories. Intertwined and juxtaposed with the direct speech exchanged by the two narrators, Nelly and Max, they individually share some of their memories only with the reader. These paradoxically contradictory and complementary memories reveal that Nelly's and Max's experiences during the time of the 1960s and their evaluations of those years differ greatly.

In a review of *Frühstück mit Max*, Reinhard Baumgart comments on the function of New York City as the location of the novel: "Es könnte aber auch der distanzierte Schauplatz dieses begeisterten Austauschs von Erinnerungen, es könnte also auch New York mitgeholfen haben, dieses Kunststück an Balance herzustellen, zwischen Heiterkeit und Hin- und Zurückgerissenwerden, zwischen Geistesgegenwart und dem Versinken in eine ferne, fremde, nahe Zeit, die den beiden noch tief im Kopf steckt" (It could be the distanced site of this enthusiastic exchange of memories, it could have been New York City that contributed to the creation of this balance between humor and remembering, between presence of mind and the long-gone past which continues to deeply shape both characters).[66] Baumgart stresses that placing the encounter in the United States rather than in Berlin creates an important distance from both home and the past. New York City as the setting prevents the drift towards either nostalgic longing or nihilistic irony and allows for a balance between the present and the past, between the here and now and the then and there. Baumgart also emphasizes that New York City is not the focal point, but serves as the backdrop of the encounter between the estranged characters and alludes to the opportunity for new beginnings and second chances.

For Max, the past does not primarily mean the burden of national history, in particular National Socialism and the Holocaust, but the experience of having grown up in a communal living project in Berlin during the late 1960s and 1970s. He detests the chaos he experienced there and is unable to forgive his father or to show any understanding for his father's attempt to raise his son in an anti-authoritarian manner. Max's first visit to New York City as a high school student leaves such a strong impression that he decides to move there as soon as he graduates. Describing his emotions retrospectively, he refers to feeling high and being turned on by its atmosphere, using language that is usually employed to describe the effects of drug use.[67] This attempt to free himself and to live in a city that not only promises personal freedom but also liberation from the burden of having grown up in Germany is at least linguistically overshadowed by implications of dependency and addiction.

New York City serves as the seemingly appropriate backdrop for a representative of the third generation. The United States seems to offer the opportunity to break away from the burden of family obligations and to make a fresh start. In Nora's terms, the immigration to the United States leads to a loss of "milieu de mémoire," of everyday experiences of remembering as lived and living traditions. However, in my reading of Max, this does not entail a utopian imagination of radical difference, since he limits himself to preserving or rather recreating a lifestyle that was already outdated in the 1960s. As his form of rebellion against his upbringing, he chooses to become an architect in order to create order and impose structure, and he lives a neatly organized and regulated life within a nuclear family. Furthermore, he does not settle in the city, but in Brooklyn. Thus, he rarely experiences the rush of emotions that led to his migration to Manhattan. The only liberation he feels is after a domestic disagreement with his wife when he is on his way to work in the city, riding his bike over the Brooklyn Bridge.[68]

For Nelly, New York City is primarily a place to visit and to explore. Even though Nelly's dreams have been shattered—she separated from Max's father and battled alcoholism and depression—she still remembers the 1960s with fondness, in particular the dreams that inspired the generation of the '68ers and her attempt to realize at least some of them in the communal living project. She comments critically on Max's alleged attempt to lead a self-determined life. When he describes his current life to her, in particular his obsession with his work, which actually leaves him very little time for anything else, including his family, she thinks that he is what they—the generation of 1968—used to call a "Fachidiot" (nerd), exposing him as a conformist adhering to the expectations of Western capitalist society.[69] In contrast to the 1960s, when the students motivated their rebellion politically, Nelly understands Max's rebellion as an adolescent phase and simply a response to his experiences with his family's history. In contrast to the members of the 1960s student movement, his experiences do not bear any political or historical ramifications. His rebellion only has a lasting impact on his personal life since he decides to leave Germany and to settle in the United States. "Space Untitled"—the name of the coffee house where Nelly and Max meet—indicates this loss of significance. The design and atmosphere of the coffee house attract all generations despite their differences, foreshadowing the loss of any historical or cultural specificity due to processes of globalization. In that sense, Manhattan as a city full of contradictions whose name means "heavenly earth" does indeed provide the space to reconcile differences, if only on the surface.[70] It is the unmarked space that serves as a site of memory filled with contradictory and complementary memories and the hope of finding common ground.

After their chance encounter Nelly and Max attempt to meet one more time. When Max arrives at the apartment where Nelly stays she cannot find the key to open the locked door. While he is waiting in front of the door, she is desperately trying to find the key, which she has misplaced inside the apartment. After Max leaves to go to work she finds the key in the refrigerator.[71] This missed opportunity to open a door and continue a relationship is not only a comment on the cold relationship between Max and Nelly. This involuntary, yet self-inflicted imprisonment also points to Nelly's ambivalent feelings about New York City and her own life.[72] It is as if she cannot leave behind the shadows that the 1960s cast.

Transcultural Encounters, Transnational Memories

The novels *Eduards Heimkehr*, *Frühstück mit Max*, and *Der Vorleser* contribute to the discourse on processes of cultural transfer and invite reflection on the construction of personal and national identities within a historical and spatial perspective. As literary texts, they emphasize the central roles of storytelling and narration within these discourses. As memory novels, they enable the study of the complex relation between the past, the present, and the future. They open poetic spaces that address remembering as well as forgetting.

The representations of the United States in novels about the 1960s challenge prevalent notions of Germany's image of "America" and call for a reevaluation of the transatlantic relationship between Germany and the United States from the perspective of the 1960s. In particular, they place the proclaimed anti-Americanism by former '68ers in a longer historical perspective. This broader context does more justice to the land of opportunity and foregrounds the United States as a land of exile for those who are persecuted in their home countries. After all, historically the United States provided safety for those who were persecuted by the Nazis and was willing to reintegrate the political activists from the 1960s from both sides of the Atlantic despite their alleged threat to Western society.

When the narrators visit the United States it is the distance from "home" that allows and challenges the literary figures to reflect on their personal as well as collective identities. The representation of the United States as both a meeting place and a site where memories of the German twentieth century are exchanged and negotiated, dialogues started, and stories told points to the fact that this process is still problematic within Germany. The creation of the United States as a literary memory space challenges prevalent notions of identity and enables a displaced discussion about identity formation in the twenty-first century in Germany, in particular with respect to the relationship between East and West Germans, between Germans and Jews, between perpetrators, bystanders, victims, survivors, and those who resisted during the Third Reich, and between those who live in contemporary Germany.

The United States in its literary representations serves as a site of memory for those who are affected by the Holocaust and its aftermath. While Eduard, Michael Berg, and many of the Germans traveling to the United States in other contemporary novels assume that the country is neutral and objective in its treatment of the Holocaust, it becomes clear that this is only true in the German imagination. Soon these travelers are confronted with the fact that since many victims emigrated to the United States either right before or right after the Holocaust, the engagement with the Holocaust is vibrant in the United States Thus, the narrators dismiss the notion of an untainted beginning, comparable to the notion of America as the uninhabited continent awaiting discovery by the Europeans. Rather, the encounters that are enabled by the configuration of the United States as the meeting space between Germans and Jews of different generations demand a radical reconsideration of personal and collective identities shaped by history and space.

Notes

1. Johann Wolfgang von Goethe, "Den Vereinigten Staaten," in *Werke* 1, ed. Erich Trunz (München: Beck, 1981): 33. "America, you're better off than/Our continent, the old./ You have no castles which are fallen/No basalt to behold./You're not disturbed within your inmost being/Right up till today's life/By useless remembering/And unreward-

ing strife." Johann Wolfgang von Goethe, "To America," in *The Permanent Goethe*, ed. Thomas Mann, trans. Stephen Spender (New York: Dial, 1948): 655.
2. From a historian's perspective, Uta Poiger undertakes a similar project with respect to the immediate postwar period. She argues that both German states understood American cultural imports as a threat to each of their distinct cultural, social, and, ultimately, political conventions and identities. Uta Poiger, *Jazz, Rock, and Rebels: Cold War Politics and American Culture in a Divided Germany* (Berkeley: University of California Press, 2000).
3. Edward Said, *Orientalism* (New York: Vintage, 1978).
4. See also Susanne Zantop's *Colonial Fantasies: Conquest, Family, and Nation in Precolonial Germany, 1770–1870* (Durham: Duke University Press, 1997).
5. For a more global approach and perspective see Carola Fink, Philipp Gassert, and Detlef Junker, ed., *1968: A World Transformed* (Cambridge: Cambridge University Press, 1998), and Arthur Marwick, *The Sixties. Cultural Revolution in Britain, France, Italy, and the United States, 1958–74* (Oxford: Oxford University Press, 1998). Both not only emphasize the transnational aspects of the movement but also its cultural rather than political nature. See also Axel Schildt and Detlef Siegfried, ed., *Between Marx and Coca-Cola: Youth Cultures in Changing European Societies, 1960–1980* (Oxford: Oxford University Press, 2005). For a focus on the transatlantic relation between Germany and the United States see Ingrid Gilcher-Holtey, *Die 68er Bewegung. Deutschland, Westeuropa, USA* (München: Beck, 2001), and Michael Schmidtke, *Der Aufbruch der jungen Intelligenz. Die 68er Jahre in der Bundesrepublik und den USA* (Frankfurt a.M.: Campus, 2003).
6. Cf. Gerard De Groot, *Student Protest. The Sixties and After* (London, New York: Longman, 1998); Ingrid Gilcher-Holtey, *Die 68er Bewegung: Deutschland, Westeuropa, USA*; Martin Klimke, *The Other Alliance: Student Protest in West Germany & the United States in the Global Sixties* (Princeton: Princeton University Press, 2010); Uta Poiger, *Jazz, Rock, and Rebels: Cold War Politics and American Culture in a Divided Germany*; and Jeremi Suri, *Power and Protest: Global Revolution and the Power of Détente* (Cambridge: Harvard University Press, 2003).
7. Alexander Stephan, ed., *The Americanization of Europe: Culture, Diplomacy, and Anti-Americanism after 1945* (New York: Berghahn Books, 2006).
8. Claus Leggewie, "'1968.' A Transatlantic Event and Its Consequences," in *The United States and Germany in the Era of the Cold War, 1945–1990. A Handbook. Volume 2: 1968–1990*, ed. Detlef Junker (Cambridge: Cambridge University Press and German Historical Institute, 2004): 421–429: 424f.
9. Philipp Gassert, "'With America against America.' Anti-Americanism in West Germany," in *The United States and Germany in the Era of the Cold War, 1945–1990. A Handbook, Volume 2: 1968–1990*, ed. Detlef Junker (Cambridge: Cambridge University Press and German Historical Institute, 2004): 502–509, 506.
10. Christina von Hodenberg and Detlef Siegfried, *Wo "1968" liegt. Reform und Revolte in der Geschichte der Bundesrepublik* (Göttingen: Vandenhoeck & Ruprecht, 2006): 11.
11. Cf. Franz Kafka's unfinished novel *Amerika* (München: K. Wolff, 1927).
12. Johann Wolfgang von Goethe, *Wilhelm Meisters Lehrjahre*, in *Werke 7*, ed. Erich Trunz (München: Beck, 1981).

13. Cf. Ferdinand Kürnberger, *Der Amerika-Müde* (1855, Frankfurt a.M.: Meidinger, 1989) and Reinhold Solger, *Anton in Amerika* (1862, Hannover: Wehrhahn, 2009).
14. The representation of the United States in German literature is well explored and continues to attract considerable interest. Compare the following by no means exhaustive references: Sigrid Bauschinger, Horst Denkler, and Wilfried Malsch, eds., *Amerika in der deutschen Literatur: Neue Welt, Nordamerika, USA* (Stuttgart: Reclam, 1975); Aminia M. Brueggemann, *Chronotopos Amerika bei Max Frisch, Peter Handke, Günter Kunert und Martin Walser* (New York: Lang, 1996); Alfred Cobbs, *The Image of America in Postwar German Literature: Reflections and Perceptions* (Bern: Lang, 1982); Manfred Durzak, *Das Amerika-Bild in der deutschen Gegenwartsliteratur* (Stuttgart: Kohlhammer, 1979); Hans Galinsky, *Amerikanisch-deutsche Sprach- und Literaturbeziehungen* (Frankfurt a.M.: Athenäum-Verlag, 1972); Christof Hamann, Ute Gerhard, and Walter Grünzweig, ed., *Amerika und die deutschsprachige Literatur nach 1848. Migration—kultureller Austausch—frühe Globalisierung* (Bielefeld: transcript Verlag, 2009); Thomas W. Kniesche, *Projektionen von Amerika. Die USA in der deutsch-jüdischen Literatur des 20. Jahrhunderts* (Bielefeld: Aisthesis, 2008); Anita Krätzer, *Studien zum Amerikabild in der neueren deutschen Literatur* (Bern: Lang, 1982); Heinz D. Osterle, ed., *Amerika!: New Images in German Literature* (New York: Lang, 1989); Wolfgang Paulsen, ed., *Die USA und Deutschland: Wechselseitige Spiegelungen in der Literatur der Gegenwart* (Bern: Francke, 1976); Alexander Ritter, ed., *Deutschlands literarisches Amerikabild: neuere Forschungen zur Amerikarezeption der deutschen Literatur.* (Hildesheim: Olms, 1977); and Richard Ruland, *America in Modern European Literature: From Image to Metaphor* (New York: New York University Press, 1976).
15. Heinz D. Osterle, "The Lost Utopia. New Images of America in German Literature," *The German Quarterly* 54.4 (Winter 1981): 427–46, 428.
16. Uwe Johnson, *Jahrestage*. (Frankfurt a.M.: Suhrkamp, 1970ff).
17. Cf. Peter Handke's *Der kurze Brief zum langen Abschied* (Frankfurt a.M.: Suhrkamp,1972). From the perspective of literary history it is revealing that Handke's attack on the literary establishment of West Germany, represented by the Gruppe 47, takes place at Princeton University in 1967 as if only the United States offered the opportunity to speak one's mind, to rebel, and to propose new ideas.
18. Cf. Erich Fried, *und Vietnam und* (Berlin: Wagenbach, 1966); Reinhard Lettau, *Täglicher Faschismus: Amerikanische Evidenz aus 6 Monaten* (München: Hanser, 1971) and Peter Weiss, *Viet Nam Diskurs* (Frankfurt a.M.: Suhrkamp, 1968).
19. Gerd Gemünden, *Framed Visions. Popular Culture, Americanization, and the Contemporary German and Austrian Imagination* (Ann Arbor: The University of Michigan Press, 1998): 31.
20. Walter Benjamin, "Ausgraben und Erinnern," *Gesammelte Schriften* IV.1, ed. Tillman Rexroth (Frankfurt a.M.: Suhrkamp, 1978): 400f.
21. Ulrike Kolb, *Frühstück mit Max* (Stuttgart: Klett-Cotta, 2000): 83f.
22. Bernhard Schlink, *Der Vorleser* (Zürich: Diogenes, 1995), chapter 12: 134–139.
23. Peter Schneider, *Eduards Heimkehr* (Berlin: Rowohlt, 1999): 355–367.
24. Pierre Nora, "Between Memory and History: Les Lieux de Mémoire," *Representations* 26.1 (1989): 7–24.
25. Ibid.: 7.

26. Ibid.: 12.
27. Leggewie, "'1968'. A Transatlantic Event and Its Consequences," points to the fact that the anti-authoritarian movement in the United States determined the themes—Vietnam and racism—and gave shape to spontaneous forms of action, such as teach-ins, go-ins, sit-ins, and happenings that were extensively adopted and imitated on the other side of the Atlantic. Gassert calls the anti-Americanism of the New Left an anti-anti-Americanism "with America against America." See Gassert, "'With America against America.' Anti-Americanism in West Germany:" 505.
28. The state investigated 3.5 million people and 10,000 of those were either not hired or laid off. See <http://www.dhm.de/ausstellungen/grundrechte/katalog/144-149.pdf> (accessed 6 June 2009).
29. See chapter 1 for a discussion of the topic in Uwe Timm's *Rot*.
30. Schlink, *Der Vorleser*, chapter 11: 199–204.
31. For an overview of the subject in German literature after 1945, cf. Sigrid Bauschinger, "Mythos Manhattan. Die Faszination einer Stadt," in *Amerika in der deutschen Literatur: Neue Welt, Nordamerika, USA*, ed. Sigrid Bauschinger, Horst Denkler, and Wilfried Malsch (Stuttgart: Reclam, 1975): 382–397. The apartment in the movie *The Reader* (2008, Dir. Stephen Daldry), which is based on the novel, forms a stark contrast to the textual description. In the movie, the apartment evokes the living space of a presumably wealthy, upper-class woman. A black maid in a white maid's uniform greets Berg, thus further emphasizing the economic success of the survivor and also adding another layer to the racial subtext of the story.
32. Schlink, *Der Vorleser*, chapter 11: 201.
33. The inscription of the Frankfurt Auschwitz trial (1963–65) in this 1968 memory novel corresponds with recent research that reassesses and confirms the significance of the trial for the history of coming to terms with the legacy of the Third Reich after 1945. See Friedrich-Martin Balzer and Werner Renz, ed., *Das Urteil im Frankfurter Auschwitz-Prozess, 1963–1965* (Bonn: Pahl-Rugenstein, 2004); Marc von Miquel, *Ahnden oder amnestieren? Westdeutsche Justiz und Vergangenheitspolitik in den sechziger Jahren* (Göttingen: Wallstein, 2004); Devin O. Pendas, *The Frankfurt Auschwitz Trial, 1963–1965: Genocide, History, and the Limits of the Law* (Cambridge: Cambridge University Press, 2006); and Rebecca E. Wittmann, *Beyond Justice: The Auschwitz Trial* (Cambridge: Harvard University Press, 2005).
34. Schlink, *Der Vorleser*, chapter 11: 202.
35. Ibid.: 203f.
36. The only direct encounter during the sixties is the law professor who was in exile for unknown reasons and who teaches the seminar that studied the Nazi trials that Berg observed as a law student.
37. Schlink, *Der Vorleser*, chapter 14: 144–147.
38. Compare the research conducted by Harald Welzer, Sabine Moller, and Karoline Tschuggnall, *"Opa war kein Nazi." Nationalsozialismus und Holocaust im Familiengedächtnis* (Frankfurt a.M.: S. Fischer, 2002). Their research stresses that many stories that are incorporated as family history are actually based on cultural representations of the Third Reich.
39. Walter Benjamin, "Berliner Chronik", in *Gesammelte Schriften* VI, ed. Tillman Rexroth (Frankfurt a.M.: Suhrkamp, 1978): 486.

40. Ibid.
41. Ibid.: 491.
42. Schneider, *Eduards Heimkehr*: 39ff.
43. Ibid.: 297–311.
44. Ibid.: 350ff.
45. Schneider, *Eduards Homecoming*: 266.
46. Schneider, *Eduards Heimkehr*: 355.
47. Schneider, *Eduards Homecoming*: 367f.
48. Schneider, *Eduards Heimkehr*: 357.
49. Ibid.: 360.
50. Ibid.: 356.
51. Schneider, *Eduards Homecoming*: 269.
52. Ibid.: 356.
53. Ibid.: 269.
54. Schneider, *Eduards Heimkehr*: 39ff.
55. Ibid.: 357.
56. Ibid.: 362.
57. Ibid.: 363ff.
58. All four characters are not completely comfortable using English, pointing to the importance of language for the purposes of identity constructions. In particular, both Berg and Hoffmann emphasize that, for them, texts written in English and conversations in English always create a distance and do not cause the same immediate affective reactions as those in German. In *Eduards Heimkehr* the language switch is not only talked about, but integrated in the text: the first couple of sentences of the dialogue between Hoffmann and Marwitz are written in English (*Eduards Heimkehr*: 356).
59. In particular in *Der Vorleser* the difference and complementary necessity of historical research, personal memories, and storytelling is emphasized: in the sixties, the survivor, whom Berg visits later in New York City, already published a book about the camp that the law students used in order to study the Holocaust.
60. Peter Schneider, "The Good Germans: Saving Konrad Latte," in *The New York Times Magazine* 13 February 2000: 26–29, 53; and Peter Schneider, *"Und wenn wir nur eine Stunde gewinnen…"Wie ein jüdischer Musiker die Nazi-Jahre überlebte* (Berlin: Rowohlt, 2001).
61. Ulrich Baer, "The Hubris of Humility: Günter Grass, Peter Schneider, and German Guilt After 1989," *The Germanic Review* 80.1 (2005): 50–73, 62.
62. Ibid.: 68.
63. Ibid.: 53.
64. Ibid.: 67.
65. Cf. Robert Boyers, "The Normality Blues," in *The Dictator's Dictation. The Politics of Novels and Novelists* (New York: Columbia University Press, 2005): 91–106, for a discussion of the comical aspects of Schneider's novel. Boyer points to the difficulties of writing comedy in Germany after 1945, in particular when literary texts revolve around the Third Reich and its legacy.
66. Reinhard Baumgart, "Ferne Zeit, ganz nah," *Die Zeit* 21, 18 May 2000: 55.
67. Kolb, *Frühstück mit Max*: 57.

68. Ibid.: 30 and 115f.
69. Ibid.: 33. Elizabeth Pfeifer describes the "Fachidioten" (specialized idiot) flyer incident that occurred at the Free University in Berlin in 1966. "Fachidiot" soon became a buzzword within the student movement as it attacked the power of the full professor and curriculum of the university which the students considered outdated and irrelevant to contemporary contexts. See Elizabeth L.B. Pfeifer, "1968 in German Political Culture, 1967–1993: From Experience to Myth," PhD diss., University of North Carolina, Chapel Hill, 1997: 130.
70. Bauschinger, "Mythos Manhattan. Die Faszination einer Stadt:" 396.
71. Kolb, *Frühstück mit Max*: 195.
72. Monika Maron narrates a similar scene of imprisonment in New York City involving the female narrator in *Animal Triste* (Frankfurt a.M.: S. Fischer, 1996).

Chapter 4

Transnational Memories: 1968 and Turkish-German Authors

> Sterne des Fatums
>
> Deine Augen harren vor meinem Leben
> Wie Nächte, die sich nach Tagen sehnen,
> Und der schwüle Traum liegt auf ihnen
> Unergründet.
>
> Seltsame Sterne starren zur Erde,
> Eisenfarb'ne mit Sehnsuchtsschweifen,
> Mit brennenden Armen, die Liebe suchen
> Und in die Kühle der Lüfte greifen.
>
> Sterne in denen das Schicksal mündet.
>
> *Else Lasker-Schüler*[1]

In April 2008, in time for the celebration of the fortieth anniversary of the student movement, *Radio Multikulti*, a Berlin-based radio station that broadcasts in a variety of languages and always from the perspective of the other within the German mainstream, hosted a series of radio shows with the title "'68 als internationale Begegnung" (68 as an international encounter).[2] The series reflected the schism that exists in current considerations and reconsiderations of 1968. On the one hand, interviews with Emine Sevgi Özdamar, Bahman Nirumand, Michael S. Cullen, Kostas Papanastasiou, and Achmed Al Sadi underscore the important contributions to 1968 and its discourse by ethnic minority Germans. Mainstream media and the public discourse commemorating the event in 2008 largely ignored these contributions. Thus, while a laudable enterprise in itself, the fact that the "international" contributions to 1968 were celebrated by a radio station that functions as a bridge between German–German and German–other discourses does not surprise.[3]

On the other hand, another series of shows by the same radio station treated the incidences of unrest in other countries in the 1960s as related, yet separate, events that were investigated by those with a non-hyphenated identity. As such, the international encounter was not an encounter between different yet equal partners, but simply another collection of parallel voices that did not engage in a dialogue with each other. This chapter asks whether fictional texts enable true encounters of those who have a stake in determining the significance of the 1960s student movement for the present and the future, whether it was either during the 1960s or in their recollections or retroactive appropriation of the rebellion. Do fictional texts have the creative power to challenge existing, and usually homogenous, notions, of the student movement in Germany in the 1960s? The analysis of Emine Sevgi Özdamar's trilogy, consisting of *Das Leben ist eine Karawanserei—hat zwei Türen—aus einer kam ich rein—aus der anderen ging ich raus, Die Brücke vom Goldenen Horn,* and *Seltsame Sterne starren zur Erde* suggests that we should understand these encounters in the light of transnationalism and as a moment of a transnational cultural memory.[4]

Hyphenated Identities in Germany in the 1990s

The emergence of a transnational cultural memory of 1968 has important repercussions for our understanding of the 1960s and of the 1990s when many of the novels about the German student movement were published. Since unification, and with renewed urgency after the terrorist attacks on September 11, 2001, the question of "identity" has resurfaced. The term "multicultural" and notions of a "diverse society" have become important themes in the reexamination of the question of what it means to be German, not only for citizens of the former FRG and the GDR and for the newly emerging German-Jewish community, but also for the ethnic minority groups in Germany.[5] The discussion of these issues has led to a reexamination of the place of different types of migrants in German society since 1945 and, even more importantly, has changed the definition of "being German."

As unified Germany enters the twenty-first century and officially declares itself a country of immigration, it is acknowledging a state of affairs which has existed de facto for at least fifty years. Germany has yet to come to terms with the legacy of the recruitment of foreign workers during the postwar economic boom. For West Germany, it is well documented that the "Anwerbestopp" (ban on recruitment) in 1973 resulted in the transformation of migrant labor into minority populations, as is the predominance of the Turkish minority. In 1973, Turks constituted a quarter of the non-German workforce, rising to a third by 1990, by which time the Turkish population numbered nearly two million.[6] However, what is still at stake is the acceptance of the contributions by hyphenated citizens to the public, political, cultural, and academic discourse in Germany.

In the 1990s, numerous attempts, mirrored in historiographical and sociological studies and oral history projects, were made to better understand Turkish–German relations. Karin Hunn wrote a history of Turkish guest workers in West Germany emphasizing the interdependency of economic, political, social, and cultural developments that determine this history.[7] Drawing on German and Turkish sources, her interdisciplinary and comparative methodology allows her to sketch the complexity of conflicting intentions and actions of the various actors involved in the process of Turkish labor immigration and the emergence of Turkish-German life.

In 1998/99, Eva Kolinsky conducted oral interviews with Turks living in Germany based on the premise "that identity cannot be traced to one event, background or cultural framework such as religion or nationality, but emerges from biography. It is shaped by the individual's experiences with the environment in which he or she is living and may change over time and between generations."[8] While Kolinsky points to distinct differences between the three generations of people of Turkish extraction by now living in Germany, she concludes that: "Turkish identity means linking German and Turkish components and traditions to create a distinctive and personal orientation."[9] Given these processes, Ayhan Kaya calls most German-Turks "transmigrants."[10]

Viola B. Georgi conducted interviews with high school students who are either born in Germany or who have German citizenship but whose parents are not German.[11] These students indicate a willingness to accept responsibility for National Socialism if that would allow them to be considered part of German society. Given the ongoing public discourse on the Nazi past in Germany, the students' notion of belonging to Germany hinged on their ability to take an interest in and to accept responsibility for that past. Yet it does pose interesting challenges both for the effect on the migrant by appropriating a past that resists easy appropriation and for the intentions of the mainstream to either include or exclude migrants in this memory work or to suggest that belonging to the national majority hinges on the acceptance of a past that defies any acceptance.

Annette Seidel Arpaci agrees with Georgi that migrants are excluded from the mainstream national remembrance culture.[12] At the same time, Arpaci points to the fallacies of the debates challenging this exclusion. They are marked not only by a further production of yet other "others," but also by a lack of interest in those migrant histories and positionalities that are prone to contradict a construed neutrality of migrants with regard to what is called the German past. Accordingly, these debates remain firmly embedded within the parameters of mainstream discourse, merely adding another participant to the dialogue allegedly taking place between Germans and Jews. The presumed detachedness of migrants from the history of Nazi Germany and the commemoration of its victims is only ever questioned for the purpose of a Europeanizing and universalizing of the Holocaust. Andreas Huyssen studies the effects of the European and increasingly global memory of the Holocaust in conjunction with German memory constructions of the past.[13] He introduces the notion of diasporic memory in order to account for the increasing engagement by non-German-Germans.

Both Arpaci and Huyssen raise important questions regarding the construction of cultural memory. How and to what effect do literary contributions by migrant authors, or by authors with identities traditionally understood as hybrid, change our understanding of the German past, bring to light the specificities of the migrants' backgrounds and place in contemporary Germany, and, thus, construct a different kind of cultural memory for Germany? Since this study is concerned with the different layers of cultural memory that are triggered by remembering 1968, the analysis of Emine Sevgi Özdamar's work will focus on the embedded memory of the Holocaust and the Third Reich through the lens of the Turkish-German author's contribution to the transnational cultural memory of 1968.

Transnational History

In contemporary discourse, the year 1968 marks the height of the student movement in Germany. Yet, as the previous chapters have argued, the German student movement was neither restricted to West Germany nor did it occur in isolation. Rather, the movement coincided with other protest movements around the world, transforming the West German student movement into an international event. Since these movements were also causally linked, they ultimately transcended national borders and formed a transnational sphere.

In contrast to internationalism, transnationalism accounts for the fact that relationships and exchanges between nations not only take place on the official level but also on the unofficial level, between groups without an official or representative mandate or without a business interest. Transnational relations are based on informal exchanges and affinities; they are carried out by groups that identify interests as shared experiences or similar political, social, or cultural goals that cannot be realized within the existing structures and that connect members of these groups across national borders and other boundaries. Conceptually, transnationalism accounts for attempts both to better understand and to subvert national boundaries. Transnationalism highlights the problematic aspects of national politics and its deficiencies since national politics always entail hegemonic and homogenous notions of identity and the state. These notions privilege the official exchanges between states. However, as the realities of many nation-states suggest, they do not account for the diversity that marks many, if not all, countries. This diversity exists because of the migration to and from nation-states and an ever-accelerated exchange of ideas between countries. Whenever these exchanges take place unofficially, such as the ones that marked the 1960s, they constitute a transnational moment.[14]

In the past, historiographical research focused on the international and global aspects of the 1960s student movements in a comparative fashion.[15] Current research employs a transnational framework in order to understand the concurrent student movements around the world in the 1960s and their transnational exchanges and interactions. Martin Klimke and Joachim Scharloth emphasize that the transnational dimension of the 1960s protest was already perceived by its contemporaries and was one of its crucial motors.[16] The editors of the Palgrave Macmillan Transnational History Series, Akira Iriye and Rana Mitter, consider one of the important aspects of 1968 to be the questioning of the presumed omnipotence of the nation and the state. The radicals were aware that their movements extended far beyond the nation-states they belonged to and claimed that national borders were still far too restrictive and thus had to be overcome. This challenge to the nation-state constitutes one element of the transnationalism of 1968.

Another transnational factor was the radicals' language use. Their similar, often identical, language provided a tie across national and linguistic borders. This point is well illustrated by the example Klimke and Scharloth provide in their introduction to *1968 in Europe: A History of Protest and Activism, 1956–1977*. In 1967, at the end of a BBC television show entitled *Students in Revolt*, for which British broadcaster Robert McKenzie invited and interviewed student leaders from across Europe, the students rose and jointly sang the Communist International in their native tongues. This incident shows that even when speaking different languages the students could revert to a shared language that transcended their native tongues and reflected their shared ideology, in this case the Communist International. This shared language, consisting of numerous cultural representations (theory, films, books, music), led to the creation of an amalgam of ideas that in turn created the New Left.

If indeed language is at the core of this movement then it is more necessary than ever to analyze the language use of the movement and its representation in all areas, including fiction. In Klimke and Scharloth's compendium, fiction as an object of research seems to be completely omitted, not an accidental oversight, I contend, since writers themselves suggested the death of literature in the 1960s. This claim led to experiments with blurred genres and so-called documentary and engaged literature. However, not even the former participants of the movement quit writing fictional texts and fiction remained as popular as ever as an art form and as an important contribution to the public discourse in Germany. Novels published in the 1990s document how 1968 and its discourse emerge as an important part of the cultural memory and as a transnational phenomenon in Germany. Fiction, in turn, shapes this discourse, and writings by hyphenated authors, such as the trilogy by Özdamar, add a layer of transnational memories to the construction of a cultural memory of 1968 in Germany and can be read within a transnational framework of 1968.

Transnational Fiction

In the twentieth century, German literary criticism often only grudgingly acknowledged experiences of (forced) migration and their aesthetic manifestations.[17] Traditionally, German literary criticism found it exceedingly difficult to study literary texts, authors, and movements that could not be analyzed strictly within national parameters and its linguistic manifestations. Recently, however, literary and cultural studies have placed an emphasis on migration studies and the experiences of various diasporas. In the 1990s, it became clear that it was not German identity that was at stake when talking about migration, but that this identity needed to be redefined in order to accommodate a population in Germany that was more diverse than ever.[18]

The history of Turkish-German literature and its reception in public and academic discourse are particularly perplexing issues. Turkish-German literature emerged in the 1960s, yet it was not recognized as such, instead categorized as *Gastarbeiterliteratur* (guest worker literature), as literature written by and about guest workers between the 1960s and 1980s. In the late 1980s this term was replaced by other, equally misleading terms, among them *Ausländer-* and *Fremdenliteratur* (foreigner literature), *Literatur der MigrantInnen* (migrants' literature), and *interkulturelle Literatur* (intercultural literature). Literature written by non German-German authors continues to be placed in a separate category to this day. This exclusion is manifest in the yearly award of the Chamisso Prize, a literature prize that has been awarded annually in Munich since 1985 to authors whose mother tongue and cultural background are non-German and whose works make an important contribution to literature written in German. The award of the Bachmann Prize to Özdamar in 1991, a literary prize traditionally awarded to German-German authors, caused a public debate over what it means to write in German and to be German. This situation was perceived as crossing deeply engrained borders that separate the German and the non-German literary space.[19]

In the twenty-first century, literary texts by so-called hyphenated authors have moved away from the margins and become a focal point in the study of German literature. As a result of this process, the definition of German literature has slowly begun changing. In *Cosmopolitical Claims. Turkish-German Literatures from Nadolny to Pamuk*, B. Venkat Mani aims to demonstrate that "recent German and Turkish novels upset normative perceptions of dominant cultural production in a nation, its language, and its literature through new forms of imaginative expressions."[20] His study explores aesthetic and political claims that unsettle concepts of home, belonging, and cultural citizenship. Through new aesthetic expressions, palpable resurgences of multiple simultaneous affiliations have emerged and shaped German fiction. Mani claims that the work of interventionist imaginations thus resists crude proverbial assimilation to and cooption by legislations of hegemonic culturalisms, regardless of whether these are mono- or multiculturalisms. What is interesting for the context of my study is the significance that Mani attributes to the imagination, specifically the creative processes in writing fiction. His study supports my own argument that fiction is an integral part of any analysis that explores historical, political, and social developments from a cultural perspective.

In *Novels of Turkish German Settlement. Cosmopolite Fictions*, Tom Cheesman argues that Turkish-German writers have become integral to the German literary scene. They include bestselling novelists Renan Demirkan and Akif Pirinçci, prestigious literary prize-winners Emine Sevgi Özdamar and Feridun Zaimoğlu, and the critically acclaimed Aras Ören and Zafer Şenocak. Cheesman focuses on these and other writers' perspectives on cosmopolitan ideals and aspirations, ranging from glib affirmation to cynical transgression and melancholy nihilism. What Cheesman calls their "literature of settlement"[21] is paradigmatic for European cultures adapting to diversity and negotiating new identities.

Both Mani and Cheesman anchor their analyses in the notion of cosmopolitanism. Despite the overwhelming interest in transnationalism in history and other disciplines, in literary criticism, book-length studies on transnationalism and German literature are still missing. Transnational approaches offer literary criticism the unique opportunity to think of the migration of people, texts, and ideas as the norm, rather than the exception, yet as a norm that inherently defies our understanding of norms as exclusionary, hierarchical, and fixed by boundaries that create homogenous spaces. Hence, transnationalism as a phenomenon and as a method encourages the spatial conceptualization of heterogeneity and fluidity in terms of identity construction and provides a new understanding of historical developments.

Furthermore, while the emphasis on transnationalism might seem to de-emphasize historical experiences represented in literary texts, just the opposite is true. Current researchers, most recently and most convincingly Leslie Adelson, point to the fact that fiction by hybrid authors does not only speak about a situation that is outside or an ultimately superfluous add-on to the German experience.[22] Rather, these texts make important contributions to debates that transcend or subvert the national context and fundamentally redefine the national context. These texts intervene because they stress the fact that with global exchanges and transfers, and national populations more diverse than ever, texts and authors that used to receive special treatment (and as such were excluded from the national discourse) are now part of the mainstream. These authors address historical events which are not considered to be their "own" but those of the nation-state they migrated to. Furthermore, they address these events in light of their own historical and cultural situation as migrants. The task at hand then is to develop an understanding of transnational literature written in German that articulates and grants equality without erasing differences between authors and their specific backgrounds.

The 1960s and 1970s lend themselves in particular to these kinds of transnational explorations that lead to a collapse of essentialist and exclusive notions of Germanness. In Germany, the student movement was marked by an engagement with the legacy of the Third Reich, a burden and responsibility young people in other countries did not face. At the same time, the German movement connected with the uprisings across the globe in their joint concern over continued oppression in and by the so-called free Western world. Thus, to authors with a hyphenated identity who were eager to be taken seriously within the German literary market and who, at the same time, were transforming it, the 1960s and 1970s offered a unique opportunity to tap into a restricted national space, the discourse on the legacy of the Third Reich, and into the most prevalent transnational aspect of the movement, the concern over exploitation in and by capitalist societies.

Sabine von Dirke claims that the issue of minority discourses is closely connected to the broader transformation of the cultural paradigm in the 1960s and 1970s. Thus, she links the emergence of what I call transnational fiction written in German directly to processes that began with the student movement and found new literary forms in the late 1970s and early 1980s. These new forms resent or distrust monoculture and totalizing paradigms and celebrate heterogeneity and plurality, mirroring postmodern thought that characterizes the political, discursive, and aesthetic landscape in the wake of the 1960s student movement.[23]

In this context, Sten Nadolny's bestseller *Selim oder Die Gabe der Rede* (Selim or The Gift of Speaking) is one of the most widely discussed examples for the representation of the 1960s student movement and its legacy by a hyphenated author.[24] In addition, the novel found critical interest because of epistemological considerations of how to anchor this text in German literary history and of how to resolve the difficulty of accounting for a text about a Turk and a German that uses one of the most recognizable events in German history, the 1960s, in order to situate the Turkish-German experience. The text juxtaposes the German and the Turk in that the latter's ability to tell stories is contrasted with the former's quest to acquire this skill. Hence, the novel emphasizes the significance of storytelling in order to anchor and transmit personal and historical experiences within a social context. Leslie Adelson argues that "Nadolny's work does not rely on direct intertextual allusions to an earlier phase of postwar German literature but probes instead the epistemological shortcomings of an altogether nonliterary form of German opposition to fascism: the student movement of the late 1960s and early 1970s."[25]

Nadolny's novel also triggered a methodological debate that foreshadowed and advanced the notion that literature by bilingual and bicultural authors should be recognized as a equal contribution to a specific discourse within Germany. Already in 1994, Adelson emphasized the need "to challenge such Turkish-German oppositions and to ask what methodological alternatives a multiculturally oriented German Studies has to offer."[26] Ülker Gökberk, however, sharply criticizes Adelson's reading of the novel and instead analyzes Nadolny's novel in light of the tension between different theoretical and methodological models that emerged in the late 1980s and 1990s, mainly *interkulturelle Germanistik* (intercultural German Studies) that became popular in Germany and a cultural studies paradigm that emerged in the U.S.[27] While many other paradigms have emerged in order to study fiction by authors with hybrid identities, attempts to integrate all writing in German remain rare and this so-called multicultural fiction continues to occupy niches, in-between spaces, or spaces completely outside the German literary imagination.

Özdamar's trilogy makes another unique contribution that highlights the importance of transnationalism for 1968 and its memory discourse and hence provides an opportunity to integrate fiction written in German into one common discourse. Her work constructs a transcultural memory of 1968 that provides unique insights into the current negotiations of time, space, and identity in Germany. This transnational memory advances our understanding of the 1960s and addresses theoretical and methodological challenges within the discourse on 1968 as well as within the discourse on Turkish-German literature. Understanding the cultural memory of 1968 as a transnational memory of 1968 broadens its scope and makes the old and tired debates of hyphenated identities obsolete. The concept of a transnational cultural memory accounts for migratory processes that are slowly delineating boundaries by creating new constellations. These processes understand the need for identity and belonging and, at the same time, the impossibility of their permanent and fixed existence. As such, the concept of a transnational memory of 1968 is a useful analytical tool and the concept that determines Özdamar's literary work.

Emine Sevgi Özdamar as a Transnational Author

Emine Sevgi Özdamar is one of the most prominent contemporary authors in Germany. As already mentioned, she has received many prizes for her work, including the Chamisso Prize (1990) and the Kleist Prize (2004). Özdamar was born in Turkey in 1946. As a young adult she came to Germany (in 1965), worked in a factory in Berlin, and lived in a hostel with other workers. She started to learn German and became interested in theatre and subsequently studied acting in Istanbul. After her return to Germany in 1976, she worked with Bertold Brecht's student Benno Besson at the *Volksbühne* in East Berlin and later in France. After the publication of her collection of stories *Mutterzunge* (Mother Tongue, 1990) she published her first novel, *Das Leben ist eine Karawanserei—hat zwei Türen—aus einer kam ich rein—aus der anderen ging ich raus*. This novel forms a trilogy together with the two successive works *Die Brücke vom Goldenen Horn* and *Seltsame Sterne starren zur Erde*. All three novels reflect on the 1960s and 1970s in both Turkey and Germany and contain autobiographical elements.[28]

Özdamar and her work have inspired interest among literary and cultural critics.[29] However, little has been written about the relation of her texts to the discourse on 1968—Elizabeth Boa and Monika Shafi are notable exceptions.[30] Shafi focuses on the second part of Özdamar's trilogy and asks to what extent the concept of generation is useful in analyzing West Germany's 1968 and its legacy as represented in Uwe Timm's novel *Rot*, Günter Grass' narrative *Mein Jahrhundert*, and Özdamar's *Die Brücke vom Goldenen Horn*.[31] She grants Özdamar's novel a special status by arguing that the text unsettles the dichotomy between the German mainstream and a 'multicultural niche' discourse. Shafi adds that the text also overcomes the restrictions of placing 1968 solely in the context of a German cultural memory.

While Shafi's interpretation provides valuable insights, I am not entirely convinced by her conclusions which seem to reinscribe essentialist notions of German, Turkish-German, mainstream, countercultural, and multicultural identities, histories, and cultures. I am proposing to shift the overall argument to a different ground and read the trilogy, and in particular its third part, *Seltsame Sterne starren zur Erde*, the least studied text of the trilogy so far, in response to Leslie Adelson's study *The Turkish Turn in Contemporary German Literature: Toward a New Critical Grammar of Migration*.

Adelson argues that prevailing analytical paradigms are inadequate to grasp the social dimensions inherent in the literature of migration. She seeks "a new critical grammar for understanding the configuration of cultural contact and Turkish presence in contemporary German literature."[32] Therefore, Adelson introduces "the concept of touching tales as an alternative organizing principle for considering Turkish lines of thought."[33] She understands Turkish lines of thought "not in terms of identity politics, ethnic difference, or national mentalities, but as figurative story lines reshaping key points of reference and orientation in German and transnational cultures through the looking glass of Turkish migration."[34]

In line with Adelson's argument, Özdamar's trilogy is not a phenomenon of the diaspora or simply an expression of the theme of transnational migration. Rather, it constitutes a contribution to the discourse on 1968 by a Turkish-German author and adds, in its specific way and from a particular narrative perspective, to the construction of a transnational memory of 1968 that is inseparable from the project of the discursive reenvisioning of 1968 in the 1990s in Germany. Adelson ascribes this "labor of imagination"[35] to literary strategies of transformation, strategies that can be observed in Özdamar's work. Like Adelson, I am not asking what the text says about the figure of the Turk, even though this is part of the analysis and certainly shapes it, but I am asking what the text narrated by the figure of the Turk says about East and West Berlin as located in the heart of central Europe and about the 1960s and 1970s, the student movement and its aftermath, the "Deutscher Herbst" (German Autumn), the height of West German terrorism in the fall of 1977. The concept of transnational memory is not only a theme in Özdamar's trilogy, but it also allows us to analyze how the representation of time and space makes use of national boundaries and histories in order to transcend and subvert them.

The narrative perspective employed in the trilogy reveals important connections to the non-hyphenated part of the discourse on the cultural memory of 1968 discussed in the first half of this study. The trilogy is told from the perspective of a first-person narrator and, within this narrative frame, invites an autobiographical reading. In addition, *Seltsame Sterne starren zur Erde* takes the form of a diary, a literary genre that creates the impression of authenticity and seems to grant access to real life experiences. Within the highly mediated frame of aesthetic expression, this literary strategy connects Özdamar's trilogy to other fictional texts written by German-German authors about the 1960s after 1989. As discussed in previous chapters, Peter Schneider and Uwe Timm shift from a third-person perspective deployed in novels published in the 1970s to the first-person perspective in the novels they write about the 1960s student movement in the 1990s. This shift reveals the changing emphasis within this discourse. In the 1990s, all three authors, Özdamar, Schneider, and Timm, chose a reflective mode of narrating, one that stresses personal remembering as an important process for the construction of a cultural memory of 1968. The construction of this kind of cultural memory serves the purpose of constructing a coherent narrative that is at the same time much less homogenous than the term cultural memory suggests. This kind of narrative is shaped by numerous and at times conflicting voices and by contrastive and complementary memories of experiences and critical reflections on them. These narratives are also always fragmented, albeit not as overtly as with Morgner's work. This fragmentation in the narrative corresponds with the process of remembering that always entails forgetting since it is impossible to remember everything. As Borges shows in his story "Funes the Memorious," a perfect memory, that is, the capacity to remember everything, prevents life from happening.[36]

Previously, Elizabeth Boa has discussed Özdamar's novels *Das Leben ist eine Karawanserei* and *Die Brücke vom Goldenen Horn* as hybrids in terms of genre, perspective, and language use: "In conveying a complex sense of transformative interchange between culturally heterogeneous countries under the impact of social and political change, both novels combat fixed national or cultural stereotypes."[37] I would like to take her analysis one step further and suggest that these texts also manifest the transnational nature of writings by hyphenated authors and by authors who emphasize the transnational nature of the student movement of 1968. Read in light of a transnational, rather than simply a national, memory of the generation of 1968, Özdamar's trilogy allows new insights into fiction writing in the twenty-first century and challenges us to develop a new critical terminology in order to account for texts, people, and ideas that transcend and subvert the national.

Das Leben ist eine Karawanserei

Özdamar's first novel, *Das Leben ist eine Karawanserei* chronicles the childhood and adolescence of a girl born at the end of the Second World War in the Anatolian city of Malatya. As Turkey modernizes, her father's repeated unemployment drives the family to Istanbul, Bursa, and Ankara. Her family's uprootedness and the increasing influence of American culture, in particular via American movies, lead the protagonist to refuse to fulfill gendered expectations connected with Muslim values. She earns money for the family as an actress; however, due to the increasing difficulty of earning a living in Turkey, the young woman decides to sign on with the Turkish government in order to migrate to Germany as a so-called guest worker. By the close of the novel she is on a train heading for Germany, sharing a compartment with a prostitute and a lesbian couple.

While this novel takes place in Turkey it foreshadows themes that gain importance throughout the world in the 1960s. The striving for personal liberation, often inspired by American cultural influences and sometimes forced by economic necessity, is accompanied by the decreased importance of traditions such as religion or class and class consciousness. In the 1960s the emerging New Left, currently often described as a social rather than a political movement, borrows from a variety of textual sources in addition to Marx in order to call for a new revolution. At first, the young girl lives in a predominantly local agricultural society, yet the numerous attempts by her father to achieve and maintain the status of middle class dislocate her into urban and increasingly cosmopolitan environments. Her quest for knowledge and education combined with the intent to become an artist seems to fail when she decides to sign on as a guest worker headed for Germany. This decision is represented as her escape from stagnation yet coincides with the loss of social standing since it emphasizes that she in fact joins the working class.

However, the working class does not seem to be determined by Marx's definition of the working class and its class consciousness. As the protagonist boards the train to Germany, the idea of the New Left is foreshadowed. Personal liberation is not solely based on solidarity among the working class, but extends to numerous individuals with a variety of backgrounds and experiences. As she shares her compartment with men and women, workers and non-workers, a prostitute and a lesbian couple, it is apparent that all migrants, regardless of their specific personal and unique identity, are united by the quest for personal liberation and by the lack of work that forces them to migrate to Germany.

This first novel of Özdamar's trilogy could be described as a Bildungsroman of the making of a female guest worker from Turkey. Pushing past the boundaries of the realistic narrative in the Bildungsroman, Özdamar also includes elements of a magic-realist style in the tradition of Jorge Luis Borges, Günter Grass, and Irmtraud Morgner. The narrator combines information and observations with accounts of dreamlike, mythic, and fairy-tale occurrences in order to confront the legacy of colonialism, the two world wars, the Armenian genocide, the Holocaust, and fascism. This dual focus of *Das Leben ist eine Karawanserei* on personal liberation and on the critical engagement with the past and historical oppression also foreshadows the 1960s. The struggle to verbalize and to fight for one's own rights was motivated by the critical engagement with the past, e.g., in Germany with the history of the Third Reich. At the same time the youthful rebellion against restrictions imposed by parents and society, as represented in schools, universities, and sites of worship, led to an increased interest in this past in the first place since the legacy of the Third Reich could be utilized as a strong weapon against the parents' generation and their (hidden and repressed) feelings of guilt and shame. As the narrator travels to Germany she is taking her own fight for liberation into a new context. While historical and local specificities still have a great significance, the novel foreshadows that young people in the 1960s were unified by their oppositional stance against the nation-state and their parents as representatives of the old order. This first part of the trilogy provides the background for the ensuing political struggle in the 1960s.

Die Brücke vom Goldenen Horn

The second part of the trilogy, *Die Brücke vom Goldenen Horn*, begins in 1966 and tells the story of the struggles of the newly arrived Turkish workers in Berlin. The narrator is a young adult now and reflects on her adolescence, in particular the constant struggle with her parents. Her parents discouraged her from becoming an actress. This desire drove her to neglect her schoolwork in favor of attending the theatre, acting, and studying her roles. Her parents also disagreed with her decision to work in a factory in Germany, since they have the aspiration that at least their children will escape the fate of a working-class existence. These reflections are interspersed with accounts of the narrator's new life in Berlin. Escaping the confinement of both home and work the narrator discovers the German theatre and the student scene in Berlin.

Boa also reads the second part of the trilogy, *Die Brücke vom Goldenen Horn*, in the context of the German student movement and the political situation in Turkey:

> *Die Brücke vom Goldenen Horn*, while telling a highly specific story, also conveys representative experiences common to a generation of young, educated people from many countries in the late 1960s who learned languages, traveled, read Marx, protested against Western imperialism, sought sexual liberation, but who would also begin in the early 1970s to question the power relations between the sexes. In Berlin and Istanbul the protagonist becomes a female apprentice, a Wilhelmine Meister with a theatrical vocation, visiting the Berliner Ensemble in Berlin and attending acting school in Istanbul where she also mixes, as the only woman, among the intellectuals who meet in the Captain's Café.[38]

The narrator's journey to Berlin is motivated by her desire for independence. She is forced to join other migrant laborers and at the same time the ability to travel, to leave home, grants her more freedom from her parents and the restrictions imposed by Turkish society. In particular the ability to travel unites her with other young people from around the world who use traveling and the experiences gained while traveling to critique their home.[39]

One of the biggest challenges for all migrant laborers is the immersion in a new language. The novel reflects this difficulty. It is written in an innovative and highly individualized language consisting of an amalgam of Turkish and German. This language manifests itself in the text in particular via the spelling of German words based on their pronunciation and the oral comprehension of the Turkish narrator. On this level, form and content converge. The novel is written in an invented language that some have characterized as a hybrid language exemplifying the situation of Turkish migrants in Germany. This particular style draws attention and invites the analysis of language and its use by the narrator and the characters in the novel. The protagonist and the other guest workers who live in a hostel for guest workers attempt to learn German. Soon, the possibilities and impossibilities of translation appear. While the Turks learn enough German in order to function at work, their understanding is shaped by their first language.

One of the hostel's supervisors, a Turkish communist, attempts to educate the mostly female workers.[40] He aims to increase their knowledge of German as well as to raise their class consciousness. However, his teaching produces mixed results. Most workers are content to be able to perform their work and to participate in the West German consumer society. They defy any attempt to further their education, let alone to raise their political awareness, with humor. They communicate by using an amalgamated language and, if this does not suffice, translators, and construct a social community within the hostel that coexists with the dominant German society. This community rests on the cultural foundation of the Turkey they left, the home they long for.

The development of the protagonist after her arrival in Berlin shows a close link between attitudes of protest and language use. Like the other workers, she rebels against her teacher, albeit not because she is satisfied with a minimal mastery of German. She rebels against him because his language, the language of the Old Left, is insufficient to quench her thirst for authentic and aesthetic experiences, namely, to lose her virginity and to become an actress.[41] She enjoys living in the hybrid linguistic space that is marked by language games. These games defy analysis and clear meanings. They privilege the play with the mother tongue within the German space and with the second language, German, within the predominantly Turkish space at the hostel. In addition, she wants to learn more about the German language and its cultural and social manifestations. The protagonist's love for literature and in particular theatre brings her in touch with another linguistic space, the language of German theatre.[42] This language allows her to bridge the abyss between her native tongue and the language of the host country. It emphasizes the performative use of language, thus allowing for personal expression within a highly mediated theatrical and aesthetic setting. Furthermore, exploring the students' nightlife in Berlin, she soon realizes that the students use a different language than her teacher at the hostel.[43] It is the sub- and counterculture of the 1960s that invites a different language, that reflects on language use and its limitations, and that ultimately, if only for a short time, declares the supremacy of the experience over the word.

This theme is closely tied to the literary discourse about the 1960s in Germany. The 1960s are marked by an attempt to find an adequate language for the students' discontent, experiences, and dreams. Thus, the experiences in a hybrid linguistic space, such as the ones the narrator in *Die Brücke vom Goldenen Horn* recounts, are a well-suited case study in order to explore the various underlying issues of the 1960s and its memory in the 1990s. In their quest for liberation, the students were also searching for a new language. The shared knowledge base that informed this movement did not so much rest on the writings of the Old Left, but on an unruly collection of texts by members of the Frankfurt School, Herbert Marcuse, Sigmund Freud, and Wilhelm Reich—to name just a few. These texts, absorbed in conjunction with global influences, e.g., the American Civil Rights movement and the post- and anti-colonial writings from South America, encouraged the students to distrust language and its claim to power. The students emphasized immediate experiences over language and preferred a language that invited self-exploration and self-discovery and resisted any claims to hegemony.

As important as finding a new language as a motivating factor for their rebellion was the students' distrust of language. The students considered language to be a tool in the hands of those in power. They claimed that language was used to silence and to keep silent rather than to liberate. These issues are skillfully addressed in *Die Brücke vom Goldenen Horn* where the Turkish migrants soon rely on the protagonist to negotiate between the German and the Turkish language spaces. The narrator turns into a translator who is soon called on even to mediate in arguments that take place in Turkish.[44] This development emphasizes the privileged position of those who speak and understand languages and who are able to negotiate between the spaces these languages construct. However, in the student movement, the focus was on transcending the boundaries that each language created. The students were searching for a liberating language that would enable them to speak about and for the oppressed without creating another border. In this process, however, the students overlooked the fact that language also enables communication with the other. Despite all opposite claims, this dialogue with the oppressed did not occur in the 1960s, a failure that is demonstrated by the students' problematic self-representations in the so-called *Väterliteratur* (literature of the fathers) of the 1970s.

Even though the German student movement did not last very long and lost momentum in the 1970s, the event itself marks the narrator's life. She decides to return to Istanbul. Inspired by the student protests in Berlin she is intent to work on political change at home.[45] However, the political situation in Turkey is significantly different and the narrator is confronted with a brutal regime. During a journey to Eastern Anatolia, the landscape reminds the visitor of previous instances of Kurdish persecution.[46] It serves as a warning for the protagonist against becoming involved with the political struggle in Turkey. Ten years after her homecoming to Turkey, the protagonist returns to Berlin. Her homecoming to Germany is recounted in the third part of the trilogy.

Seltsame Sterne starren zur Erde

In *Seltsame Sterne starren zur Erde*, the narrator is not only distinguished by her Turkish background, but also by her audacious self-insertion into the German geographical, historical, and political space in the 1970s. Her return to the divided Berlin in the aftermath of the German student movement initiates her active negotiation between the Turkish and German factors that constitute her life. Their poetic transformation, through a "labor of imagination"[47] performed by the narrator, marks this hybrid text as an important contribution to the discourse of 1968 and changes the cultural memory of 1968 to a transnational memory. The text is informed by the narrator's Turkish-German background and by the attempt to contribute to the "reworking of cultural matter"[48] that shapes the future understanding of German history. Therefore, instead of creating a kind of a parallel world that occupies a niche in an otherwise German context, this text by a Turkish-German author contributes to the numerous debates about the German past and its function and place in Germany's future. These debates marked the 1990s in Germany and mediated 1968 and the Third Reich through layers of remembrance. "In Deutschland zu leben, ist ein Beruf" (To live in Germany is a profession)[49] the narrator observes on a cold and overcast day in East Berlin. In response, she pursues a career as a writer, actress, and theatre director. These creative professions allow her to work with personal as well as with historical experiences by turning both of them into poetic expressions. *Seltsame Sterne starren zur Erde* chronicles and reflects these first beginnings of the narrator's professional life in order to contribute transnational memories to the memories of 1968.

The text encompasses the time between the fall of 1976 and January of 1978. The narrator leaves her hometown, Istanbul, her family, and her husband and moves to Berlin in order to begin an internship at the *Volksbühne* in East Berlin. While she is waiting for her visa, she lives in a communal post-1968 living project in the working-class district Wedding, in West Berlin, where the political events of the *Deutscher Herbst* serve as the backdrop for her experiences with members of the New Left. In the first part of the book, references to chronology and historical events are presented as quotes from newspaper headlines and movie announcements. In the second part, the book takes the form of a diary and work log where personal observations intersect with notes and drawings from her documentation of the rehearsals for Fritz Marquardt's production of Heiner Müller's *Die Bauern*. The insertion of quotes and references indicate her familiarity with German literary and intellectual history and emphasize her attempt to situate herself within this context. This kind of intertextuality suggests that attempts to categorize this literature as Turkish-German and as somehow suspended in an in-between space are obsolete. Already the title—a quote taken from Else Lasker-Schüler's poem *Sterne des Fatum*—indicates that the kind of imaginative labor the narrator undertakes creates connections instead of borders and thus challenges the notion of fixed identities, be they personal or national. Rather than adhering to the notion of the autonomous subject placed in between the Turkish and the German worlds or experiencing the diaspora, the narrator contributes to the rewriting of German history for the twenty-first century. This rewriting strongly suggests that the notion of identity takes on a new meaning.

Furthermore, since the narrator as an artist works with a variety of media—writing, drawing, and performing/directing—the artist is not defined by the genre that she is working in, but claims a poetic existence and creates her own life as an expression of this poetic work. The narrative blurs the line between the genre of the diary and the autobiographical account that only serves a personal function. This hybrid form of autobiography and work diary points to the text's important task of documenting the work process as well as providing a space to negotiate the different subject positions between East and West, Turkey and Germany, and the different positions among the New and the Old Left. This purposeful play with genre and identity suggests that texts not only serve as an archive for memories but also that texts are important sites of negotiating conflicting and competing memories, be they national or transnational.

The narrator in *Seltsame Sterne starren zur Erde* inserts herself into the German cultural and geographical space by remembering the German division during the Cold War and by responding, through the mediation of the 1960s and 1970s, to the legacy of the Third Reich and the Holocaust. Taking the step, at the time unusual, of working in the East, the narrator juxtaposes her experiences in East and West Berlin. As in *Eduards Heimkehr*, the Berlin Wall takes on a significant meaning. Like Eduard, the Turkish-German narrator expresses a certain nostalgic longing for the Wall. For Eduard, the Wall provided a clear demarcation line that provided orientation through the jungle of the city during the Cold War. For the narrator in *Seltsame Sterne starren zur Erde*, the Wall served as a true "Schutzwall" (protective barrier) insofar as it allowed her to begin her theatre career by working with some of the most famous representatives of the (East) German theatre scene and to create a poetic existence for herself while staying in East Berlin.[50]

In contrast to the West German mainstream, the Turkish-German memory suggests that East Berlin enabled an existence less inhibited by commercialism and by the daily demands and grinding routine of life. The narrator lives a life for and immersed in the arts, spending her days at the theatre, reading, and experiencing the cityscape. With her roommate in East Berlin she studies Italian, a language associated in Germany with a longing for the south, as immortalized by Goethe's Italian voyages. In addition to creating a truly transnational landscape of memories, the narrator, in the tradition of the cultural politics of the GDR, evokes the literary heritage of Germany untainted by the wars in the twentieth century and the Holocaust. This creates an idyllic space within East Berlin that is void of any engagement with the political or social situation in the GDR.

In contrast, West Berlin does not become a home for the narrator. The political atmosphere in West Berlin is overshadowed by the German Autumn and the violent confrontation between the state and the so-called sympathizers with the terrorists. The narrator does not develop any true friendships in the communal living project. She engages in an affair with one of its members.[51] However, as soon as she moves to East Berlin, his girlfriend moves in, as the female members of the commune inform her gleefully during one of the phone conversations that serve as a reminder of how close and how far East and West Berlin were from each other during the Cold War.[52]

The narrator's sexual experiences are juxtaposed with the refusal of the other female members of the commune to have sexual relations. Their claim, that sexual relations between men and women are always exploitive, is in turn juxtaposed with the reality of the brothel two floors down from the communal living project. Furthermore, exploitation in the Marxian sense of the word is also part of their neighborhood as the commune observes workers in a sweatshop from their kitchen window. Thus, the economic, social, as well as political situation in West Berlin poses so many challenges that the narrator never truly identifies with the West. This disconnect with West Berlin intensifies her understanding of the Berlin Wall as a protection rather than a manifestation of the German division during the Cold War. This depiction of the Wall is one of the moments that most clearly demonstrate how this text about the 1960s, written in the 1990s by a hyphenated author, interrupts and dislodges the mainstream understanding of German history.[53]

In addition to inserting herself into the German landscape by narrating the Wall, the text references the Holocaust and its legacy. It does so indirectly, like other novels that constitute the genre of 1968 memory novels, by addressing the Holocaust via the 1960s and 1970s, responding and contributing to the several layers of remembering and forgetting that already constitute its cultural memory. Very specific instances illustrate how the Holocaust is mediated through the 1960s and 1970s. Peter, the narrator's lover in the commune in West Berlin, reads poems by German-Jewish author Else Lasker-Schüler to her. He prefaces his reading by briefly recounting Lasker-Schüler's life which ended in exile in Israel because she was threatened by the Nazis.[54] As discussed in the previous chapter, only in the 1960s did exile literature become a topic of interest in Germany. Before then, numerous attempts document how the thought of exile was excluded in order to facilitate the process of reconstruction in Germany. Thus, the student protests in the 1960s did indeed initiate fundamental changes in academia and the public discourse, in particular with respect to which topics were addressed and how they were studied.

Another example of the text's engagement with the German twentieth century fuses the Wall with the legacy of the Second World War. Approaching the Berlin Wall from the West, the narrator observes the writing on the Wall that stems from student protests in the 1960s. The graffiti warns against the danger of a third global war by recounting the number of deaths in previous wars. However, the figures only recount civilian deaths and do not mention the victims of the Holocaust explicitly.[55] In a similar vein, during her stay at the commune, its members persistently hint that they need to differentiate themselves from their own parents due to their past crimes. The narrator refuses to respond to this generational posturing which discursively obscures perpetrators and victims. Instead, she is reminded of the devastating situation after the military coup in Turkey in 1960.[56] All these examples point to the fact that, as Mani suggests: "National history or national literary history will only slouch in lurking memories as allusions to the history of the host nation or the nation of birth are placed before the reader and then instantly displaced."[57] Furthermore, as all examples pertaining to the appropriation of German history by a Turkish-German author demonstrate, even the 1960s with their self-proclaimed intention to work through the legacy of the Holocaust once and for all have failed. It is simply impossible to write or say concluding words; instead, remembering (and forgetting) and the continuous reworking of cultural memories are appropriate in order to give the Holocaust and its legacy the place it deserves.

Seltsame Sterne starren zur Erde is less concerned with the dangers of forgetting the past than it is with the creation of new conditions for remembering twentieth-century Germany in the present. As this process is mediated by numerous layers, most dominantly by the 1960s and 1970s and the legacy of the Third Reich and the Holocaust, it combines the construction of memories with their recuperation. Since many German-German authors are more interested in normalcy, in appeasing unsettling memories, and in creating their own literary legacy, it is no coincidence that the project of approaching the past and the "work" of engaging with the past in the 1990s is conducted by a Turkish-German author. The narrator in *Seltsame Sterne starren zur Erde* responds to the social presence in the newly unified state by recognizing that a multitude of people, more diverse than ever, actually live in contemporary Germany: children and grandchildren of victims, perpetrators, and bystanders, former East and West Germans, the "real" Germans and those of a non-German heritage and tradition. This diversity allows her to shape one particular site in the transnational memories of 1968 that references the German division and the Holocaust.

The narrator not only inserts herself in the German memory landscape, but she also creates close textual, albeit fragmented and abbreviated, connections between the urban spaces of Berlin and Istanbul. And while Istanbul, as a city between Europe and Asia, between West and East, is of course the perfect literary topos for a discussion of transience as well as the *Raumzeit* (space time)[58] of historical developments and geopolitical constellations, the discursive convergences of the two cities that Özdamar creates seem to foreshadow the wars that mark the beginning of the twenty-first century—fueled by religious and ethnic struggles and seemingly insurmountable cultural differences between the West and the rest of the world. With the insertion of Istanbul in the text, *Seltsame Sterne starren zur Erde* not only reconfigures the memory of Germany into a transnational cultural memory, but also adds to our understanding of the significance of remembering for the foreshadowing of the future.

In addition to creating a transnational memory landscape, Özdamar inscribes the narrator into this landscape. The narrator gains the status of a subject who is able to transcend her initial response that to live in Germany is work, referencing work as a burden, a meaningless occupation, an alienated job, or an exploitive situation in a capitalist system. Instead, the narrator turns work into a productive, poetic, transforming, and transformative labor of the imagination that takes on a significant meaning for the individual. This transformation could also be read as an attempt to rescue the individual's subject position from vanishing in the postmodern sphere by granting him or her the privileged status of juggling the processes of remembering and forgetting in national and transnational contexts.

Despite all the literary and cultural repercussions that shape Özdamar's text, the narrator maintains her independence and takes control of her narrative by making her voice heard. Yet it is not a voice that states or refutes claims; it is not a voice that attempts to be heard within multicultural identity politics. It is a voice that is radically individualized, and at times even essentialized, without obscuring her various alliances: Turkish-German migrant, artist, student, woman, holder of an East German visa, illegal resident of West Berlin, member of a West Berlin commune, granddaughter, sister, wife, friend.

In her role as narrator, director, actress, and visual artist, the narrator is the involved observer and engaged chronicler of the historical developments in East and West during the Cold War. This status guarantees her narrative control and shapes her unique insights and perspectives with respect to the events in Germany. This narrative situation also informs the construction of a transnational cultural memory of the 1960s. This particular narrative perspective is most clearly expressed in the narrator's relation to the left. Even though the narrator clearly sympathizes with the New Left, she also distances herself: she asserts that they speak a different language—too theoretical, too political, too abstract. She exposes the self-indulgence of members of the New Left in both East and West, especially in comparison with the political situation of the left in Turkey. This estrangement from the German New Left assures the individualized subject position the narrator occupies. The following two examples highlight this strategy. In the West, one evening, sitting around the dinner table with the members of the communal living project, the narrator records the conversation as if it were a play. The conversation is triggered by the word "deprimierend" (depressing)[59] which sets the stage for each of the participants-turned-actors to recite predictable lines about specific German *Befindlichkeiten* (mental states) either popular among the students of the 1970s or among those criticizing the rebellious youth: "Die junge Generation, die nach Westberlin abgehauen ist, kann sich nicht mit dem Kalten Krieg identifizieren. ... Hier sind die jungen Leute entweder links oder in Psychobewegungen. ... Wir wollen eins zu eins leben. Wir haben keine Karriereabsichten. Wir wollen experimentell leben" (The young generation that left for West Berlin cannot identify with the Cold War… Here, young people are either left or in consciousness raising groups… We want to live authentically. We do not want to climb the corporate ladder. We want to experiment).[60] In the vein of a Socratic dialogue in which each rhetorical move is predetermined and predictable, the narrator assigns each of her friends a specific role as she listens to and records their conversation. In an ironic twist, the narrator in the meantime washes the dishes. This scene unmasks the members of the New Left as stuck in a theoretical and mainly rhetorical posturing at the expense of meaningful or sometimes just necessary productivity—like washing the dishes! In contrast to the second part of the trilogy, the utopian trust in the immediacy of the experience and its privilege over language has declined and been replaced by the artist's attempt to capture experience in the highly mediated work of art.

In the East, the narrator is able to share her love for the theatre and to start a career as a German-speaking actress and director. Yet she remains an observer, and she takes on the role of the student, which is further complicated by the rather traditional gender dynamic. All of her role models and teachers are male, and while the narrator wonders why she does not have sex with them or anyone else in the East for that matter, she seems to be content to play the role of the exotic and female other in need of an education. This gendered aspect of the narrator's situation in East Berlin is reinforced by the prominent references to Else Lasker-Schüler and to Berthold Brecht. Else Lasker-Schüler also suffered from oblivion in German literary history and the fact that she has a German-Jewish background and was in exile seems to be only reinforced by the fact that she is also a female author. Berthold Brecht, on the other hand, has come under scrutiny due to research that argues that many of his plays were actually co-written by female authors who have been omitted as authors. While the narrator seems to point to these problematic aspects of German literary history and its exclusion of female authors, she herself seems to accept an auxiliary position vis-a-vis the more prominent male authors and directors, thus reinforcing rather traditional and exclusionary gender lines between female and male artists.[61]

This essentially feminine position is further reinforced by her disinterest in politics. Even though the narrator meets many of the political dissidents in East Germany, she is not really interested in their political lives. Political events and debates in East Berlin serve only as the background for the narrator's personal and professional development. In line with one of the central aspects of the discourse on 1968, the critique of language and its hegemonic use, the narrator claims that the dissidents' language is a foreign language to her.[62] While these attempts to disassociate could be read as naiveté on the part of the narrator, I propose to read them as a strategy to de-center and refashion events from the perspective of a Turkish-German voice. After all, identity is not something the narrator possesses as a fixed quality, but rather identity emerges through interactional, performative, and discursive practices. Processes of identity formation cannot be neatly bifurcated as individual or social. Interconnections between individual and social levels pervade both processes and products of identity construction. The narrator's distance from the left in East and West and from the Old and New Left reinforces her attempt to inscribe a self-confident and autonomous, albeit heterogeneous, subject position into the transnational memories of 1968.

Shafi comments on this narrative strategy in *Die Brücke vom Goldenen Horn* and understands the narrator's ironic distancing as an indication that she is outside of the movement itself.[63] However, I read the narrator's position in *Seltsame Sterne starren zur Erde* as both outside and inside. She is not outside because of her origin, yet she is outside because she maintains her own self. She is inside because she is able to add another perspective to the experiences of the aftermath of 1968 on both sides of the Iron Curtain. This inside-outside position creates a transnational moment of cultural memories: the narrator with a Turkish background appropriates and reflects the German experiences in the twentieth century. They are not foreign experiences but rather they are the experiences as they become available to her in her unique position as someone who is an illegal resident in West Berlin, a legal visitor in East Berlin, and a Turkish citizen unwilling and unable to live in Istanbul. The creative appropriation of the German past, the Third Reich, the GRD and the old FRG, and the Cold War through the lens of the events of 1968 turns *Seltsame Sterne starren zur Erde* into a novel that belongs to the genre of 1968 memory novels that emphasizes the importance of transnational exchange and transnational memories.

A Transnational Cultural Memory of 1968

Encompassing and expanding multicultural identity politics, transnationalism points to the importance of border-crossing and across-the-border interaction while questioning the narrative and legitimacy of the nation-state. Reading Özdamar's trilogy proffers an insight into the convergence of the concept of transnationalism with the discourse on 1968. The novels subvert the idea of the nation-state by adding another voice and other experiences that challenge the dominant narrative of the German past, e.g., how the narrator understands and experiences the Berlin Wall, the German 1960s and 1970s, and the numerous attempts to come to terms with the Nazi past. The texts add another important aspect to this narrative by pointing to 1968 as a central experience for the narrator.

My understanding of a transnational cultural memory of 1968 emphasizes that memory has to be understood in its chronological as well as its spatial dimension and their intersections. While space separates, the need for dialogue to facilitate understanding beyond this spatial divide historicizes the experience and thus opens up avenues for understanding. The hybrid genre responds to these complex demands by allowing the narrator to create her poetic existence within literary traditions.

The genre of 1968 memory novels provides insight into the relationship between fiction and the public discourse in Germany and thus connects literary studies to other disciplines. Albeit a small group, Turkish-German authors make important contributions to the discourse on 1968 in the 1990s. I read these texts as examples of a transnational moment of cultural memory rather than as diasporic texts by authors with hyphenated identities. These novels simultaneously shape and reflect the discourse on 1968 in Germany. The protagonist's wanderings from Istanbul to West and East Berlin challenge the stories provided by the '68ers in West Berlin and transform 1968 into the site of identity construction and reconfiguration in Germany in the twenty-first century.

Notes

1. Stars of Fate. Your eyes before my life/Like nights, that long for the day,/And the humid dream lies on top of them/Unfathomed. Strange stars stare to the earth,/Iron-colored with trails of desire,/With burning arms, that are looking for love/And reach for the cool of the air./Stars in which the fate flows. Else Lasker-Schüler, *Gedichte 1902–1943. Gesammelte Werke 1*, ed. Friedhelm Kemp (München: Kösel-Verlag, 1959): 45.
2. The broadcast took place between 7 and 11 April 2008.
3. Contributions included: Author Emine Özdamar; Iranian-German author Bahman Nirumand, who wrote the book *Persien: Modell eines Entwicklungslandes oder die Diktatur der freien Welt* (Reinbek: Rowohlt, 1967, translated into English as *Iran: The new Imperialism in Action*); city historian Michael S. Cullen, owner of the café "Terzo Mondo," one of the most prominent meeting places in the 1960s and 1970s; Kostas Papanastasiou, actor in the German TV series "Lindenstraße;" and refugee worker and teacher Ahmed Al Sadi.
4. Emine S. Özdamar, *Das Leben ist eine Karawanserei—hat zwei Türen—aus einer kam ich rein—aus der anderen ging ich raus* (Köln: Kiepenheuer & Witsch, 1992); *Life Is a Caravanserai: Has Two Doors I Came in One I Went Out the Other,* trans. Luise Von Flotow-Evans (London: Middlesex University Press, 2000*); Die Brücke vom Goldenen Horn* (Köln: Kiepenheuer & Witsch, 1998); *The Bridge of the Golden Horn*, trans. Martin Chalmers (London: Serpent's Tail, 2009); *Seltsame Sterne starren zur Erde* (Köln: Kiepenheuer & Witsch, 2003).
5. Mostly examined in the context of West Germany, the issue of foreign-born workers and their continued presence in East Germany has been largely excluded from this discourse. Research focusing on the 1990s as a post-unification period has mostly assumed, at least discursively, the homogeneity of an East German population that was pitted against West Germans who were, albeit reluctantly, defined as "multicultural."

6. The Turkish population of Germany stabilized during the 1990s. However, in the new millennium, the population has continued to shrink (from 2,107,400 in 1997 to 2,053,564 in 1999 and to 1,713,551 in 2007) according to the Statistisches Bundesamt Deutschland. No explanations for the causes are given; it is possible that the declining birth rate as well as the changed citizen law have contributed to this change. <http://www.destatis.de/jetspeed/portal/cms/Sites/destatis/Internet/DE/Content/Statistiken/Bevoelkerung/AuslaendischeBevoelkerung/Tabellen/Content50/TOP10,templateId=renderPrint.psml> (accessed 12 June 2009).
7. Karin Hunn, *"Nächstes Jahr kehren wir zurück...": Die Geschichte der türkischen "Gastarbeiter" in der Bundesrepublik* (Göttingen: Wallstein, 2005).
8. Eva Kolinsky, "Migration Experiences and the Construction of Identity among Turks Living in Germany," in *Recasting German Identity. Culture, Politics, and Literature in the Berlin Republic*, ed. Stuart Taberner and Frank Finlay (Rochester, NY: Camden House, 2002): 205–218, 206.
9. Kolinsky, "Migration Experiences and the Construction of Identity among Turks Living in Germany:" 214.
10. Ayhan Kaya, "German-Turkish Transnational Space: A Separate Space of Their Own," *German Studies Review* 30.3 (2007): 483–502, 483.
11. Viola B. Georgi, *Entliehene Erinnerung. Geschichtsbilder junger Migranten in Deutschland* (Hamburg: Hamburger Edition, 2003).
12. Annette Arpaci Seidel, "National Memory's *Schlüsselkinder*: Migration, Pedagogy, and German Remembrance Culture," in *German Culture, Politics, and Literature into the Twenty-First Century: Beyond Normalization*, ed. Stuart Taberner and Paul Cooke (Rochester, NY: Camden House, 2006): 105–120.
13. Andreas Huyssen, "Diaspora and Nation: Migration Into Other Pasts," *New German Critique* 88 (Winter 2003): 147–164.
14. I am thinking here of the inspiration of the U.S. student movement for the German activists or the linkages that were created via theoretical ideas that travelled the continents, such as writings by Frantz Fanon, Herbert Marcuse, and Wilhelm Reich.
15. Gerard J. DeGroot's research (*Student Protest; The Sixties Unplugged*) presents a comparative overview of the international student movement of the 1960s and its common themes and struggles.
16. Martin Klimke and Joachim Scharloth, *1968 in Europe: A History of Protest and Activism, 1956–1977* (New York: Berghahn, 2008).
17. Cf., for example, the delayed and problematic reception of the so-called "Exilliteratur" in Germany after 1945.
18. Compare research conducted by Leslie Adelson, Jeffrey Peck, and Azade Seyhan, to name just three of the most prolific literary critics and theorists who emphasize the new, much more diverse and as a result much more complex situation that emerges in Germany at the turn of the new millennium. See: Leslie Adelson, *The Turkish Turn in Contemporary German Literature: Toward a New Critical Grammar of Migration* (New York: Palgrave Macmillan, 2005); Jeffery Peck, *Being Jewish in the New Germany* (New Brunswick: Rutgers University Press, 2006); Azade Seyhan, *Writing Outside the Nation* (Princeton: Princeton University Press, 2001).
19. Cf. Karen Jankowsky, "'German' Literature Contested: The 1991 Ingeborg-Bachmann-Prize Debate, 'Cultural Diversity,' and Emine Sevgi Ozdamar," *The German Quarterly* 70.3 (Summer 1997): 261–276.

20. B. Venkat Mani, *Cosmopolitical Claims. Turkish-German Literatures from Nadolny to Pamuk* (Iowa City: University of Iowa Press, 2007): 7.
21. Tom Cheesman, *Novels of Turkish German Settlement: Cosmopolite Fictions* (Rochester, NY: Camden House, 2007): vii.
22. Leslie Adelson, *The Turkish Turn in Contemporary German Literature: Toward a New Critical Grammar of Migration* (New York: Palgrave Macmillan, 2005).
23. Sabine von Dirke, "West Meets East: Narrative Construction of the Foreigner and Postmodern Orientalism in Sten Nadolny's *Selim oder Die Gabe der Rede*," *The Germanic Review* 69.2 (1994): 61–69.
24. Sten Nadolny, *Selim oder Die Gabe der Rede* (München: Piper, 1990). For the author's comments on this process see Sten Nadonly, "Wir und Die–Erzählen über Fremde," in *Schreiben zwischen den Kulturen: Beiträge zur deutschsprachigen Gegenwartsliteratur*, ed. Paul Michael Lützeler (Frankfurt a.M.: S. Fischer, 1996): 65–74.
25. Leslie A. Adelson, "Opposing Oppositions: Turkish-German Questions in Contemporary German Studies," *German Studies Review* 17.2 (1994): 305–330, 312.
26. Ibid.: 306.
27. Ülker Gökberk, "Culture Studies und die Türken: Sten Nadolnys *Selim oder Die Gabe der Rede* im Lichte einer Methodendiskussion," *The German Quarterly* 70.2 (Spring 1997): 97–122. See also Leslie Adelson's "Response to Ülker Gökberk, 'Culture Studies und die Türken,'" *The German Quarterly* 70.3 (Summer 1997): 277–282.
28. Emine Sevgi Özdamar, *Mutterzunge* (Berlin: Rotbuch Verlag, 1990).
29. In addition to those already mentioned, see also Margaret Littler's discussion of emerging identity formation in the Turkish-German diaspora as exemplified in the literary work of Emine Sevgi Özdamar. Margaret Littler, "Diasporic Identity in Emine Sevgi Özdamar's *Mutterzunge*," in *Recasting German Identity. Culture, Politics, and Literature in the Berlin Republic*, ed. Stuart Taberner and Frank Finlay (Rochester, NY: Camden House, 2002): 219–234.
30. Elizabeth Boa, "Özdamar's Autobiographical Fictions: Trans-National Identity and Literary Form," *German Life and Letters* 59.4 (2006): 526–539, and Monika Shafi, "Talkin' 'Bout My Generation: Memories of 1968 in Recent German Novels," *German Life and Letters* 59.2 (2006): 201–216.
31. Uwe Timm's novel *Rot* (Köln: Kiepenheuer & Witsch, 2001); Günter Grass's narrative *Mein Jahrhundert* (Göttingen: Steidl, 1999); and Özdamar's *Die Brücke vom Goldenen Horn*.
32. Adelson, *The Turkish Turn*: 5.
33. Ibid.: 20.
34. Ibid.: 21–22.
35. Ibid.: 14.
36. Jorge Luis Borges, *Labyrinths: Selected Stories and Other Writings* (New York: New Directions Publishing Co., 1964).
37. Boa, "Özdamar's Autobiographical Fictions: Trans-National Identity and Literary Form:" 526.
38. Ibid.: 536.
39. The importance of travel is also evident in Morgner's trilogy.
40. Özdamar, *Die Brücke vom Goldenen Horn*: 31f.

41. Ibid.: 36.
42. Ibid.: 146–172.
43. Ibid.
44. Ibid.: 111ff.
45. Ibid.: 175.
46. Ibid.: 247–291.
47. Adelson, *The Turkish Turn*: 14.
48. Ibid.
49. Özdamar, *Seltsame Sterne starren zur Erde*: 213.
50. Ibid.: 17ff.
51. Ibid.: 58f.
52. Ibid.: 80.
53. Ibid.: 61.
54. Ibid.: 58f.
55. Ibid.: 67ff.
56. Ibid.: 65.
57. Mani, *Cosmopolitical Claims*: 105.
58. I am referencing Benjamin's notions of *Raumzeit* and *Schauplatz* which carry important implications for the construct of cultural memory—see chapter 3. "Berliner Chronik." *Gesammelte Schriften* VI, ed. Tillman Rexroth (Frankfurt a.M.: Suhrkamp, 1978): 465–519; and "Ursprung des deutschen Trauerspiels" *Gesammelte Schriften* I.1, ed. Tillman Rexroth (Frankfurt a.M.: Suhrkamp, 1978): 203–409.
59. Özdamar, *Seltsame Sterne starren zur Erde*: 51.
60. Ibid.: 52.
61. Ibid.: 118, 120, 164, 177.
62. Ibid.: 182, 202.
63. Shafi, "Talkin' 'Bout My Generation."

Conclusion

Continued Taboos, Confirmed Canons

> Andenken
>
> Also was die siebziger Jahre betrifft,
> kann ich mich kurz fassen.
> Die Auskunft war immer besetzt.
> Die wundersame Brotvermehrung
> beschränkte sich auf Düsseldorf und Umgebung.
> Die furchtbare Nachricht lief über den Ticker,
> wurde zur Kenntnis genommen und archiviert.
>
> Widerstandslos, im großen und ganzen,
> haben sie sich selber verschluckt,
> die siebziger Jahre,
> ohne Gewähr für Nachgeborene,
> Türken und Arbeitslose.
> Daß irgendwer ihrer mit Nachsicht gedächte,
> wäre zuviel verlangt.
>
> *Hans Magnus Enzensberger*[1]

The relationship between "Geist" (intellect), "Macht" (power), and "Tat" (deed) receives a lot of attention in Germany. Most recently, Stuart Parkes asks how writers, literary texts, and public discourse reconcile these apparently contradictory positions throughout the twentieth century and particularly after 1945.[2] As this study shows, the distinction between the literary text as a simple representation of historical events and the political sphere where power and action are located is obsolete. The interpretation of the 1968 memory novels in this study supports the notion that literary texts actively engage in the recuperation as well as the recherché of the past for the aesthetic and educational benefit of the present. Hans Christoph Buch asserts that the novel about the student movement, just like the novel about the fall of the Berlin Wall, is still missing.[3] However, read together, numerous novels that deal with the 1960s student movement in Germany and beyond paint an image of the event in order to dissect its significance. As culturally and socially mediated texts, 1968 memory novels act by contributing to the discourse about, and cultural memory of, 1968.

Novels discussed in this study unearth the past of 1968, National Socialism, and the Holocaust by digging through the various layers of memories that cover these events. This excavation leads to the rediscovery of hidden, silenced, and repressed pasts and to the reconsideration of various conflicting and complementary recollections. The literary memory of 1968 recovers historical events as unfinished matter from which a new kind of politics could emerge. This process is complicated by the understanding that it is impossible to completely or simply recuperate the authentic past events. Instead, the process of recuperation is always accompanied by a recherché that is a reconstruction of the past that is marked by remembering, rereading, and revisiting past events from the present perspective. Therefore, the process of remembering that informs these novels is always a participatory act within the (power) structures of public discourse.

Studying 1968 through fiction addresses questions of representation and narrativity; however, it also poses epistemological challenges. These challenges, in particular whether and how these novels create new knowledge about 1968, change our understanding of the event and participate in its historicization by triggering numerous, often antagonistic, debates about 1968. If literary texts created a kitsch memory that did not address the multiple, often conflicting recollections of 1968, these novels would indeed not receive as much attention as they do in the public discourse in Germany. The difference between fiction that engages in this critical memory work and other art forms, texts, and disciplines that explore this past lies in the methods that literary texts employ in order to construct and reconstruct stories of 1968. In particular, 1968 memory novels avoid the iconoclastic representation of the time period as focused on a few male and female leaders who have come to symbolize the student movement and subsequent terrorism through their representation in the media and in the visual arts. In a break from traditional representations of history, contemporary fiction represents a diverse spectrum of activists and social movements in order to memorialize and commemorate all participants and their concerns and goals. While the focus on a few leaders of the movement might enable the broader identification with them to create a coherent and persuasive story, remembering the wide spectrum of protest and rebellion in the 1960s and 1970s puts into practice one of the goals of the movement, namely the focus on the individual and his or her liberation and insertion into history.

Eduards Heimkehr, *Rot*, the *Salman* trilogy, *Seltsame Sterne starren zur Erde*, and *Der Vorleser* are among those texts that contribute to the genre of 1968 memory novels. As a genre, these novels construct the transnational cultural memory of 1968. These texts employ the first-person perspective that creates their reflective and self-reflective mode. They work with temporal layers of various recollections, build sites of remembering, and reflect on the significance of language, identity, and history in order to foreshadow a future that cannot be approached without knowledge of the past. These novels encourage rereading, revisiting, and reinscribing as activities that memorialize and historicize in order to spur and satisfy the human desire for freedom, equality, and justice. Without being moralistic, the novels acknowledge the moral and ethical dilemmas of remembering and forgetting by narrating tales of 1968 that span the twentieth century and create transnational connections. The trilogies by Morgner and Özdamar explore transnational dimensions in both narrative and plot. Suspended between Paris and Prague (Morgner) and amongst Turkey, Berlin, and Paris (Özdamar) these trilogies call into question hegemonic sites for remembering that exclude some members of the population in contemporary Germany. As trilogies, they span decades of history and consciously attempt to inscribe memories by East Germans, Turkish-Germans, and women into a cultural memory of 1968 by mirroring the form that Peter Schneider chose in order to narrate life in Berlin between the construction of the Berlin Wall in 1961 and its fall in 1989 in his Berlin trilogy consisting of *Der Mauerspringer*, *Paarungen*, and *Eduards Heimkehr*.[4] 1968 memory novels avoid the trap of aestheticizing death, injustice and loss, and emphasize that there is no closure for remembering the 1960s. Thus, these memory novels do not provide a pacified site for remembering and forgetting, but they create narrative spaces to ensure that memories impinge in order to bear on the present and the future.

And yet, despite the novels' numerous attempts to break silences, to encourage dialogues, and to break taboos, they nevertheless are embedded in a cycle of perpetuating silences and taboos.[5] Let me provide three examples. In *Eduards Heimkehr*, Eduard Hoffmann engages in an illicit love affair that can be read as a symbolic tryst with the German nation and its cultural heritage. This affair alludes to the turn to the political right that some of the former activists underwent. Furthermore, it points to the need to renegotiate the Germans' relationship with their state and nation after 1989, a point that this study addresses by tracing a shift in the representations of the 1960s student movement from the exclusive focus on the West German movement to include manifestations of upheaval in East Germany in the 1960s. Furthermore, my reading encourages a transnational understanding of the cultural memory of 1968. Both the representation of the United States as a site of the German imagination and the U.S. as the meeting space for Germans and Jews and as well as the numerous authors with hybrid identities who inscribe their experiences of 1968 within a cultural memory of 1968 contribute to this transnational dimension of 1968 memory novels.

Eduard's affair with a woman who invites him to spend a weekend in Weimar with her serves as a reminder that the 1968 memory novels are embedded in the German cultural and literary heritage. This has important repercussions for these concluding remarks that shift the ground to a slightly less optimistic outlook with respect to the Germans' ability to adjust to and to live up to the expectations of the fundamental changes of identity and identity politics in the twenty-first century. Even though Eduard is tantalized by the woman, who obscures her identity and appears either as a siren or an erinys, he ultimately decides to stay with his wife and thus to remain in the familiar constellation that has determined the negotiations of the past in Germany since 1945: the former West Berlin '68er, married to the Jewish survivor, who, after a stint in the U.S., returns to a unified Berlin in order to pursue the same opportunities there that other globalized cities in the twenty-first century offer. This move is symbolized by the newly constructed Potsdamer Platz in the center of Berlin where Eduard's wife Jenny finds a job as a public relations manager—a significant contrast to Eduard whose work is located in the former East. The couple settles in the former West Berlin and even finds a solution to their sexual problems. Read on the political level, the union between Eduard and Jenny cannot be disturbed by outsiders. Thus, the discourse of the recollections of 1968 and of the memories and postmemories of National Socialism and the Holocaust remains firmly in the hands of the former activist, and, albeit reluctantly, the Jewish survivor. Outsiders, like the tantalizing seductress presumably from the former East Germany who is trying to lure Eduard back into the heritage of the German "Kulturnation,"[6] the idea of a shared understanding of national literature, music, art, and philosophy that provides a cultural identity untainted by German history, do not gain entry to this discourse. *Eduard's Heimkehr* seems to suggest that the discourse of the former West Germany as a narrative of Westernization and, increasingly, globalization, prevails as the dominant discourse for the unified Germany.

Der Vorleser offers another example of the perpetuating taboos rendered seemingly obsolete by the changes attributed to the 1960s student movement. After Hanna's conviction, Michael Berg does not visit her in prison; however, he does send her tapes of stories he records for her. His text choice consists of the traditional canon of German literature, since he claims that both Hanna and he do not need any more experiments, and thus he does not include any literature outside the canon or published after the beginning of the twentieth century. This decision not only makes a political statement by alluding to German chancellor Konrad Adenauer's reelection campaign in 1957, which famously relied on the slogan "Keine Experimente!" (No experiments!) but also it alludes to the continued existence and validity of the conventional German literary canon and, as such, regresses to aesthetic positions that existed prior to the 1960s student movement. The narrator in *Der Vorleser* seems to suggest that in order to fill the vacuum left by the Third Reich one must construct a personal and national identity based on what is genuinely German. In order to do so Berg, unlike Eduard Hoffmann, relies on the notion of "Kulturnation" even though this shared communal space is in itself problematic, as the end of the novel makes clear: The narrator questions himself constantly, and every single assertion is contradicted by numerous considerations and rhetorical questions which are not answered and remain unanswered despite his reading of the traditional canon of German literature. Furthermore, the attempt to rely on this canon cannot "save" Hanna, redeem her guilt, or replace a dialogue between Berg and her—even after she is able to read and write and has listened to many of the tapes he sent, she still decides to commit suicide the day before she is released from prison.[7]

The third taboo addresses the issue of sexuality that, despite all opposite assertions and appearances, remains a taboo. In *Frühstück mit Max*, the breakfast that Max and Nelly share is preceded by a night they spent together, albeit twenty-some years ago. Without sharing his memories with Nelly, Max recalls for the reader of the novel that he visited Nelly's apartment in Berlin one night. Taking advantage of her unconscious state, induced by valium, he slips into her bed. While others claim that the text remains ambiguous about the events that follow I interpret this scene as describing a sexual act that has to be understood as a rape since Nelly is unconscious.[8] The topic of sexual violence, in particular against women, is represented as a moment of telling silence in some of the novels. In Schlink's *Der Vorleser*, Hanna Schmitz is accused of selecting young and beautiful women as readers, insinuating an at least homoerotic desire on her part, and in Özdamar's trilogy, violence against women is attributed to and sanctioned by the male-dominated agrarian society of premodern Turkey. In *Frühstück mit Max*, the rape is not only associated with sexual desire and sexual violence but also with the incest taboo. In this context, the role and function of family relations, in particular those between parents and children, remains undertheorized. While Max accuses Nelly and his father of parental neglect, Nelly recalls her own insecurities and the discussions she endured in the commune since she was not Max's birth mother. While the student activists attacked the biologism that spurred the privileging of the birth mother, they completely misunderstood the importance of the bond between children and parents, regardless of whether the parents are indeed the biological parents or assume that role, e.g., via adoption. Nelly recalls that she was never able to form a nurturing bond with Max even though she would have liked to, because the activists in the 1960s rejected bonding between parents and children in favor of communal child-rearing practices and in order to encourage children's self-determination while growing up. This representation of the complex relation between sexuality, violence, and education in *Frühstück mit Max* serves as a powerful reminder that the ghosts of the 1960s lurk in hidden memories that contribute to the narratives of the cultural memory of 1968.

The creation and reflection of taboos, represented as the mingling of love, sex, and violence, is embedded in notions of writing and reading as preeminent activities in order to remember and to address forgetting and to negotiate identity on the personal and political level. Reading and writing also refer to the importance of the discourse that shaped the 1960s and to the theories and methodologies that originated from this time period that challenged the notion of a canon that could supply and support fixed notions of identity. Timm's novel *Rot* places this discussion in the context of the advent of postmodernity. Linde, the narrator, claims that while he belongs to the generation that read everything in the original, the next generation lives by digestible quotes that are suitable to blend and mirror the fragmentation of the individual after 1968. Morgner also plays with the notion of the original when the figure of the communist Alain first learns German in order to be able to read Karl Marx in the language in which he wrote. This trust in authenticity and true origins takes on an absurd meaning when Beatriz takes Alain's trust in all things German one step further and decides to move to East Germany, where utopian expectations and hopes are supposed to come true. These inherent tensions in 1968 memory novels are probably the most important reason why literary texts, with their unique ability to narrate stories, are so centrally located within the transnational cultural memory of 1968 in Germany.

A considerable number of contributions to the discourse on 1968 declare the events of the 1960s and 1970s as a failed enterprise that was undertaken for all the wrong reasons and led nowhere. This narrative of failure represents 1968 as a topic of the past in order to undermine its political ramifications in the future. As my discussion of taboos shows, 1968 memory novels do not completely succeed in breaking free from the patterns of silence and oppression that dominated the discourse in divided Germany before 1989. This assessment counters the overall optimistic reading of these texts that suggests that in our daily lives as well as in cultural representations thereof we have finally arrived in the twenty-first century, marked by the recognition of individual and societal plurality and by a commitment to human rights, including the freedom of movement which requires a new understanding of migration and heterogeneity. And yet, despite their shortcomings, these novels construct opportune moments to come clean, to make a fresh start, and to achieve greater authenticity amidst a world that is not black and white, yet nevertheless trusts and enforces ethical and moral standards. In contrast to other contributions to and appropriations of the discourse of the 1960s and 1970s, 1968 memory novels question the sanitized version of the 1960s student movement that allows global corporations to market the event as the "summer of love" in order to sell their products.[9] 1968 memory novels included in this study point to 1968 as a contradictory, messy, and most of all, radical political event that gains new significance in its literary manifestations and makes an important contribution to Germany's identity.

In the 1960s, the student activists pushed art from its bourgeois pedestal and called for art's reintegration into life by conceptualizing it as an emancipatory practice. If the 1960s' critique of capitalism, imperialism, and militarism and its fight for equality, democracy, and peace foreshadow the contemporary critique of globalization and the struggle over human rights, then maybe the novels suggest that the fourth generation can learn from their grandparents in order to avoid committing the mistake the latter identified in the aftermath of the 1960s as: "Wir sind nicht radikal gewesen!" (We were not radical!).[10] 1968 memory novels point to traces of 1968 that are relevant for shaping our individual and social life in the twenty-first century; they create a noisy silence that highlights people and issues that are usually kept in the dark corners of historical and public discourses; and they invite controversy, heterogeneity, and the creation of productive intersections of history, memory, and fiction which ask: is it art? And is it radical enough?

Notes

1. Memory. In reference to the 1970s,/it is possible to be brief./The directory assistance was always busy./The miracle of the feeding of the five thousand/only took place in Düsseldorf and surroundings./The terrible news came across the ticker/was read and archived. Without resistance overall/did they swallow themselves/ the 1970s,/ without assurances for the next generation,/Turks or the unemployed./That someone would remember them with clemency/would be asked too much. Hans Magnus Enzensberger, *Die Furie des Verschwindens* (Frankfurt a.M.: Suhrkamp, 1980): 9.
2. Stuart Parkes, *Writers and Politics in Germany, 1945–2008* (Rochester, NY: Camden House, 2009): 2.
3. "Der große Roman über die Berliner Mauer ist bis heute nicht geschrieben worden, genausowenig wie der große Roman über die französische Revolution oder die Studentenrevolte von 1968. Und der große Roman über den Tag, an dem die Mauer fiel, wird vielleicht nie geschrieben werden. Solche historischen Ereignisse haben Schriftsteller als Chronisten nicht nötig; sie beschreiben sich sozusagen selbst, in Form von Augenzeugenberichten und Interviews, die im Fernsehen gesendet und in Zeitungen gedruckt oder kommentiert werden; und sie bringen ihre eigene Poesie hervor, die sich in Flugblättern, Transparenten und Slogans wie 'Die Phantasie an die Macht' oder 'Wir sind das Volk!' ausdrückt." (The great novel about the Berlin Wall has not been written yet, just like the great novel about the French Revolution or the student protests from 1968. And the great novel about the day when the Berlin Wall fell might possibly never be written. Such historical events do not need writers as chroniclers; they describe themselves in the form of eyewitness accounts and interviews which are shown on TV and printed in newspapers; they create their own poetry which expresses itself in flyers and slogans such as "All Power to the Imagination" and "We are the People!") Hans Christoph Buch, "Die Berliner Mauer und die deutsche Literatur," in *war jewesen. West-Berlin 1961–89*, ed. Detlef Holland-Moritz and Gabriela Wachter (Berlin: parthas verlag, 2009): 46.
4. Peter Schneider, *Der Mauerspringer* (Darmstadt: Luchterhand, 1982); *The Walljumper* (New York: Pantheon Books, 1983); *Paarungen* (Berlin: Rowohlt, 1992); *Couplings* (New York: Farrar, Straus and Giroux, 1996); *Eduards Heimkehr* (Berlin: Rowohlt, 1999); and *Eduard's Homecoming* (New York: Farrar, Straus and Giroux, 2000).
5. Numerous topics are absent from the discourse, e.g., drugs; AIDS/HIV; the constructive discussion of anti-Semitism among the left; the instrumentalization of the so-called "Third World"; and the far-reaching implications of the nature vs. nurture debate in particular for education.
6. For a discussion of that concept cf. Stephen Brockmann, *Literature and German Reunification* (Cambridge: Cambridge University Press, 1999): 5–10.
7. Morgner's and Özdamar's trilogies provide very different appropriations of the canon: Morgner's trilogy constitutes a creative subversion of the German and Eu-

ropean canon and Özdamar's Turkish narrator becomes an actress and director in Germany and demonstrates an expert familiarity with German drama and theatre.
8. For a discussion and different interpretations of this scene, see Burghard Damerau, "Muttersöhne. Die Konstruktion einer Art von Männern bei Ulrike Kolb," *Literatur für Leser* 24.3 (2001): 179–191; and David Horton, "Space Untitled: Past and Present in Ulrike Kolb's *Frühstück mit Max*," *Neophilologus* 90 (2006): 87–105. Damerau compares the motif of the "schlafend empfangenden Frau" (sleeping and sexually abused woman who conceives during this intercourse) to Heinrich von Kleist's novella *Die Marquise von O...* .
9. See, for example, the marketing campaigns by GAP and Target in the United States in the summer of 2009.
10. Peter Schneider, "Wir haben Fehler gemacht," presentation at the Free University Berlin on May 5, 1967. <http://www.glasnost.de/hist/apo/1967.html> (accessed April 15, 2005).

Bibliography

Adelson, Leslie A. "Opposing Oppositions: Turkish-German Questions in Contemporary German Studies." *German Studies Review* 17.2 (1994): 305–330.
———. "Response to Ülker Gökberk, 'Culture Studies und die Türken.'" *The German Quarterly* 70.3 (Summer 1997): 277–282.
———. *The Turkish Turn in Contemporary German Literature: Toward a New Critical Grammar of Migration*. New York: Palgrave Macmillan, 2005.
Adorno, Theodor W. "Kulturkritik und Gesellschaft." *Gesammelte Schriften* 10.1. Ed. Rolf Tiedemann. Frankfurt a.M.: Suhrkamp, 1986: 11–30.
———. "Was bedeutet: Aufarbeitung der Vergangenheit?" *Gesammelte Schriften* 10.2. Ed. Rolf Tiedemann. Frankfurt a.M.: Suhrkamp, 1986: 555–572.
Albrecht, Clemens. "Die Dialektik der Vergangenheitsbewältigung oder: Wie die Bundesrepublik zur Geschichtsnation wurde, ohne es zu merken." *Die intellektuelle Gründung der Bundesrepublik. Eine Wirkungsgeschichte der Frankfurter Schule*. Ed. Clemens Albrecht, Guenter C. Behrmann, Michael Bock, Harald Homann, and Friedrich H. Tenbruck. Frankfurt a.M.: Campus, 1999: 567–572.
Albrecht, Clemens, Guenter C. Behrmann, Michael Bock, Harald Homann, and Friedrich H. Tenbruck, ed. *Die intellektuelle Gründung der Bundesrepublik. Eine Wirkungsgeschichte der Frankfurter Schule*. Frankfurt a.M.: Campus, 1999.
Allertz, Robert. *Die RAF und das MfS. Fakten und Fiktionen*. Berlin: edition ost, 2008.
Aly, Götz. *Unser Kampf. 1968—ein irritierter Blick zurück*. Frankfurt a.M.: S. Fischer, 2008.
Andersch, Alfred. *Die Rote*. Olten/Freiburg: Walter, 1960.
Arpaci Seidel, Annette. "National Memory's *Schlüsselkinder*: Migration, Pedagogy, and German Remembrance Culture." *German Culture, Politics, and Literature into the Twenty-First Century: Beyond Normalization*. Ed. Stuart Taberner and Paul Cooke. Rochester, NY: Camden House, 2006: 105–120.
Assmann, Aleida. *Erinnerungsräume. Formen und Wandlungen des kulturellen Gedächtnisses*. München: Beck, 1999.
Assmann, Aleida and Jan Assman. "Das Gestern im Heute. Medien und soziales Gedächtnis." *Studienbegleitbrief zur Studieneinheit 11 des Funkkollegs Medien und Kommunikation*. Weinheim: Beltz, 1991: 41–82.
Baer, Ulrich. "The Hubris of Humility: Günter Grass, Peter Schneider, and German Guilt After 1989." *The Germanic Review* 80.1 (2005): 50–73.

Baier, Lothar, Wilfried Gottschalck, Reimut Reiche, Thomas Schmid, Joscha Schmierer, Barbara Sichtermann, and Adriano Sofri. *Die Früchte der Revolte. Über die Veränderung der politischen Kultur durch die Studentenbewegung.* Berlin: Wagenbach, 1988.

Balzer, Friedrich-Martin and Werner Renz, ed. *Das Urteil im Frankfurter Auschwitz-Prozess, 1963–1965.* Bonn: Pahl-Rugenstein, 2004.

Bammer, Angelika. "The American Feminist Reception of GDR Literature (with a Glance at West Germany)." *GDR Bulletin* 16.2 (1990): 18–24.

Bauschinger, Sigrid. "Mythos Manhattan. Die Faszination einer Stadt." *Amerika in der deutschen Literatur: Neue Welt, Nordamerika, USA.* Ed. Sigrid Bauschinger, Horst Denkler, and Wilfried Malsch. Stuttgart: Reclam, 1975: 382–397.

Bauschinger, Sigrid, Horst Denkler, and Wilfried Malsch, ed. *Amerika in der deutschen Literatur: Neue Welt, Nordamerika, USA.* Stuttgart: Reclam, 1975.

Becker, Thomas P. and Ute Schröder, ed. *Die Studentenproteste der 60er Jahre. Archivführer-Chronik-Bibliographie.* Köln: Böhlau, 2000.

Bendkowski, Halina. *Wie weit flog die Tomate? Eine 68erinnen-Gala der Reflexion.* Berlin: Heinrich-Böll-Stiftung, 1999.

Benjamin, Walter. "Ursprung des deutschen Trauerspiels." *Gesammelte Schriften.* I.1. Ed. Tillman Rexroth. Frankfurt a.M.: Suhrkamp, 1978: 203–409.

———. "Der Erzähler." *Gesammelte Schriften.* II.2. Ed. Rolf Tiedemann and Hermann Schweppenhäuser. Frankfurt a.M.: Suhrkamp, 1977: 438–465.

———. "Ausgraben und Erinnern." *Gesammelte Schriften.* IV.1. Ed. Tillman Rexroth. Frankfurt a.M.: Suhrkamp, 1978: 400f.

———. "Berliner Chronik." *Gesammelte Schriften.* IV.1. Ed. Tillman Rexroth. Frankfurt a.M.: Suhrkamp, 1978: 465–519.

———. *Selected Writings.* Ed. Michael W. Jennings and Howard Eiland, trans. Edmund Jephcott, Howard Eiland, and others. Cambridge, London: The Belknap Press of Harvard University Press, 2002.

Bergmann, Werner. "Kommunikationslatenz und Vergangenheitsbewältigung." *Vergangenheitsbewältigung am Ende des 20. Jahrhunderts.* Ed. Helmut König, Michael Kohlstruck, and Andreas Wöll. Opladen: Westdeutscher Verlag, 1998: 393–408.

Berman, Paul. *Power and the Idealists. Or, The Passion of Joschka Fischer.* Berkeley: Soft Skull Press, 2005.

Beutin, Wolfgang, ed. *Deutsche Literaturgeschichte. Von den Anfängen bis zur Gegenwart.* 7th ed. Stuttgart: Metzler, 2008.

Bieling, Rainer. *Die Tränen der Revolution. Die 68er zwanzig Jahre danach.* Berlin: Siedler, 1988.

Biermann, Wolf. *Alle Lieder.* Köln: Kiepenheuer & Witsch, 1991.

Bloch, Ernst. *Das Prinzip Hoffnung.* Frankfurt a.M.: Suhrkamp, 1959.

Boa, Elizabeth. "Özdamar's Autobiographical Fictions: Trans-National Identity and Literary Form." *German Life and Letters* 59.4 (2006): 526–539.

Böll, Heinrich. *Wo warst du, Adam?* Opladen: Friedrich Middelhauve, 1951.
Borges, Jorge Luis. *Labyrinths: Selected Stories and Other Writings.* New York: New Directions Publishing Co., 1964.
Born, Nicolas. *Die erdabgewandte Seite der Geschichte.* Reinbek: Rowohlt, 1976.
Boyers, Robert. "The Normality Blues." *The Dictator's Dictation. The Politics of Novels and Novelists.* New York: Columbia University Press, 2005: 91–106.
Brasch, Thomas. *Vor den Vätern sterben die Söhne.* Berlin: Rotbuch Verlag, 1977.
Bren, Paulina. "1968 East and West: Visions of Political Change and Student Protest from across the Iron Curtain." *Transnational Moments of Change. Europe 1945, 1968, 1989.* Ed. Gerd-Rainer Horn and Padraic Kenney. Lanham: Rowman and Littlefield, 2003: 119–135.
Bridge, Helen. *Women's Writing and Historiography in the GDR.* Oxford: Clarendon Press, 2002.
Briegleb, Klaus and Sigrid Weigel, ed. *Gegenwartsliteratur seit 1968. Hansers Sozialgeschichte der deutschen Literatur 12.* München: Hanser, 1992: 21–72.
Brinkmann, Rolf Dieter. *Keiner weiß mehr.* Köln: Kiepenheuer & Witsch, 1968.
Brockmann, Stephen. *Literature and German Reunification.* Cambridge: Cambridge University Press, 1999.
Brown, Timothy. "1968 East and West: Divided Germany as a Case Study in Transnational History." *The American Historical Review* 114.1 (2009): 69–96.
Brueggemann, Aminia M. *Chronotopos Amerika bei Max Frisch, Peter Handke, Günter Kunert und Martin Walser.* New York: Lang, 1996.
Buch, Hans Christoph. "Die Berliner Mauer und die deutsche Literatur." *war jewesen. West-Berlin 1961–89.* Ed. Detlef Holland-Moritz and Gabriela Wachter. Berlin: parthas verlag, 2009: 44–50.
Büchner, Georg. *Lenz.* Stuttgart: Reclam, 1957.
Buselmeier, Michael. "Nach der Revolte. Die literarische Verarbeitung der Studentenbewegung." *Literatur und Studentenbewegung. Eine Zwischenbilanz.* Ed. Martin W. Lüdke. Opladen: Westdeutscher Verlag, 1977: 158–185.
Cailloux, Bernd. *Das Geschäftsjahr 1968/69.* Frankfurt a.M.: Suhrkamp, 2005.
Cardinal, Agnès. "'Be Realistic: Demand the Impossible.' On Irmtraud Morgner's *Salman* Trilogy." *Socialism and the Literary Imagination. Essays on East German Writers.* Ed. Martin Kane. New York, Oxford: Berg, 1991: 147–161.
Cheesman, Tom. *Novels of Turkish German Settlement: Cosmopolite Fictions.* Rochester, NY: Camden House, 2007.
Cobbs, Alfred. *The Image of America in Postwar German Literature: Reflections and Perceptions.* Bern: Lang, 1982.
Cohn-Bendit, Daniel and Reinhard Mohr. *1968. Die letzte Revolution, die noch nichts vom Ozonloch wußte.* Berlin: Wagenbach, 1988.
Cornils, Ingo. "Romantic Relapse? The Literary Representation of the German Student Movement." *German Studies Towards the Millenium. Selected Pa-*

pers from the Conference of University Teachers of German, University of Keele, September 1999. Ed. Christopher Hall and David Rock. New York: Lang, 2000: 107–123.

———. "Successful Failure? The Impact of the German Student Movement on the Federal Republic of Germany." *Recasting German Identity. Culture, Politics, and Literature in the Berlin Republic.* Ed. Stuart Taberner and Frank Finlay. Rochester, NY: Camden House, 2002: 106–122.

———. "Long Memories: The German Student Movement in Recent Fiction." *German Life and Letters* 56.1 (2003): 89–101.

———. "Writing the Revolution: the Literary Representation of the German Student Movement as Counter-Culture." *Counter-Cultures in Germany and Central Europe.* Ed. Steve Giles and Maike Oergel. Bern: Lang, 2003: 295–314.

Cornils, Ingo and Frank Finlay, ed. *"(Un-)Erfüllte Wirklichkeit." Neue Studien zu Uwe Timms Werk.* Würzburg: Königshausen & Neumann, 2006.

Cornils, Ingo and Sarah Waters, ed. *Memories of 1968. International Perspectives.* Oxford: Lang, 2010.

Costabile-Heming, Carol Anne. "Tracing History through Berlin's Topography: Historical Memories and Post-1989 Berlin Narratives." *German Life and Letters* 58.3 (2005): 344–356.

Damerau, Burghard. "Muttersöhne. Die Konstruktion einer Art von Männern bei Ulrike Kolb." *Literatur für Leser* 24.3 (2001): 179–191.

Dannenberg, Sophie. *Das bleiche Herz der Revolution.* München: Deutsche Verlagsanstalt, 2004.

Davis, Belinda, Wilfried Mausbach, Martin Klimke, and Carla MacDougall, ed. *Changing the World, Changing Oneself: Political Protest and Collective Identities in 1960s/70s West Germany and the U.S.* New York: Berghahn, 2010.

DeGroot, Gerard J., ed. *Student Protest. The Sixties and After.* London, New York: Longman, 1998.

———. *The Sixties Unplugged. A Kaleidoscopic History of a Disorderly Decade.* Cambridge: Harvard University Press, 2008.

Delius, Friedrich Christian. *Amerikahaus und der Tanz um die Frauen.* Reinbek: Rowohlt, 1997.

———. *Mein Jahr als Mörder.* Berlin: Berlin Verlag, 2004.

De Lorent, Peter. *Die Hexenjagd.* Köln: Weltkreis, 1987.

Donahue, William Collins. "Elusive '68: The Challenge to Pedagogy." *Die Unterrichtspraxis/Teaching German* 41.2 (2008): 113–123.

Dudek, Peter. "'Vergangenheitsbewältigung.' Zur Problematik eines umstrittenen Begriffs." *Aus Politik und Zeitgeschichte* B 1-2 (3 January 1992): 44–53.

Durzak, Manfred. *Das Amerika-Bild in der deutschen Gegenwartsliteratur.* Stuttgart: Kohlhammer, 1979.

Eco, Umberto. "An *Art Oblivionalis*? Forget It!" *Publication of the Modern Language Association of America* 103 (1988): 254–261.

Eigler, Friederike. *Gedächtnis und Geschichte in Generationenromanen seit der Wende.* Berlin: Erich Schmidt, 2005.
Eley, Geoff. "Telling Stories about Sixty-Eight: Troublemaking, Political Passions, and Enabling Democracy." *German Studies Association Newsletter* XXXIII.2 (2008/9): 39–50.
Emmerich, Wolfgang. "Affirmation-Utopie-Melancholie. Versuch einer Bilanz von vierzig Jahren DDR-Literatur." *German Studies Review* 14.2 (1991): 325–344.
———. *Kleine Literaturgeschichte der DDR. Erweiterte Neuausgabe.* Leipzig: Gustav Kiepenheuer Verlag, 1996.
Enzensberger, Hans Magnus. "Gemeinplätze, die Neueste Literatur betreffend." *Kursbuch* 15 (1968): 187–197.
———. *Die Furie des Verschwindens.* Frankfurt a.M.: Suhrkamp, 1980.
Erdle, Birgit and Sigrid Weigel, ed. *Fünfzig Jahre danach. Zur Nachgeschichte des Nationalsozialismus.* Zürich: vdf, 1996.
Fahlenbrach, Kathrin. *Protest-Inszenierungen. Visuelle Kommunikation und kollektive Identitäten in Protestbewegungen.* Wiesbaden: Westdeutscher Verlag, 2002.
Fink, Carole, Philipp Gassert, and Detlef Junker, ed. *1968: A World Transformed.* Cambridge: Cambridge University Press, 1998.
Fleischer, Helmut. "Mit der Vergangenheit umgehen. Prolegomena zu einer Analytik des Geschichtsbewußtseins." *Vergangenheitsbewältigung am Ende des 20. Jahrhunderts.* Ed. Helmut König, Michael Kohlstruck, and Andreas Wöll. Opladen: Westdeutscher Verlag, 1998: 409–432.
Fox, Thomas C. "Germanistik and GDR Studies: (Re)Reading a Censored Literature." *Monatshefte* 85.3 (1993): 284–294.
Frese, Matthias et al., ed. *Demokratisierung und gesellschaftlicher Aufbruch. Die sechziger Jahre als Wendezeit der Bundesrepublik.* Paderborn: Ferdinand Schöningh, 2003.
Freud, Sigmund. "Konstruktionen in der Analyse." *Gesammelte Werke* 16. Frankfurt a.M.: S. Fischer, 1950: 41–56.
Frevert, Ute. "Umbruch der Geschlechterverhältnisse? Die 60er Jahre als geschlechterpolitischer Experimentierraum." *Dynamische Zeiten. Die 60er Jahre in den beiden deutschen Gesellschaften.* Ed. Karl Christian Lammers, Axel Schildt, and Detlef Siegfried. Hamburg: Christians, 2000: 642–660.
Fried, Erich. *und Vietnam und.* Berlin: Wagenbach, 1966.
Fuchs, Anne. *Phantoms of War in Contemporary German Literature, Film and Discourse: The Politics of Memory.* New York: Palgrave Macmillan, 2008.
Galinsky, Hans. *Amerikanisch-deutsche Sprach- und Literaturbeziehungen.* Frankfurt a.M.: Athenäum-Verlag, 1972.
Galtung, Johan. "Violence, Peace, and Peace Research." *Journal of Peace Research* 6 (1969): 167–191.

Gassert, Philipp. "'With America against America.' Anti-Americanism in West Germany." *The United States and Germany in the Era of the Cold War, 1945–1990. A Handbook*, Volume 2: 1968–1990. Ed. Detlef Junker. Cambridge: Cambridge University Press and German Historical Institute, 2004: 502–509.

Gassert, Philipp and Martin Klimke, ed. "1968: Memories and Legacies of a Global Revolt." *Bulletin of the German Historical Institute* Supplement 6 (2009): 5–24.

Gassert, Philipp and Pavel A. Richter. *1968 in West Germany: A Guide to Resources and Literature of the Extra-Parliamentarian Opposition*. Washington D.C.: German Historical Institute, 1998.

Gehrig, Sebastian, Barbara Mittler, and Felix Wemheuer, ed. *Kulturrevolution als Vorbild? Maoismen im deutschsprachigen Raum*. Frankfurt a.M.: Lang, 2008.

Gehrke, Bernd. "1968—das unscheinbare Schlüsseljahr der DDR." *1968 und die Arbeiter. Studien zum proletarischen Mai in Europa*. Ed. Bernd Gehrke and Gerd-Rainer Horn. Hamburg: VSA-Verlag, 2007: 103–130.

———. "1968. Die 68-er Proteste in der DDR." *Aus Politik und Zeitgeschichte* 14–15 (31 March 2008): 40–46.

Gemünden, Gerd. *Framed Visions. Popular Culture, Americanization, and the Contemporary German and Austrian Imagination*. Ann Arbor: The University of Michigan Press, 1998.

Genazino, Wilhelm. *Eine Frau, eine Wohnung, ein Roman*. München: Hanser, 2003.

Georgi, Viola B. *Entliehene Erinnerung. Geschichtsbilder junger Migranten in Deutschland*. Hamburg: Hamburger Edition, 2003.

Gerschmann, Karl-Heinz. "Wenn Dunkelmänner Briefe schreiben…" *Neophilologus* 81 (1997): 89–103.

Gerstenberger, Katharina. *Writing the New Berlin: The German Capital in Post-Wall Literature*. Rochester, NY: Camden House, 2008.

Gilcher-Holtey, Ingrid. *Die 68er Bewegung: Deutschland, Westeuropa, USA*. München: Beck, 2001.

Giles, Steve and Maike Oergel, ed. *Counter-Cultures in Germany and Central Europe. From Sturm und Drang to Baader-Meinhof*. Oxford: Lang, 2003.

Gitlin, Todd. *The Whole World is Watching: Mass Media in the Making and Unmaking of the New Left*. Berkeley: University of California Press, 1980.

Goethe, Johann Wolfgang von. "Den Vereinigten Staaten." *Werke* 1. Ed. Erich Trunz. München: Beck, 1981.

———. "To America." *The Permanent Goethe*. Ed. Thomas Mann, trans. Stephen Spender. New York: Dial, 1948.

———. *Wilhelm Meisters Lehrjahre*, in *Werke* 7, ed. Erich Trunz. München: Beck, 1981.

Gökberk, Ülker. "Culture Studies und die Türken: Sten Nadolnys *Selim oder Die Gabe der Rede* im Lichte einer Methodendiskussion." *The German Quarterly* 70.2 (Spring 1997): 97–122.

Götze, Karl-Heinz. "Gedächtnis. Romane über die Studentenbewegung." *Das Argument* 127 (1981): 367–382.

Goldhagen, Daniel Jonah. *Hitler's Willing Executioners: Ordinary Germans and the Holocaust.* New York: Knopf, 1996.

Grass, Günter. *Mein Jahrhundert.* Göttingen: Steidl, 1999.

Härtling, Peter. *Nachgetragene Liebe.* Darmstadt: Luchterhand, 1980.

Hakemi, Sara. *Anschlag und Spektakel. Flugblätter der Kommune I, Erklärungen von Ensslin/Baader und der frühen RAF.* Bochum: Posth Verlag, 2008.

Halbwachs, Maurice. *The Collective Memory.* Trans. Francis J. Ditter, Jr. and Vida Yazdi Ditter. New York: Harper & Row, 1980.

Hamann, Christof, Ute Gerhard, and Walter Grünzweig, ed. *Amerika und die deutschsprachige Literatur nach 1848. Migration—kultureller Austausch—frühe Globalisierung.* Bielefeld: transcript Verlag, 2009.

Handke, Peter. *Der kurze Brief zum langen Abschied.* Frankfurt a.M.: Suhrkamp, 1972.

Hartung, Klaus. "Die Repression wird zum Milieu. Die Beredsamkeit linker Literatur." *Literaturmagazin* 11 (1979): 52–79.

Havemann, Florian. *Havemann. Eine Behauptung.* Frankfurt a.M.: Suhrkamp, 2007.

Herminghouse, Patricia A. "Die Frau und das Phantastische in der neueren DDR-Literatur. Der Fall Irmtraud Morgner." *Die Frau als Heldin und Autorin: neue kritische Ansätze zur deutschen Literatur.* Ed. Wolfgang Paulsen. Bern: Francke, 1979: 248–266.

———. "New Contexts for GDR Literature: An American Perspective." *Cultural Transformations in the New Germany: American and German Perspectives.* Ed. Friederike Eigler and Peter C. Pfeiffer. Rochester, NY: Camden House, 1993: 93–101.

Herzog, Dagmar. *Sex after Fascism: Memory and Morality in Twentieth-Century Germany.* Princeton: Princeton University Press, 2005.

Hirsch, Marianne. *Family Frames: Photography, Narrative, and Postmemory.* Cambridge: Harvard University Press, 1997.

Hofmann, Klaus. "Poetry after Auschwitz—Adorno's Dictum." *German Life and Letters* 58.2 (2005): 182–94.

Hofmann, Michael. "'Solidarität mit Prag. Arbeiterproteste 1968 in der DDR." *1968 und die Arbeiter. Studien zum proletarischen Mai in Europa.* Ed. Bernd Gehrke and Gerd-Rainer Horn. Hamburg: VSA-Verlag, 2007: 92–102.

Horn, Gerd-Rainer and Padraic Kenney, ed. *Transnational Moments of Change. Europe 1945, 1968, 1989.* Lanham: Rowman and Littlefield, 2003.

Hörnigk, Frank. "Die Literatur bleibt zuständig: Ein Versuch über das Verhältnis von Literatur, Utopie und Politik in der DDR–am Ende der DDR." *The Germanic Review* 67.3 (1992): 99–105.

Horton, David. "Space Untitled: Past and Present in Ulrike Kolb's *Frühstück mit Max*." *Neophilologus* 90 (2006): 87–105.

Hosfeld, Rolf and Helmut Peitsch. "'Weil uns diese Aktionen innerlich verändern, sind sie politisch.' Bemerkungen zu vier Romanen über die Studentenbewegung." *Basis. Jahrbuch für deutsche Gegenwartsliteratur* 8 (1978): 92–126.

Huber, Martin. *Politisierung der Literatur–Ästhetisierung der Politik*. Bern: Lang, 1992.

Hunn, Karin. *"Nächstes Jahr kehren wir zurück…": Die Geschichte der türkischen "Gastarbeiter" in der Bundesrepublik*. Göttingen: Wallstein, 2005.

Huyssen, Andreas. "Diaspora and Nation: Migration Into Other Pasts." *New German Critique* 88 (Winter 2003): 147–164.

Jankowsky, Karen. "'German' Literature Contested: The 1991 Ingeborg-Bachmann-Prize Debate, 'Cultural Diversity,' and Emine Sevgi Ozdamar." *The German Quarterly* 70.3 (Summer 1997): 261–276.

Janssen, Doris. *"Blue-Note-Akrobatik." Irmtraud Morgner im kulturellen Kontext der sechziger Jahre*. Marburg: Tectum Verlag, 1998.

Jarausch, Konrad H. "1968 and 1989: Caesuras, Comparisons, and Connections." *1968: A World Transformed*. Ed. Carole Fink, Philipp Gassert, and Detlef Junker. Cambridge, Cambridge University Press, 1998: 461–477.

———. *After Hitler. Recivilizing Germans, 1945–1995*. Oxford: Oxford University Press, 2006.

Jarausch, Konrad H. and Michael Geyer. *Shattered Past: Reconstructing German Histories*. Princeton: Princeton University Press, 2002.

Jenny, Zoë. *Das Blütenstaubzimmer*. Frankfurt a.M.: Frankfurter Verlagsanstalt, 1997.

Johnson, Uwe. *Jahrestage*. Frankfurt a.M.: Suhrkamp, 1970ff.

Kätzel, Ute. *Die 68erinnen. Portrait einer rebellischen Frauengeneration*. Berlin: Rowohlt, 2002.

Kafka, Franz. *Amerika*. München: K. Wolff, 1927.

Kailitz, Susanne. *Von den Worten zu den Waffen? Frankfurter Schule, Studentenbewegung, RAF und die Gewaltfrage*. Wiesbaden: VS Verlag für Sozialwissenschaften, 2007.

Kaiser, Paul and Claudia Petzold, ed. *Boheme und Diktatur in der DDR. Gruppen, Konflikte, Quartiere. 1970-1989*. Berlin: Verlag Fannei & Walz, 1997.

Kaminer, Wladimir. *Schönhauser Allee*. München: Manhattan, 2001.

Katsiaficas, George. *The Imagination of the New Left: A Global Analysis of 1968*. Boston: South End Press, 1987.

Kaufmann, Eva. "Interview mit Irmtraud Morgner". *Weimarer Beiträge* 30 (1984): 1494–1514.

Kaya, Ayhan. "German-Turkish Transnational Space: A Separate Space of Their Own." *German Studies Review* 30.3 (2007): 483–502.

Kehrer, Jürgen. *Das Kappenstein-Projekt.* Dortmund: Grafit, 1997.

Kinder, Hermann. *Der Schleiftrog.* Zürich: Diogenes, 1977.

Klimke, Martin. *The Other Alliance: Student Protest in West Germany and the United States in the Global Sixties.* Princeton: Princeton University Press, 2010.

———. "Revisiting the Revolution: 1968 in Transnational Cultural Memory." *Memories of 1968. International Perspectives.* Ed. Ingo Cornils and Sarah Waters. Oxford: Lang, 2010: 25–48.

Klimke, Martin and Joachim Scharloth, ed. *Handbuch 1968 zur Kultur- und Mediengeschichte der Studentenbewegung.* Stuttgart: Metzler, 2007.

———. *1968 in Europe: A History of Protest and Activism, 1956–1977.* New York: Berghahn, 2008.

Klingenstein, Grete. "Über Herkunft und Verwendung des Wortes 'Vergangenheitsbewältigung.'" *Geschichte und Gegenwart* 4 (1988): 301–312.

Kniesche, Thomas W. *Projektionen von Amerika. Die USA in der deutsch-jüdischen Literatur des 20. Jahrhunderts.* Bielefeld: Aisthesis, 2008.

Köhler, Barbara. "A la recherché de la révolution perdue. Ein innerdeutscher Monolog." *Women and the Wende: Social Effects and Cultural Reflections of the German Unification Process: Proceedings of a Conference held by Women in German Studies, 9–11 Sept 1993 at the University of Nottingham.* Ed. Elizabeth Boa and Janet Wharton. Amsterdam, Atlanta: Rodopi, 1994: 1–5.

König, Helmut. "Von der Diktatur zur Demokratie oder Was ist Vergangenheitsbewältigung." *Vergangenheitsbewältigung am Ende des 20. Jahrhunderts.* Ed. Helmut König, Michael Kohlstruck, and Andreas Wöll. Opladen: Westdeutscher Verlag, 1998: 371–392.

König, Helmut, Michael Kohlstruck, and Andreas Wöll, ed. *Vergangenheitsbewältigung am Ende des 20. Jahrhunderts.* Opladen: Westdeutscher Verlag, 1998.

Koenen, Gerd. *Das rote Jahrzehnt. Unsere kleine deutsche Kulturrevolution 1967–77.* Köln: Kiepenheuer & Witsch, 2001.

Kohlstruck, Michael. *Zwischen Erinnerung und Geschichte. Der Nationalsozialismus und die jungen Deutschen.* Berlin: Metropol, 1997.

Kolb, Ulrike. *Eine Liebe zu ihrer Zeit.* Reinbek: Rowohlt, 1995.

———. *Frühstück mit Max.* Stuttgart: Klett-Cotta, 2000.

Kolinsky, Eva. "Migration Experiences and the Construction of Identity among Turks Living in Germany." *Recasting German Identity. Culture, Politics, and Literature in the Berlin Republic.* Ed. Stuart Taberner and Frank Finlay. Rochester, NY: Camden House, 2002: 205–218.

Komfort-Hein, Susanne. "'1968:' Literarische Konstruktionen einer Generation." *GeNarrationen. Variationen zum Verhältnis von Generation und

Geschlecht. Ed. Eveline Kilian and Susanne Komfort-Hein. Tübingen: Attempto, 1999: 191–215.

Korn, Salomon. *Geteilte Erinnerung. Beiträge zur 'deutsch-jüdischen' Gegenwart.* Berlin: Philo, 1999.

Kowalczuk, Ilko-Sascha. "'Wer sich nicht in Gefahr begibt …' Protestaktionen gegen die Intervention in Prag und die Folgen von 1968 für die DDR-Opposition." *Widerstand und Opposition in der DDR.* Ed. Klaus-Dietmar Henke, Peter Steinbach, and Johannes Tuchel. Köln, Weimar, Wien: Böhlau, 1999: 257–274.

Krätzer, Anita. *Studien zum Amerikabild in der neueren deutschen Literatur.* Bern: Lang, 1982.

Kraushaar, Wolfgang. *1968 als Mythos, Chiffre und Zäsur.* Hamburg: Hamburger Edition, 2000.

———. *Achtundsechzig. Eine Bilanz.* Berlin: Propyläen, 2008.

Kürnberger, Ferdinand. *Der Amerika-Müde.* Frankfurt a. M.: Meidinger, 1855, repr. 1989.

Kundnani, Hans. *Utopia or Auschwitz. Germany's 1968 Generation and the Holocaust.* New York: Columbia University Press, 2009.

LaCapra, Dominick. *History, Theory, Trauma: Representing the Holocaust.* Ithaca: Cornell University Press, 1994.

Lasker-Schüler, Else. *Gedichte 1902–1943. Gesammelte Werke* 1. Ed. Friedhelm Kemp. München: Kösel-Verlag, 1959.

Leggewie, Claus. "'1968.' A Transatlantic Event and Its Consequences." *The United States and Germany in the Era of the Cold War, 1945–1990. A Handbook.* Volume 2: 1968–1990. Ed. Detlef Junker. Cambridge: Cambridge University Press and German Historical Institute, 2004: 421–429.

Lettau, Reinhard. *Täglicher Faschismus: Amerikanische Evidenz aus 6 Monaten.* München: Hanser, 1971.

Linklater, Beth V. *"Und immer zügelloser wird die Lust:" Constructions of Sexuality in East German Literatures; with special reference to Irmtraud Morgner and Gabriele Stötzer-Kachold.* Bern: Lang, 1997.

Littler, Margaret. "Diasporic Identity in Emine Sevgi Özdamar's *Mutterzunge.*" *Recasting German Identity. Culture, Politics, and Literature in the Berlin Republic.* Ed. Stuart Taberner and Frank Finlay. Rochester, NY: Camden House, 2002: 219–234.

Luckscheiter, Roman. *Der postmoderne Impuls: Die Krise der Literatur um 1968 und ihre Überwindung.* Berlin: Duncker und Humblot, 2001.

Ludwig, Janine. *Heiner Müller, Ikone West.* Frankfurt a.M.: Lang, 2009.

Ludwig, Janine and Mirjam Meuser, ed. *Literatur ohne Land? Schreibstrategien einer DDR-Literatur im vereinten Deutschland.* Freiburg: FWPF, 2009.

Lüdke, Martin W., ed. *Literatur und Studentenbewegung. Eine Zwischenbilanz.* Opladen: Westdeutscher Verlag, 1977.

Lützeler, Paul Michael. "Literatur als Selbstverständigungsmedium einer Generation." *Zeitschrift für Literaturwissenschaft und Linguistik* 124 (2001): 56–64.

———. "'Postmetropolis:' Peter Schneiders Berlin-Trilogie." *Gegenwartsliteratur* 4 (2005): 91–110.

Magenau, Jörg. "Literatur als Selbstverständigungsmedium einer Generation." *Zeitschrift für Literaturwissenschaft und Linguistik* 124 (2001): 56–64.

Mani, B. Venkat. *Cosmopolitical Claims. Turkish-German Literatures from Nadolny to Pamuk.* Iowa City: University of Iowa Press, 2007.

Markgraf, Nikolaus. "Die Feministin der DDR." *Irmtraud Morgner. Texte, Daten, Bilder.* Ed. Marlis Gerhardt. Frankfurt a.M.: Luchterhand, 1990: 150–155.

Maron, Monika. *Animal Triste.* Frankfurt a.M.: S. Fischer, 1996.

Marwick, Arthur. *The Sixties. Cultural Revolution in Britain, France, Italy, and the United States, 1958–1974.* Oxford: Oxford University Press, 1998.

Mausbach, Wilfried. "Wende um 360 Grad? Nationalsozialismus und Judenvernichtung in der 'zweiten Gründungsphase' der Bundesrepublik." *Wo "1968" liegt. Reform und Revolte in der Geschichte der Bundesrepublik.* Ed. Christina von Hodenberg and Detlef Siegfried. Göttingen: Vandenhoeck & Ruprecht, 2006: 15–47.

McCormick, Richard. *Politics of the Self: Feminism and the Postmodern in West German Literature and Film.* Princeton: Princeton University Press, 1991.

McDougall, Alan. *Youth Politics in East Germany: The Free German Youth Movement 1946–1968.* Oxford: Clarendon Press, 2004.

McGlothlin, Erin. *Second-Generation Holocaust Literature: Legacies of Survival and Perpetration.* Rochester, NY: Camden House, 2006.

Meckel, Christoph. *Suchbild. Über meinen Vater.* Düsseldorf: Claassen, 1980.

Mehl, James V. "Language, Class and Mimic Satire in the Characterization of Correspondents in the *Epistolae obscurorum virorum*," *Sixteenth Century Journal* XXV.2 (1994): 289–305.

Meier, Georg. *Alle waren in Woodstock, außer mir und den Beatles.* Berlin: Dittrich, 2008.

Merkel, Ina. "The GDR–A Normal Country in the Centre of Europe." *Power and Society in the GDR, 1961–1979. The 'Normalisation of Rule'?* Ed. Mary Fulbrook. New York: Berghahn Books, 2009: 194–203.

Merkel, Rainer. *Das Gefühl am Morgen.* Frankfurt a.M.: S. Fischer, 2005.

Mews, Siegfried. "The Desire to Achieve 'Normalcy'–Peter Schneider's Post-Wall Berlin Novel *Eduard's Homecoming.*" *Studies in Twentieth and Twenty First Century Literature* 28.1 (2004): 258–285.

Minnerup, Günter. "Germany 1968 and 1989: The Marginalized Intelligentsia against the Cold War." *Student Protest. The Sixties and After.* Ed. Gerard J. DeGroot. London, New York: Longman, 1998: 201–215.

Mitscherlich, Alexander. *Auf dem Weg zur vaterlosen Gesellschaft. Ideen zur Sozialpsychologie.* München: Piper, 1963.

Modick, Klaus. *Der Flügel.* Frankfurt: S. Fischer, 1994.
Morgner, Irmtraud. *Leben und Abenteuer der Trobadora Beatriz nach Zeugnissen ihrer Spielfrau Laura: Roman in dreizehn Büchern und sieben Intermezzos.* Darmstadt: Luchterhand, 1974.
———. *Amanda: ein Hexenroman.* Darmstadt: Luchterhand, 1983.
———. *Der Schöne und das Tier: eine Liebesgeschichte.* Darmstadt: Luchterhand, 1991.
———. *Das heroische Testament: Roman in Fragmenten.* Ed. Rudolf Bussmann. München: Luchterhand, 1998.
———. *The Life and Adventures of Trobadora Beatrice as Chronicled by her Minstrel Laura: A Novel in Thirteen Books and Seven Intermezzos.* Trans. Jeanette Clausen, ed. Jeanette Clausen and Silke von der Emde. Lincoln: University of Nebraska Press, 2000.
Mosler, Peter. *Was wir wollten, was wir wurden. Studentenrevolte, zehn Jahre danach.* Reinbek: Rowohlt, 1977.
Mündemann, Tobias. *Die 68er ... und was aus ihnen geworden ist.* München: W. Heyne Verlag, 1988.
Nadolny, Sten. *Selim oder die Gabe der Rede.* München: Piper, 1990.
———. "Wir und Die–Erzählen über Fremde." *Schreiben zwischen den Kulturen: Beiträge zur deutschsprachigen Gegenwartsliteratur.* Ed. Paul Michael Lützeler. Frankfurt a.M.: S. Fischer, 1996: 65–74.
Niekus-Moore, Cornelia. *Patterned Lives: The Lutheran Funeral Biography in Early Modern Germany.* Wiesbaden: Harrassowitz, 2006.
Nirumand, Bahman. *Persien: Modell eines Entwicklungslandes oder die Diktatur der freien Welt.* Reinbek: Rowohlt, 1967.
Nora, Pierre. "Between Memory and History: Les Lieux de Mémoire." *Representations* 26.1 (1989): 7–24.
Özdamar, Emine S. *Mutterzunge.* Berlin: Rotbuch Verlag, 1990.
———. *Das Leben ist eine Karawanserei—hat zwei Türen—aus einer kam ich rein—aus der anderen ging ich raus.* Köln: Kiepenheuer & Witsch, 1992.
———. *Die Brücke vom Goldenen Horn.* Köln: Kiepenheuer & Witsch, 1998.
———. *Life Is a Caravanserai: Has Two Doors I Came in One I Went Out the Other.* Trans. Luise Von Flotow-Evans. London: Middlesex University Press, 2000.
———. *Seltsame Sterne starren zur Erde.* Köln: Kiepenheuer & Witsch, 2003.
———. *The Bridge of the Golden Horn.* Trans. Martin Chalmers. London: Serpent's Tail, 2009.
Ohse, Marc-Dietrich. *Jugend nach dem Mauerbau: Anpassung, Protest und Eigensinn (DDR 1961–1974).* Berlin: Ch. Links Verlag, 2003.
Osterle, Heinz D. "The Lost Utopia. New Images of America in German Literature." *The German Quarterly* 54.4 (Winter 1981): 427–446.
Osterle, Heinz D., ed. *Amerika!: New Images in German Literature.* New York: Lang, 1989.

Ott, Ulrich and Roman Luckscheiter, ed. *Belles lettres/ Graffiti. Soziale Phantasien und Ausdrucksformen der Achtundsechziger.* Göttingen: Wallstein, 2001.
Ott, Ulrich and Friedrich Pfäfflin, ed. *Protest! Literatur um 1968.* Marbach: Deutsche Schillergesellschaft, 1998.
Otto, Karl A., ed. *APO: Außerparlamentarische Opposition in Quellen und Dokumenten (1960–1970).* Köln: Pahl-Rugenstein, 1989.
Parkes, Stuart. *Writers and Politics in Germany, 1945-2008.* Rochester, NY: Camden House, 2009.
Paulsen, Wolfgang, ed. *Die USA und Deutschland: Wechselseitige Spiegelungen in der Literatur der Gegenwart.* Bern: Francke, 1976.
Peck, Jeffrey. *Being Jewish in the New Germany.* New Brunswick: Rutgers University Press, 2006.
Pendas, Devin O. *The Frankfurt Auschwitz Trial, 1963–1965: Genocide, History, and the Limits of the Law.* Cambridge: Cambridge University Press, 2006.
Pfeifer, Elizabeth L.B. "1968 in German Political Culture, 1967–1993: From Experience to Myth." PhD diss., University of North Carolina, Chapel Hill, 1997.
Plenzdorf, Ulrich. *Die neuen Leiden des jungen W.* Rostock: Hinstorff, 1973.
Poiger, Uta G. *Jazz, Rock, and Rebels: Cold War Politics and American Culture in a Divided Germany.* Berkeley: University of California Press, 2000.
Prell, Uwe and Lothar Wilker, ed. *Die Freie Universität Berlin 1948–1968–1988. Ansichten und Einsichten.* Berlin: Berlin Verlag, 1989.
Prinz, Alois. *Der poetische Mensch im Schatten der Utopie. Zur politisch-weltanschaulichen Idee der 68'er Studentenbewegung und deren Auswirkung auf die Literatur.* Würzburg: Königshausen & Neumann, 1990.
Rehmann, Ruth. *Der Mann auf der Kanzel. Fragen an einen Vater.* München: Hanser, 1979.
Reichel, Peter. *Vergangenheitsbewältigung in Deutschland. Die Auseinandersetzung mit der NS-Diktatur von 1945 bis heute.* München: Beck, 2001.
Renz, Peter. *Vorläufige Beruhigung.* Hamburg: Hoffmann & Campe, 1980.
Ritter, Alexander, ed. *Deutschlands literarisches Amerikabild: neuere Forschungen zur Amerikarezeption der deutschen Literatur.* Hildesheim: Olms, 1977.
Ruland, Richard. *America in Modern European Literature: From Image to Metaphor.* New York: New York University Press, 1976.
Rummel, Erika. *Scheming Papists and Lutheran Fools. Five Reformation Satires.* New York: Fordham University Press, 1993.
Said, Edward. *Orientalism.* New York: Vintage, 1978.
Schaumann, Caroline. *Memory Matters: Generational Responses to Germany's Nazi Past in Recent Women's Literature.* Berlin: Walter de Gruyter, 2008.
Schildt, Axel and Detlef Siegfried, ed. *Between Marx and Coca-Cola: Youth Cultures in Changing European Societies, 1960–1980.* Oxford: Oxford University Press, 2005.
Schindel, Robert. *Gebürtig. Roman.* Frankfurt a.M.: Suhrkamp, 1992.

Schlant, Ernestine. *The Language of Silence: West German Literature and the Holocaust.* New York: Routledge, 1999.
Schlink, Bernhard. "Recht–Schuld–Zukunft." *Geschichte–Schuld–Zukunft.* Ed. Jörg Calließ. Loccum: Evangelische Akademie, 1988: 57–78.
———. *Der Vorleser.* Zürich: Diogenes, 1995.
———. "Die Bewältigung von Vergangenheit durch Recht." *Vergangenheitsbewältigung am Ende des 20. Jahrhunderts.* Ed. Helmut König, Michael Kohlstruck, and Andreas Wöll. Opladen: Westdeutscher Verlag, 1998: 433–450.
———. *Vergangenheitsschuld und gegenwärtiges Recht.* Frankfurt a.M.: Suhrkamp, 2002.
Schmidtke, Michael A. *Der Aufbruch der jungen Intelligenz. Die 68er Jahre in der Bundesrepublik und den USA.* Frankfurt a.M.: Campus, 2003.
Schmitter, Elke. *Leichte Verfehlungen.* Berlin: Berlin Verlag, 2002.
Schneider, Peter. *Lenz.* Berlin: Rotbuch, 1973.
———. *...schon bist Du ein Verfassungsfeind.* Berlin: Rotbuch, 1975.
———. *Der Mauerspringer.* Darmstadt: Luchterhand, 1982.
———. *The Walljumper.* Trans. Leigh Hafrey. New York: Pantheon Books, 1983.
———. *Paarungen.* Berlin: Rowohlt, 1992.
———. *Couplings.* New York: Farrar, Straus and Giroux, 1996.
———. *Eduards Heimkehr.* Berlin: Rowohlt, 1999.
———. *Eduard's Homecoming.* Trans. John Brownjohn. New York: Farrar, Straus and Giroux, 2000.
———. *"Und wenn wir nur eine Stunde gewinnen..." Wie ein jüdischer Musiker die Nazi-Jahre überlebte.* Berlin: Rowohlt, 2001.
———. *Skylla.* Berlin: Rowohlt, 2005.
———. *Rebellion und Wahn. Mein '68.* Köln: Kiepenheuer & Witsch, 2008.
Scholz, Leander. *Das Rosenfest.* München: Hanser, 2001.
Schwaiger, Brigitte. *Lange Abwesenheit.* Wien, Hamburg: Zsolnay, 1980.
Seyfried, Gerhard. *Der schwarze Stern der Tupamaros.* Berlin: Eichborn, 2004.
Seyhan, Azade. *Writing Outside the Nation.* Princeton: Princeton University Press, 2001.
Shafi, Monika. "Talkin' 'Bout My Generation: Memories of 1968 in Recent German Novels." *German Life and Letters* 59.2 (2006): 201–216.
Solger, Reinhold. *Anton in Amerika.* Hannover: Wehrhahn, 1862, repr. 2009.
Sonner, Franz Maria. *Als die Beatles Rudi Dutschke erschossen.* München: Kunstmann, 1996.
———. *Die Bibliothek des Attentäters.* München: Kunstmann, 2001.
Stephan, Alexander, ed. *The Americanization of Europe: Culture, Diplomacy, and Anti-Americanism after 1945.* New York: Berghahn Books, 2006.
Strobl, Ingrid. *Ende der Nacht.* Berlin: Orlanda, 2005.
Suri, Jeremi. *Power and Protest: Global Revolution and the Power of Détente.* Cambridge: Harvard University Press, 2003.

Taberner, Stuart. "Introduction: German Literature in the Age of Globalisation." *German Literature in the Age of Globalisation.* Ed. Stuart Taberner. Birmingham: Birmingham University Press, 2004: 1–24.
Timm, Uwe. *Heißer Sommer.* München: Bertelsmann, 1974.
———. *Kerbels Flucht.* München: Verlag Autoren-Edition, 1980.
———. *Rot.* Köln: Kiepenheuer & Witsch, 2001.
———. *Der Freund und der Fremde.* Köln: Kiepenheuer & Witsch, 2005.
Varon, Jeremy. *Bringing the War Home: The Weather Underground, the Red Army Faction, and Revolutionary Violence in the Sixties and Seventies.* Berkeley: University of California Press, 2004.
Vesper, Bernward. *Die Reise.* Frankfurt a.M.: Zweitausendeins, 1977.
Von der Emde, Silke. "Places of Wonder: Fantasy and Utopia in Irmtraud Morgner's Salman Trilogy." *New German Critique* 82 (Winter 2001): 167–192.
Von Dirke, Sabine. "West Meets East: Narrative Construction of the Foreigner and Postmodern Orientalism in Sten Nadolny's *Selim oder Die Gabe der Rede.*" *The Germanic Review* 69.2 (1994): 61–69.
———. *"All Power to the Imagination!" The West German Counterculture from the Student Movement to the Greens.* Lincoln: University of Nebraska Press, 1997.
Von Hodenberg, Christina and Detlef Siegfried, ed. *Wo "1968" liegt. Reform und Revolte in der Geschichte der Bundesrepublik.* Göttingen: Vandenhoeck & Ruprecht, 2006.
Von Lange, Alexa Hennig. *Peace.* Köln: DuMont, 2009.
Von Lucke, Albrecht. *68 oder ein neues Biedermeier. Der Kampf um die Deutungsmacht.* Berlin: Wagenbach, 2008.
Von Miquel, Marc. *Ahnden oder amnestieren? Westdeutsche Justiz und Vergangenheitspolitik in den sechziger Jahren.* Göttingen: Wallstein, 2004.
Wackwitz, Stephan. *Neue Menschen. Bildungsroman.* Frankfurt a.M.: S. Fischer, 2005.
Walter, Joachim. "Interview mit Irmtraud Morgner." *Weltbühne* 32 (1972): 10–11.
Weigel, Sigrid. "Shylocks Wiederkehr. Die Verwandlung von Schuld in Schulden oder: Zum symbolischen Tausch der Wiedergutmachung." *Fünfzig Jahre danach. Zur Nachgeschichte des Nationalsozialismus.* Ed. Birgit Erdle and Sigrid Weigel Zürich: vdf, 1996: 165–192.
———. "'Generation' as a Symbolic Form: On the Genealogical Discourse of Memory since 1945." *Germanic Review* 77.4 (2002): 264–278.
———. *Genea-Logik. Generation, Tradition und Evolution zwischen Kultur- und Naturwissenschaften.* München: Wilhelm Fink Verlag, 2006.
Weinrich, Harald. *Lethe. Kunst und Kritik des Vergessens.* München: Beck, 1997.
Weiss, Heipe. *Fuchstanz. Roman.* Frankfurt: Dipa-Verlag, 1996.
Weiss, Peter. *Viet Nam Diskurs.* Frankfurt a.M.: Suhrkamp, 1968.

Welzer, Harald, Sabine Moller, and Karoline Tschuggnall. *"Opa war kein Nazi." Nationalsozialismus und Holocaust im Familiengedächtnis.* Frankfurt a.M.: S. Fischer, 2002.

Wierling, Dorothee. "How do the 1929ers and the 1949ers differ?" *Power and Society in the GDR. 1961-1979. The 'Normalisation of Rule'?* Ed. Mary Fulbrook. New York: Berghahn Books, 2009: 204–219.

Wildner, Siegrun. *Experimentum Mundi: Utopie als ästhetisches Prinzip: zur Funktion utopischer Entwürfe in Irmtraud Morgners Romanwerk.* St. Ingbert: Röhrig, 2000.

Winkler, Willi. *Die Geschichte der RAF.* Berlin: Rowohlt, 2007.

Wittmann, Rebecca E. *Beyond Justice: The Auschwitz Trial.* Cambridge: Harvard University Press, 2005.

Woelk, Ulrich. *Rückspiel.* Frankfurt a.M.: S. Fischer, 1993.

———. *Die letzte Vorstellung.* Hamburg: Hoffmann & Campe, 2002.

Wölfel, Ute. *Rede-Welten. Zur Erzählung von Geschlecht und Sozialismus in der Prosa Irmtraud Morgners.* Trier: Wissenschaftlicher Verlag, 2007.

Wolff, Frank and Eberhard Windaus, ed. *Studentenbewegung 1967–69. Protokolle und Materialien.* Frankfurt a.M.: Verlag Roter Stern, 1977.

Wolfrum, Edgar. "'1968' in der gegenwärtigen deutschen Geschichtspolitik." *Aus Politik und Zeitgeschichte* B 22-23/2001. (accessed 11 October 2011) http://www.bpb.de/publikationen/27NG0I,0,1968_in_der_gegenw%E4rtigen_deutschen_Geschichtspolitik.html

Young, James E. *The Texture of Memory. Holocaust Memorials and Meaning.* New Haven, London: Yale University Press, 1993.

———. *At Memory's Edge: After-Images of the Holocaust in Contemporary Art and Architecture.* New Haven: Yale University Press, 2000.

Zantop, Susanne. *Colonial Fantasies: Conquest, Family, and Nation in Precolonial Germany, 1770–1870.* Durham: Duke University Press, 1997.

Index

1968
    anniversaries in 1998 and 2008, 2, 5–6, 121
    in East and West, 5, 16, 57–63, 136–142
    as global caesura, 6
    as psychological condition, 50
    as symbolic marker and discourse, 5
    shift from 1960s student movement to generation of 1968, 17, 34–35, 41–51
1968ers' appropriation of victim position, 46–48, 101, 103–112
    schizophrenic split and delusion, 50
    self-perceptions, 10–14, 34, 42–44, 48–50, 57–63, 98, 114

America, 94–96
    See also United States of America
Americanization, 95
anarchism, 45–46
anti-Americanism, 95–97
anti-Semitism, 107
art, 12–19
    collaboration, 64, 81–85
    creative process, 82–85, 126
    fragmentation, 82–85
    happening, 81–82
    and memory, 16–19
    montage, 82–85
    relationship between the aesthetic and the political, 17, 36–49, 82–86
    as resistance, 61, 82–83
    See also memory and art
    See also storytelling
Assmann, Aleida and Jan, 15

Benjamin, Walter, 15, 99
Berlin, 43–45
    Berlin Republic, 7
    Berlin Wall as demarcation of East and West, 45
    site of 1960s student protest, 58–60, 65
    site of memory, 46, 67–69, 75–77, 136–142
Biermann, Wolf, 83
Bitterfelder Weg, 83

civil disobedience, 2, 20, 103
Civil Rights movement, 3, 59, 67, 91, 103, 135
Cold War, 13, 67, 95, 137
coming to terms with the past, 32, 46–48, 100–101, 104
    1968 as third coming to terms with the past, 6–9
    responsibility of the second and third generation, 101
    See also Vergangenheitsbewältigung
cultural heritage, 70–72, 80, 138–139, 149–150
    as family history, 47
    as historical responsibility, 7, 15, 101
    as inheritance, 45, 107, 111

death of literature, 16–17, 125
Deutscher Herbst, 130, 136
diversity, 14, 43, 124–127
bilingualism, 2, 128
multiculturalism 2, 122–129, 140–143
Dunkelmännerbriefe, 79
Dutschke, Rudi, 2–3

East–West conflict, 45, 58, 76–77
   See also Cold War
encounter, 94–96, 105–114
   border crossing, 20, 126, 142
   transatlantic encounter, 97–99, 103, 115
   as transnational sphere, 74, 97, 99, 122
   travel, 68
   as trope of memory, 95, 106
Europe, 2, 4, 16–19, 59, 68–69, 125
exile, 95, 104–112
   See also United States of America
eyewitness, 10–15, 107, 111
   as source of memory, 47

family conflicts, 19, 34, 42, 46–48, 89, 100–101, 106–114, 131–136, 151
family novels, 12
Fischer, Joschka, 5
Freud, Sigmund, 135
Fuchs, Anne, 32

gender, 48, 59, 65–67, 75–82, 141
   female storytelling, 110
generation, 35–36
   generational conflict, 34, 49–51, 58, 102
   intragenerational struggle, 34, 49
   See also memory
genre, 17, 82–85, 125, 137
   1968 memory novels, 13, 16–19, 41–42, 143, 148
   Bildungsroman, 39–40
   eulogy, 42
   hybrid genre, 11, 125, 131
   magic realism, 132
German Democratic Republic (GDR), 57–63
   GDR fiction, 2, 63–67
German unification, 5–8, 57–63, 122–124
globalization, 114, 150, 152
guilt, 7, 32, 98, 111–112, 150
   collective guilt, 46–48
   as debt/economic obligation, 45
   See also sexuality

Halbwachs, Maurice, 14, 101
Hamburg as site of 1960s student protest, 1, 36
Herzog, Dagmar, 48
hippie, 71
Hirsch, Marianne, 15, 107
history, 3, 19, 43
   family history, 108–110
   fragmentary knowledge of history, 49
   historical documents as sources of memory, 47, 107, 110
   historiography of unified Germany after 1989, 7, 51
   See also memory
Holocaust, 3–7, 14, 19, 31–40, 101–111, 123–124, 137–139, 140
   See also memory
houses as sites of memory, 10, 46, 108

identity, 20, 76, 105–109, 130, 137–143, 148–152
   in Germany, 2, 36, 50, 122
   identity struggle, 2, 20, 122–129
   language and identity, 109
   national identity, 12, 16, 94, 102
ideology, 8, 45, 59, 77, 125
Istanbul, 129–143

Koenen, Gerd, 10–16
Kraushaar, Wolfgang, 10–16
Kurras, Karl Heinz, 2

language, 14, 18, 134–137, 140–141
   and identity, 109–110
   insufficiency of, and the creation of a new language, 83, 135
   learning, German, 134, 152
   learning, Italian, 137
   as tool of power and domination, 74, 135
   use, 73, 113, 125
life as poetic existence, 137, 143
   creation of life, 82
   in a communal living project, 112–114, 136–140
love, 69, 72–73, 110–111

entanglement of political and sexual revolution, 48
free love, 48
sexual and political liberation as an act of resistance, 81
symbolic significance, 48–49, 149–152

Marx, Karl, 37, 152
media, 6, 8, 59, 69–71, 76–77
  as tool in political conflicts, 45, 76–77
memory
  1968 memory novel, 13, 16–19, 41–42, 143, 148
  as archive, 12, 107
  as construction of the past, 4, 11–19, 43, 108, 123, 142, 148
  contest, 2–3, 16–18, 32–33, 42–44, 46
  cultural, 14–16
  as discourse on spatiality, 10–13, 101–102, 106, 114–115
  as discourse on temporality, 13–16, 46, 99–101, 106, 148
  and family history, 108–110
  and fiction, 2–14
  layers, 2–3, 11–16, 138–139, 148
  memory work as archeology, 29n77, 47
  milieux and lieux de mémoire, 101–102
  moral and ethical obligation, 15, 31–32
  relationship between historiography, fiction, memory, 4, 11–19
  remembering and forgetting, 11–14, 41, 100–102, 138, 149
  remembering and storytelling, 13–14, 41–42, 85, 114
  sites of memory, 13, 46, 102, 106, 137, 149
  as tool, 15, 102, 129
  topography of memory, 10
  transnational, 14–16
migrant, 1–4, 43, 104–105, 122–132

migration, 4, 124–129, 152
narrative perspective, 11, 17, 43–45, 130–131
narratives of 1968, 8–10
new left/old left, 7, 40, 136–137, 140–142
New York City, 104–105, 112–114
Nora, Pierre, 101
normalization, 7
nostalgia, 6, 8, 113, 137

Ohnesorg, Benno, 2–3
ownership, 45, 107

palimpsest of memories, 2, 15, 20, 96, 99, 101–102
Paris, 64–77
political participation, 66
postmemory, 9, 14–17, 47–48, 62, 100–102, 106–107
  See also memory
Prague, 59–62, 74–75
  Prague Defenestration, 74
  Prague Spring, 60, 74
protest as generational struggle, 8, 45–49, 58
  as posturing, 46
  as revolutionary change, 3, 49

Reich, Wilhelm, 47, 135
revolution, 9, 36, 39, 49,
  revolutionary art, 70–71
  revolutionary attitude as an adolescent phase, 49
  sexual revolution, 48, 81
  short lived and failed, 34, 75
  as simulacrum, 45
romantic relationship, 37–38, 48
  illicit affair, 48, 149
  See also love
  See also sexuality
  See also the personal is the political

SDS (German Student Organization), 37, 39, 65
September 11, 2001, 2, 122

sexuality, 36–38, 48, 73, 80–81, 138, 151
   abortion, 38, 65
   guilt and shame, 48, 104, 111, 133
   incest, 49, 151
   married couples, 47–48, 150
   pregnancy, 49
   sexual relations between Germans and Holocaust survivors, 48, 150
   sexual relations involving Holocaust perpetrators, 48, 105–106
   sexual secrets, 48
   sexual taboo, 151
   sexual violence, 69
   sexuality as commodity, 70
silence, 31–33, 38, 41–44, 99–101, 111, 135, 148–152
   as exclusion and omission, 14, 17
   theory and practice, 80–83
social movements, 2–3, 12–13, 61, 67, 148
squatters, 45–49, 107
storytelling, 12–14, 41–42, 83–85, 114
   female, 110
   as political participation, 63, 83–85
   Turkish–German, 128

taboo, 48, 149–152
terrorism, 3, 5–6, 73, 81, 130, 148
the personal is the political, 39–40, 46–48, 65, 69, 73, 99, 114–115, 132, 141, 150–151
transnational fiction, 125–129
Turkish–German literature, 126–130

United States of America, 94–96, 114–115
   in the 1960s, 103–104
   as land of exile, 104
   as meeting place, 96, 102, 110, 112
   as site of generational conflict, 102–103
   as utopian imagination, 112–114
utopia, 7, 16, 39, 66–87, 112–114

Vergangenheitsbewältigung, 7, 32
   See also coming to terms with the past
Vietnam War, 3, 20, 67, 95
violence, 6, 39, 40–45, 60, 73, 81, 151
   revolutionary counter-violence, 3
   sexual violence, 69–70

westernization, 61, 95, 97, 150